The Who
The Official History

Ben Marshall
with **Pete Townshend**
and **Roger Daltrey**

The Who
The Official History

HARPER
DESIGN
An Imprint of HarperCollins Publishers

Introduction
A Real Life Rock Opera

All stories are supposed to have a beginning, a journey and an end. The beginning for me was December 1970 when I joined Track Records at the invitation of my two lifelong friends, Mike Shaw and Chris Stamp. Schoolboy pals and fellow Mods, the common ingredient that flowed through our veins was a love of music and an obsession with fashion. It seemed, therefore, that for me to leap into the Track world was a 'No Brainer'!

Everything was immediate in those days, chew it up and spit it out then on to the next course of the banquet that the 60s and 70s served up. Never did I dream that I would be writing about and still working with band, The Who some forty-five years later.

From the beginning, small clubs and an eventual residency at The Marquee Club in Wardour Street, engineered by Chris Stamp and Kit Lambert, an Amazing Journey soon began to unfold. They were very quickly adopted by the youth of the UK and Europe, the peacocks of the Mod movement. Then, following a couple of minor tours and sorties into the US, a tremendous breakthrough occurred in the shape of several festivals – Monterey, Woodstock and the Isle of Wight. Spectaculars that catapulted The Who onto the world stage, and a huge, universal mass audience.

However, for me, it was the 70s that served up the most interesting, explosive, and in-depth performances. With the incredible song-writing talent of Pete Townshend having come to the fore, they now had works such as *Tommy*, *Who's Next* and *Quadrophenia*, from which they could choose great songs and create a superb set.

To witness a Who performance over the next two decades was to experience greatness, and a unique dynamic unrivalled by any rock band since. Pete Townshend, with his whirlwind, malevolent, leaping presence, one of the greatest of modern guitarists. Roger Daltrey, the iconic blonde powerhouse, the voice of Townshend's incredible lyrics and anthems, aimed at a questioning and disenchanted generation. Alongside them, a multi-instrumentalist bass player in John Entwistle, who played as if he was a lead guitarist, and a lunatic drummer, Keith Moon, who played by no conventional rules. HOW COULD THEY FAIL!

For them to be considered the 'Greatest Live Rock Band' by many critics is well deserved.

Of course, no opera worthy of the name can be devoid of drama or tragedy. That, we as a band have experienced. Pete Meaden, original discoverer of the band, then The High Numbers, Kit Lambert, Chris Stamp, Mike Shaw, John Entwistle, Keith Moon, all have passed away over the years. Amongst these, if the Madcap Moon was predictable, Entwistle's death was both unexpected and unnecessary. None of us realising that his heart problem, that he was so flippant about, could have fatal consequences.

One cannot single out certain performances as being better than others, when all Who concerts are of a level few other rock bands ever attain. What is clear is that this 2014/2015 touring cycle is still a part of the Amazing Journey, one more act in the Real Life Opera that has enveloped our lives.

As for the end? Not written yet!

Myself, I am eternally grateful to have a played a small part in what has been a spectacular life experience, in which I have shared a passion for music, friendships and family bonds of which I never dreamed.

Beyond belief. Enjoy!

— Bill Curbishley
June 2015

1944 — 1955

1

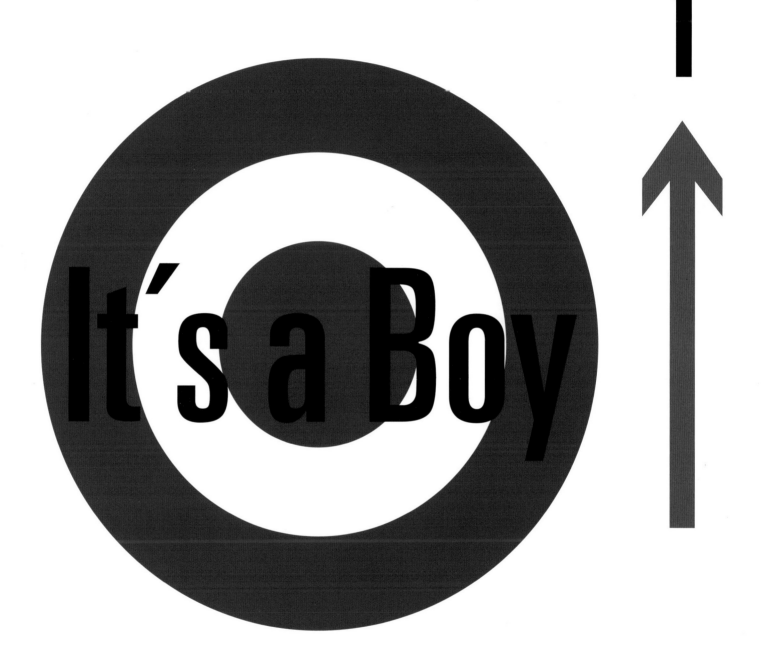

It's a Boy

War Babies and
Baby Boomers

What do you see when you look at a picture of yourself as a child?

Probably not much, just a kid you have been told was once you. That's the way most of us do it. Most of us look at childhood pictures of ourselves in a distant, uncomprehending way, as if we were looking at pictures of someone else, which in a sense we are. Occasionally we might wonder what happened to that person, how we ever were that person, but we rarely go the extra mile and ask how that person became the person we are today. Pete Townshend has spent a lifetime trying to answer that question. He began by asking that question and then asked how a whole generation came to be.

Pete Townshend was born into a family of itinerant, heavy-drinking musicians on 19 May 1945, just two weeks after VE Day and four months before VJ Day brought to an end the greatest conflagration humanity had ever known. War, and Pete's childhood, haunt The Who. The band's themes – unresolved conflict, aggression expressed and repressed, introspection and self-hate bordering on self-harm, idealism battling with cynicism – all these can be attributed to those times. In his autobiography, *Who I Am,* Pete says he sensed both conflict and music (the two always go together with The Who) even before he was born:

'... war and its syncopated echoes – the klaxons and saxophones, the big bands and bomb shelters, V2s and violins, clarinets and Messerschmitts, mood-indigo lullabies and satin-doll serenades, the wails, strafes, sirens, booms and blasts – carouse, waltz and unsettle me while I am still in my mother's womb.'

The Second World War is The Who's war. It is not a war we readily associate with rock 'n' roll. The rock 'n' roll war was Vietnam, which began with rock 'n' roll's birth and ended as it came of age. And it *looked* rock 'n' roll, thanks to the lurid colour photographs of Tim Page, who deemed war glamorous and who inspired the verdant greens and fiery, blood reds of Francis Ford Coppola's *Apocalypse Now*.

Vietnam wasn't just the war scored by rock 'n' roll, it was the war the rock generation believed it could stop. This was back in a time when music and youth were arrogant and naïve enough to believe they were capable of anything – of stopping wars and starting revolutions, of upending the status quo and entirely redefining society. Well, no one quite had the answer to that. Everyone believed the times they were a-changin'. Truly *everyone*. Acid guru Timothy Leary believed it just as surely as FBI Director J. Edgar Hoover. President Nixon was as certain of it as were Bob Dylan and Joan Baez. Both Charles Manson and Roman Polanski saw the times a-changin'. The Who, like some of the other bands who burst onto the scene over the next couple of years – The Beatles, The Rolling Stones, The Kinks, The Yardbirds and The Small Faces – also believed rock 'n' roll could change the world. And for a while it could and did. For a while The Who, antagonistic, anthemic and idealistic, led the charge.

The Who helped to make the world we live in now. But what they made of the colour war, the rock 'n' roll war, was filtered through the one they were born into. The war The Who's generation tried so hard to stop was for Townshend a loud echo of that previous formative convulsion. Nonetheless, their staggeringly violent live performances, their notorious infighting, their nihilistic 'art of auto-destruct', their emphatic rejection of their parents' values all spoke acutely to a generation who regarded themselves as being at war with the establishment and at war with war itself. The Who may have been looking back at the bombsites of working-class West London, but more than any other band of their generation they held up a mirror to a society in turmoil.

TOP Ration queue at the London Food Office in Acton, 1948.
RIGHT Keith looking angelic as a toddler.

Pete Townshend's war was the one his father and Roger Daltrey's and John Entwistle's fathers had helped to fight, and that Pete kept fighting in different ways for decades to follow. The Second World War cost Britain in lives more than half a million and in money around £120 billion. It also cost the country an empire. When Britain had gone to war with Germany in 1939 it had been the most powerful country on the planet. By 1945 it was a country in penury, unable to come to terms with itself or what it had lost. It was a country with an ex-identity. The financial austerity that followed the Second World War was terrible; debts the country incurred were so profound that by the time Britain had repaid them half of The Who were dead (Keith Moon in 1978, John Entwistle in 2002) and rave music was considered passé. Pete Townshend was ten years old before his mother was able to throw away her ration book.

But the austerity produced by the war was not just financial; there was also an emotional austerity. Roger and Pete remember fathers, uncles and friends of the family flatly refusing to discuss anything that had happened 'over there' – in Germany, or Italy, or North Africa or, much worse, Japan. It had happened but it could not be spoken about. Could not even be asked about. And then there were the people who had been sent away from London, Liverpool, Manchester and any other city within range of Hitler's Luftwaffe. More than 3.5 million people, mainly children, were evacuated from the cities to the safety of the countryside. Parents gave instructions to their children: 'don't complain', 'grin and bear it', 'look after your sister', 'write home as soon as you can'. It was arranged that the country's most vulnerable should be evacuated over a 96-hour period. When Roger Daltrey's father Harry was drafted overseas, Roger and his mother were evacuated to Scotland.

Broadly speaking, the four-day official exodus worked surprisingly well. The real problems came in the reception areas, where arrangements for the children's arrival and care had been left to local authorities, with little more than an injunction to do their best. And from there things went from bad to worse.

When the children returned home many of them, perhaps the majority, had experienced some form of bullying, while for a small yet significant proportion the bullying had turned into something more sinister. But when they tried to tell their parents, or their teachers or even friends and siblings they were told to shut up, to keep quiet, to thank their lucky stars they hadn't been blown to bits in the Blitz. This was more than just the stiff British upper lip, it was a code of silence, a very British version of the Sicilian mafia concept of *omertà*. And it affected Pete Townshend deeply. In The Who's 1969 album *Tommy,* when a toddler, a war baby, sees something he shouldn't have, his parents scream at the terrified child, 'You didn't see it, you didn't hear it, you won't say nothing to no one, not ever in your life.' Effectively the child is made blind, deaf and dumb, forced by fear of punishment into a state of unreachable insensibility.

OPPOSITE ABOVE Roger Daltrey. **OPPOSITE BELOW** John Entwistle with his mum and dad, who would later divorce. **RIGHT** A group of children on their way to school in West London, fully equipped for an evacuation rehearsal, 1939. **BELOW** Evacuee children, carrying their gas masks, seen boarding a bus to leave London for the countryside a few days before Britain entered the Second World War.

This then was the world Pete Townshend, Roger Daltrey, John Entwistle and Keith Moon (the youngest of The Who, born a year after the end of the war) inhabited in their formative years – austere, impecunious, emotionally stunted, violent and silent. Pete and John both came from broken homes, although Pete's mum Betty would eventually, after a series of affairs, be reconciled with his dad Clifford. John's parents Herbert and Maud (known as Queenie) separated when he was just eighteen months old. Pete Townshend's sense of loss and anger with his mother in particular is evident in many of The Who's songs. Even John, whose reserved nature is often attributed to his parents' early split, uses songs to address childhood bullying and sex abuse, most notably in 'Cousin Kevin' from *Tommy*, 'When I Was a Boy' and more obliquely in 'Trick of the Light', which deals with sexual inadequacy.

Roger and Keith came from what could be regarded as stable families. Both were staunchly working class. Keith's parents in particular seemed almost to take pride in just how boring they were; even years later, when their notorious millionaire son offered to buy them a house, they refused, preferring to carry on living in the home where Keith had grown up. Biographers of the band often make much of the fact that rock 'n' roll's most notorious animal should have come from such steadfastly conservative stock, suggesting it is an irony of almost cosmic proportions. The truth is, though, that The Who, especially to begin with, were a visceral rejection of the past, as loud, gobby and shocking as punk rock would be a generation later.

The music before The Who, before rock 'n' roll, the music Pete's mother and father had performed before the war and were still performing, during and after the war, was sweet and smooth; it exemplified a romanticism and escapism – in Pete's later view a sort of wishful thinking bordering on denial. As a child he had played in bombsites where he and his friends had found human bones. In 2013, at a question and answer session following a reading from his autobiography, he said the book was 'the story of the boy out in the crowd, lost amid post-war life, who represented boys and girls in West London, who had been changed by the times'. Pete does not regard the travails of his early life as particularly exceptional, which is why he felt so profoundly uneasy about the music his parents played and listened to. It seemed to draw a veil over the truth.

'You weren't asked to do anything – just to shut up,' said Pete. But shutting up was just about the only thing The Who wouldn't do. The Who set out to make a generation audible, then deafening.

OPPOSITE More than one million London homes were destroyed or damaged during the war. **ABOVE** Gas mask drill in Richmond, London, 1941.

Introducing Roger Harry Daltrey

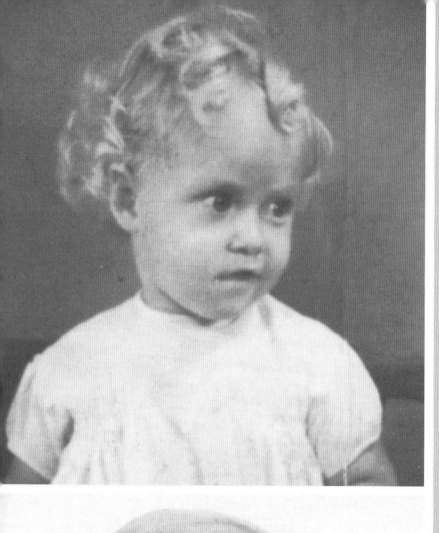

Roger Daltrey was born on 1 March 1944 at Hammersmith Hospital, East Acton, during a heavy bombing raid. He is one of three children born to parents Irene and Harry Daltrey. His dad worked as an insurance clerk, while his mum Irene was on sick benefits due to losing a kidney and contracting polio shortly before Roger was born. When Harry was drafted overseas, Roger and his mum were evacuated to a Scottish farm, and there the pair saw out the remainder of the war, at the end of which the family were immediately reunited. Like Pete Townshend and John Entwistle, Roger grew up in Acton, first attending Victoria Primary School and then Acton County Grammar School along with Pete and John. Roger showed huge academic promise, ranking at the top of his class in the Eleven Plus exam, which led to his enrolment at the Acton County Grammar School. His mum and dad hoped he would eventually go on to university, but by his early teens Roger was wearing the uniform of the Teddy Boy, Britain's first youth cult and still one of its most notorious.

Daltrey became a sheet metal worker during the day. His real interest, though, was rock 'n' roll. He was fascinated by Elvis Presley, Cliff Richard and The Shadows and the skiffle artist Lonnie Donegan. 'It was Donegan that made me think I could do it,' says Roger. At night after work Roger practised on a home-made guitar and performed in pubs and working men's clubs.

'Back then all I wanted to be was rich and famous, and I make absolutely no apology for that.' In this Roger was no different to thousands of British teenagers. It would take a meeting with John Entwistle, several band name and line-up changes and almost a decade to make his dream come true. And by the time it did come true the dream would have changed.

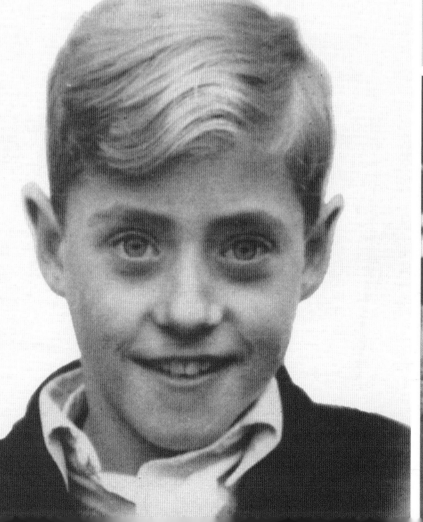

Introducing John Alec Entwistle

John Entwistle was born on 9 October 1944 in Chiswick, West London. He was an only child. John's dad Herbert was in the Royal Navy and his mum 'Queenie' Maud worked as a tax clerk. His parents' marriage failed soon after he was born, and he was brought up mostly by his grandparents in South Acton. Although broken homes were not uncommon in the immediate post-war era, there is no doubt in anyone's mind that divorce had a profound effect on John, contributing to a reserved nature he only really shook off in the very final years of his life.

By the age of seven John had started piano lessons and soon after that his father Herbert bought him a trumpet and began teaching him to play. John did not enjoy the piano at all, but his brief period learning it did teach him how to read and write music. At twelve years old after passing the Eleven Plus exam he went to Acton County Grammar School.

In his second year there he met Pete Townshend, who was at the time learning to play the banjo. They shared a similarly dark sense of humour and a love of Dixieland jazz, which was unusually popular in that part of London. The two would spend what little money they had going to the gigs of Cy Laurie and Ken Colyer in Soho. Together the two formed The Confederates. The group only played one gig together before they decided that rock 'n' roll was a more attractive prospect.

Entwistle later claimed that he could never hear his trumpet when the band played. He decided to switch to guitar but, owing to his large hands, that didn't particularly suit him. Eventually, in part out of his fondness for the low guitar tones of Duane Eddy, he decided to take up the bass. He made his own instrument at home from a block of wood to which he glued a square-backed neck. It later snapped, giving him an 'instant four-string harp.'

OPPOSITE BELOW Seaside holidays played a big part in the early lives of The Who. **LEFT** John played bugle in the Boys' Brigade. **BOTTOM LEFT** John, on the left, learned to box at school. **BOTTOM RIGHT** John with his adored mum Queenie.

Introducing Peter Dennis Blandford Townshend

Pete Townshend was born on 19 May 1945 at Chiswick Hospital, West London, ten days after Nazi Germany surrendered. His dad Cliff Townshend was a professional alto saxophonist in the Royal Air Force's dance band The Squadronaires and his mum Betty was a singer with the Sydney Torch and Les Douglass Orchestras. Cliff and Betty had what can be most kindly described as a volatile marriage. Pete devotes a substantial part of his autobiography to describing the arguments the pair had. Both drank heavily and had savage tempers. Cliff was often away from his family touring with his band while Betty carried on affairs with other men.

The couple split when Pete was a toddler and he was sent to live with his maternal grandmother Emma Dennis, whom Pete later descrnibed as 'clinically insane'.

After Pete had spent two nightmarishly bizarre years with his grandmother, Cliff and Betty were reconciled and he returned to Acton. Shy and solitary, he lost himself in books, fascinated by the works of Jonathan Swift and Robert Louis Stevenson.

Like Roger, Pete passed the Eleven Plus exam and enrolled at Acton County Grammar School. At school, he was frequently bullied because he had a large nose, and this continued when he got home. Pete's close friend Richard Evans, who designed many of The Who's most famous record sleeves and has known him for forty years, says the taunts of the women closest to him as a child still echo in his ears to this day. 'This seemed to be the biggest thing in my life,' Pete told *Rolling Stone's* Jann Wenner years later. 'It was the reason I did everything. The reason I picked up a guitar.'

Nevertheless he loved his mum and dad and especially loved their trips to the English seaside and the Isle of Man. It was on one such trip that he saw *Rock Around the Clock*, the Bill Haley movie that took Britain by storm.

'*Rock Around the Clock* did it for me,' he recalls. 'Up till then I hadn't been that into rock 'n' roll. After that I wanted to get a guitar.' Though the film ignited his interest in rock 'n' roll, he still felt a deep sense of loyalty towards the music his parents played, precisely because they played it. While at school he joined a short-lived trad jazz band with his school-mate John Entwistle. Called The Confederates it featured Pete on banjo, John on horns, Phil Rhodes on clarinet and Chris Sherwin on drums. 'I'd been buggering about for two years on banjo and guitar without getting anywhere. I knew they expected me to be able to play,

Pete My dad was the business: handsome, cool, great sax player and convivial drinker.

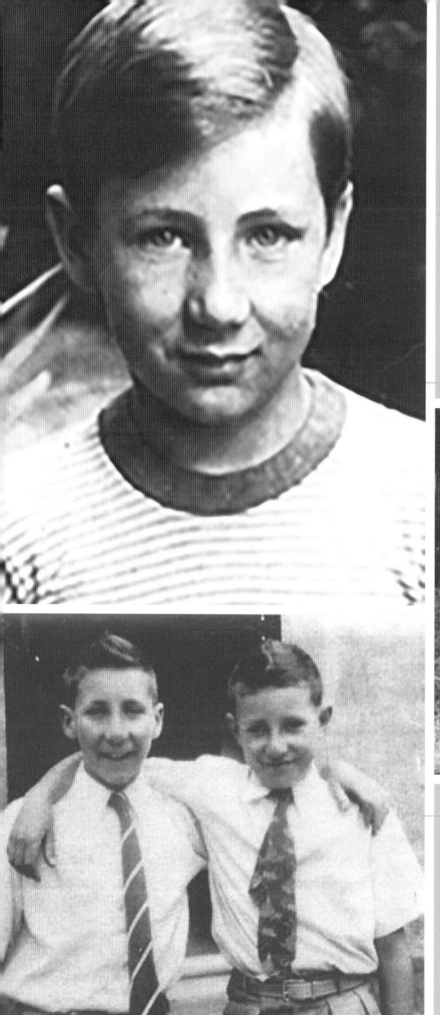

so I went out and bought a chord book. They were really impressed, which I thought was weird. Perhaps they thought if you could play three chords you could play them all.'

Pete failed to get into university, and so was faced with a choice between art school, music school or work. He decided like so many musicians after him to go to art school, enrolling at Ealing Art College in 1961 to study graphic design. At Ealing, Townshend studied alongside future Rolling Stones guitarist Ronnie Wood and future Queen singer Freddie Mercury. Just as importantly, one of his teachers was the auto-destructive art pioneer Gustav Metzger. Metzger unwittingly gave Townshend a way to fight back.

Pete I hated this picture. A local photographer knocked at the door and got my mum to comb my hair.

Pete This is not a picture of me, but it will serve its purpose (it's of my brother Paul). We all sat on those things at one time or other.

Pete Just think, I could have been a hairdresser. My first creation: 'The Tent'. Applied to my best friend Jimpy a little more aggressively than I applied it to myself.

Introducing Keith John Moon

Keith Moon was born to Alfred Charles (Alf) and Kathleen Winifred (Kit) Moon on 23 August 1946 at Central Middlesex Hospital in north-West London, and grew up in Wembley. His dad was a motor mechanic and his mum a part-time domestic cleaner. Both parents were staunchly working-class, small 'c' conservatives who kept themselves to themselves.

Keith by contrast was an extreme extrovert, hyperactive and restless. There is a photograph of Keith's class at Barham Primary School. In it the children are standing with backs straight, smiling politely into the camera. Looking at the picture you can practically hear the photographer and teacher tell the children to behave. And all of them do apart from Keith, who is wild eyed, gurning and pulling a face. He was seven years old and that picture already tells us so much about what and who he would become.

Unlike all the other members of The Who, Keith failed his Eleven Plus exam. In the Britain of the 1950s this early failure would normally condemn you to a life of manual drudgery. Most of Keith's mates didn't even think he would make it that far. At Alperton Secondary School for Boys, school work came a very poor second to practical jokes that reduced his teachers to despair and his mates to fits of laughter. He was interested in practical jokes and home science kits, with a particular fondness for explosions. His art teacher said in a report: 'Retarded artistically. Idiotic in other respects.' His music teacher wrote that Moon 'has great ability, but must guard against a tendency to show off'. In the documentary *Keith Moon: His Final Hours,* the common consensus was that Moon would become a thief or criminal, or amount to even less.

After leaving school at fifteen, Keith took a job in the printing room at the National Council for Social Services. He didn't last long. At sixteen his dad bought him his first proper drum kit, a Blue Pearl Premier, for £25 on hire purchase (essentially rent to buy). Moon infuriated his parents' neighbours by practising at all hours. But he was good, eventually taking lessons from local hero Carlo Little of The Savages, who were Screaming Lord Sutch's backing group. Other than drumming and messing about, the only thing Keith excelled at was boxing. There is a local newspaper report with a photo of a teenage Keith Moon leaning menacingly over the unconscious body of an opponent he has actually punched out of the ring.

Boxing's physical commitments (the endless hours of training) proved too much for the easily distracted Keith. However, he continued to audition and play in a number of bands, including Mark Twain and The Strangers. Mark Evans, who became the band's bassist, remembers auditioning alongside Moon. 'This audition was being held in someone's front room up in Rickmansworth, and there was Keith behind the drums. I thought this kid's young, but then he started playing. I said, "If you can get hold of that drummer I'll join the band".'

When the band were offered six months' work playing US Army bases in Germany, Keith's age precluded him from going. After several more stints with local bands he finally joined surf outfit The Beachcombers. At the time he was just about holding down a job as a trainee electrician. As he later told *Rolling Stone* magazine's Jerry Hopkins, 'That was the first of twenty-three jobs I started within two years. With my knowledge and personality I was always considered management material.'

OPPOSITE BELOW Keith drumming in The Beachcombers. **ABOVE LEFT** Keith's first serious group, Mark Twain and The Strangers. **ABOVE RIGHT** Keith pulling faces for the school photograph. **LEFT** Keith monkeying about.

1954 — 1958

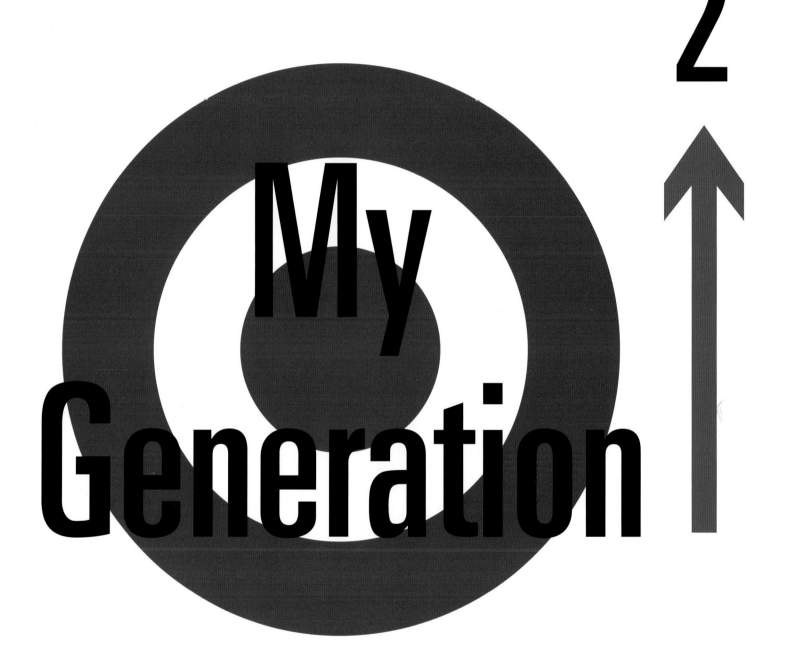

2

My Generation

How Baby Boomers Invented the Generation Gap

It is impossible to overstate the seismic shock of rock 'n' roll.

Nonetheless nearly sixty years on it can be easy to overlook the cultural impact the music had on its audience and, more broadly, society. It changed everything – from the way in which popular music was produced and sold, to the way in which it was socially received, through to how young people dressed, behaved and even thought.

Before rock 'n' roll, popular music had essentially been about theatre songs, novelty songs (derived mostly from music hall and vaudeville), Hollywood hits and (slightly more radically) crooners like Perry Como, Bing Crosby and Frank Sinatra. The music, in fact, that Pete Townshend's mother and father loved and played and towards which the young Townshend felt such fierce devotion. When the first rock 'n' roll records appeared, popular music became a radically different proposition, as writer and Social Sciences professor Michael Billig explains:

'It sounded different from anything previous generations had listened to. The whine of the electric guitar, the crisp drumming, the echo effects and, later, more complex mixtures of electric and acoustic instruments, all made rock 'n' roll a new sound. The generation that had lived through the hard times of the Depression and the Second World War preferred its music soft and romantic. Their children, growing up in safer, more affluent times, wanted to hear more dangerous music. They responded to simple chords, a jumping beat and loud electric guitars.'

In Britain the leader of this revolution came in the most unlikely form of the tubby, genial Bill Haley. A former country singer raised in America's rust belt, Haley was by today's standards as 'fake' as any *X Factor* contestant, turning to rock 'n' roll out of sheer expediency. Country music hadn't worked out and rock 'n' roll seemed to be where the money was. Fake or not, Haley briefly became one of the most controversial figures on the planet. His song 'Rock Around the Clock' was the theme to the notorious inner-city school drama *Blackboard Jungle*. The movie, a template for the 'dedicated teacher reaches troubled kids in a ghetto school' genre, was released to instant controversy in 1955. *The New York Times* was shocked by its explicit violence: 'The picture begins with the feeling that the class-room is a bloody battleground, and then proceeds to present a series of episodes that bear out this grim anxiety.' The reviewer concluded that the film's 'emphasis is wholly upon impudence, rebellion and violence'. Which of course is what made it so attractive to young men.

What kept them coming back, though, was Bill Haley's anthemic song. John Mothersole, a London teenager in 1955, remembers seeing the movie half a dozen times. 'The film itself was fine,' he recalls. 'A sort of well-meaning if somewhat heavy-handed tribute to teachers. But that song? If all your life all you've heard is Bing. That's what obsessed me. Me and my mates would go to the pictures just to hear it. We were going along just to watch the title sequence. It was our first taste of rock 'n' roll and it blew our minds. We just couldn't get enough. For millions of teenagers it was a mental jailbreak.'

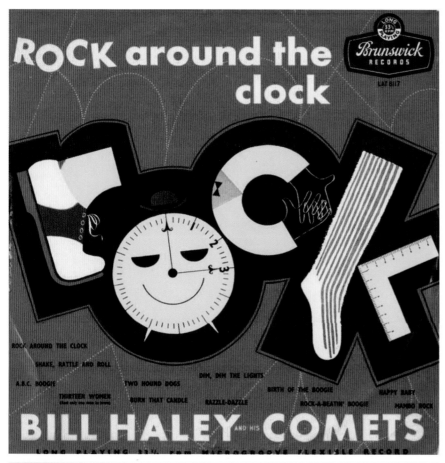

The film studio Metro Goldwyn Mayer, clearly aware of the impact of Bill Haley, followed *Blackboard Jungle* up a year later with *Rock Around the Clock*. The new film was essentially a vehicle for Haley and was bereft of the violence and left-leaning politics of *Blackboard Jungle*, but it proved to be a far bigger hit. Pete Townshend, Roger Daltrey, John Entwistle and Keith Moon, along with practically every other even slightly rebellious teenager in the UK, went to see it. Pete was taken along by his dad during one of their many summer seaside excursions. John Mothersole again: 'Basically, you had three stations: the Home Service, which was a news service; the BBC Third Programme that was so clever and up its own arse it was pretty much incomprehensible to anyone without a degree from Oxford; and supplying the music you had BBC Light Programme, which was presented by a feller in a dinner jacket who played Bing Crosby records. Radio Luxemburg was there too, but reception was really bad. So the atmosphere was utterly stifling. The BBC were never gonna play rock 'n' roll, 'cos at the time they felt, like the government felt, that they had this patrician duty to inform and educate, in their words. So rock 'n' roll was, if anything, something they wanted to protect us from. Fuck, it was practically in their charter. So when these movies came along – first *Blackboard*, then *Rock Around the Clock* – we had to go and see it every time we wanted to hear the fucking song. To me *Rock Around the Clock's* not the greatest rock 'n' roll record ever made, but it was the first for most British kids and sixty years later it still sends shivers down my spine when I hear it played.'

When in 1956 the movie was first screened in Britain, it resulted in a string of violent disturbances. Cinema seats were torn out and in several major cities youths were arrested and later fined for aggressive or insulting behaviour as they left cinemas. Disturbances were also reported in Toronto, Sydney and in Auckland, New Zealand. Across Europe, reactions to *Rock Around the Clock* were even more extreme. In Holland, where the movie was banned in several major cities, young people took to the streets to demonstrate for their right to see the film. In the West German city of Hamburg the film inspired a full-scale riot, with cars being overturned and burned, and shop fronts and street signs smashed by teenagers, forcing the police to turn water cannons on the youth in an attempt to quell the disturbances.

Rock 'n' roll with all its sexual allure and subversive promise was what their future looked like

Bill Haley's music clearly generated a great deal of excitement with kids like John Mothersole and the youthful members of The Who. Haley's image, however, was a whole lot harder to love. He and his band The Comets may have helped to create a moral panic and with it a generation gap (something rock and pop doesn't just thrive on but actually requires to deliver on its promise), but they looked like a bunch of plump, affable, ageing and alarmingly energetic uncles. They could never hope to inspire much identification among Britain's boys or romantic adulation among girls.

But then came Chuck Berry, Little Richard and Elvis Presley. All three would have a huge long-term cultural impact. But it was Elvis who effected the most change. His manager Colonel Tom Parker had always said that if he could find a white kid who could sing like a black man he would make his fortune. What Parker could never have predicted was how Elvis would change the course of history. In the US, most Americans had some notion of the singer's provenance. Many already loved the blues and country music, and those that weren't familiar with them at least knew such things existed. In poor, war-blighted Britain, both the music and the appearance of Elvis, with his anthracite quiff, huge baby eyes, Cupid's-bow lips set somewhere between a pout and sneer and the suggestive thrust and wiggle as he performed, was like nothing anyone had seen before. His cocky and androgynous looks, the way he danced, with that aggressively sexual gyration of the hips, and even the way he spoke, with that Southern-fried drawl – to British ears and eyes it was all so utterly alien that Elvis might as well have dropped from the sky. To British teenagers he was a way of both switching off and switching on. To the young Roger Daltrey, Pete Townshend, John Entwistle and Keith Moon he appeared like some angel of salvation, pointing a clear way out of the ennui of early 1950s Britain. Elvis, and more generally rock 'n' roll with all its sexual allure and subversive promise, was to them not just what the future looked like but what their specific future looked like. Later Roger would freely admit that he'd actually wanted to *be* Elvis.

ABOVE The phenomenon of girls screaming at concerts had begun with Frank Sinatra, but with the arrival of Elvis hysteria became de rigueur.
OPPOSITE Presley's gyrations and vocal style, which borrowed heavily from African-American blues singers, so shocked and appalled middle America, he was only allowed to be filmed from the hips up. **OVERLEAF** Teds bopping.

When Elvis Presley began to record rock 'n' roll songs for Sun Records, he quite consciously imitated African-American performers, with all the authentic rawness and emotion that was missing in the work of other white rock 'n' roll artists. It was Presley who was instrumental in what one critic called 'the sexual seduction of whites into blackness'. This seduction was further enhanced by Presley's image, which teenagers across the world, including the young Roger Daltrey and Keith Moon, imitated. His stage performances were spectacular in a way quite unknown to white audiences. Youth and sex had never been mixed so potently. Elvis signalled the arrival of the new teenage pop idol, burying the notion of a pop star of indeterminate age for at least as long as it took his fans to grow into adulthood and old age.

On his own, though, Elvis could not have succeeded. In the mid-1950s a whole series of social, economic and technological changes took place, creating a perfect storm from which rock 'n' roll could be born. Presley for instance first reached a nationwide audience in the US through television. Indeed, in the case of young teenagers outside of the US, Presley remained an essentially mediated star. Globally people experienced him via television and his numerous films. TV also helped create the moral panic and generational clashes that would swiftly become central to rock 'n' roll's appeal. Just as no one can quite foresee what effects the internet will have on the young minds of today, no one had any idea how television would affect the teenagers of the 1950s. Presley's TV appearances on the *The Dorsey Brothers' Stage Show* in early 1956 passed largely without comment perhaps because they were seen by relatively small audiences or because Elvis's dancing was filmed from the waist up, rendering his famous gyrations less obvious. However, when he appeared on *The Milton Berle Show* in June that year, his dancing was both more

extreme and seemed, to a scandalised America, to go on forever (in fact, it lasted just half of his performance of 'Hound Dog'). The reaction of professional critics and the self-appointed guardians of morality alike was swift and harsh. The furious public outcry nearly caused NBC to cancel Elvis's next scheduled TV appearance. These news stories, along with clips of Elvis, filtered back to the UK, where kids devoured them. TV first showed what would outrage, then reported on the outrage and round and round it went, this circle of provocation. The Who, always something of a meta-band, knew very early on that provocation, often brutal, foul-mouthed provocation, would be central to their appeal.

However, it wasn't simply what Elvis did that appealed. It is what his fans did. Nearly all early footage of 'The King' includes shots of his fans. Not long shots, where the kids appear as some amorphous mass, but tight close-ups. The faces of the young people are hysterical, near orgasmic, out of control. TV was showing kids the effect Elvis had and how they in turn should respond. And they responded with dutiful derangement. Elvis wasn't the first singer to inspire screaming; that honour probably goes to Frank Sinatra. But Elvis was the first, via television, to make it global and, because of his gyrations, to make it seem explicitly sexual. All of which added to the sense of a generation gap, with parents, teachers and preachers asking what sort of black magic was being cast on their sons and daughters. Well, mostly their daughters. By 1964, when The Beatles led the British invasion, there had been ten years' worth of film charting teenagers seemingly losing their minds at rock 'n' roll shows. Everyone knew how to react. Beatlemania was just Elvis mania refined and massively amplified. By the time The Who arrived in the US, their reputation for smashing their instruments preceding them, again TV had primed American teenagers.

OPPOSITE CLOCKWISE FROM TOP LEFT Lonnie Donegan, Johnny Kidd & The Pirates, Cliff Richard and Buddy Holly.

Along with new technology came new wealth and new ideas about how British society might work. The immediate post-war years and the 1950s were undoubtedly a time of extreme austerity, but this was also a period when Britain set about rebuilding itself. In five years, more than a million homes were built to replace the 700,000 that had been destroyed in the Blitz. London and Britain's other big cities were littered with bombsites (many of which would survive into the 1980s), giving the country a desperately broken appearance. Colour photographs of these rubble-strewn places, which doubled as makeshift playgrounds, look to the contemporary eye more like Bosnia or the Gaza Strip than London. Meanwhile, Clement Attlee's Labour government, which had won a landslide election, was putting socialist ideas into action, nationalising key industries and introducing the National Health Service. Families that had been devastated by war and had voted for socialism now dedicated themselves to building a better world for their children. John Mothersole again: 'I think our parents had this sense that we were all lucky to be alive, so I had a very happy childhood. My mum and dad didn't have much money, but what little they did have went on us kids. I wouldn't say we were spoilt, but we were indulged.'

This applied to Pete Townshend, whose parents and grandmother though emotionally all over the place, bought him musical instruments, to John Entwistle, whose dad bought him a clarinet, and even Keith Moon, who was bought a drum kit in his teens. In fact, of the four Who members, only Roger Daltrey was not bought an instrument by his parents.

Optimism and pessimism, emotional distance and material indulgence, dreams of utopia and the reality of a country that six years of war had practically bankrupted rubbed up against one another. By the 1950s the tension between what was and what might be was making the country a living, breathing paradox. Food was still rationed and yet in 1951 a study proclaimed poverty to be at an end. That was debatable – and has been much debated since – but what was certainly true was that between the late 1950s right up until the mid-1970s Britain enjoyed a period of unusual economic prosperity. John Clinton, then a young Teddy Boy from Bethnal Green in London's East End, remembers walking out of a job at lunchtime and finding a new one that very afternoon.

'Like a lot of kids I left school at fifteen and I worked as a bricklayer. There was so much work around you could call the shots. If you didn't like your boss, or just fancied a change, you left and went elsewhere. With the amount of building work going on in my part of London, I wouldn't have to walk more than a hundred yards to find another job. People talk about it being austere, but I always had money in my pocket.'

ABOVE Keith in his surf band The Beachcombers. **OPPOSITE** John practising on his home-made guitar, at home with his mum.

1950s BESTSELLING RECORDS

Albums

1 *South Pacific* Soundtrack 1958

2 *My Fair Lady* Broadway cast 1956

3 *The King and I* Soundtrack 1956

4 *A Swingin' Affair,* Frank Sinatra1957

5 *Pal Joey* Soundtrack 1957

6 *King Creole,* Elvis Presley 1958

7 *Carousel* Soundtrack 1956

8 *Songs for Swingin' Lovers,* Frank Sinatra 1956

9 *This is Sinatra!,* Frank Sinatra 1956

10 *The Tommy Steele Story,* Tommy Steele 1957

Singles

1 'Rock Around the Clock', Bill Haley & His Comets 1955

2 'Diana', Paul Anka 1957

3 'Mary's Boy Child', Harry Belafonte 1957

4 'The Harry Lime Theme' (from *The Third Man*), Anton Karas 1950

5 'What Do You Want to Make Those Eyes at Me For', Emile Ford & the Checkmates 1959

6 'Jailhouse Rock', Elvis Presley 1957

7 'What Do You Want', Adam Faith 1959

8 'Living Doll', Cliff Richard 1959

9 'All Shook Up', Elvis Presley 1957

10 'All I Have to Do is Dream' / 'Claudette', The Everly Brothers 1958

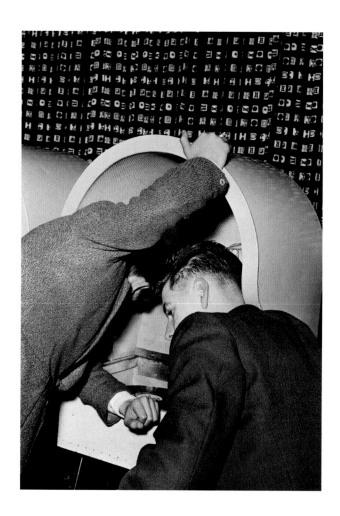

LEFT Teenagers in record shops shut into their soundproof listening booths. **OPPOSITE** The Beachcombers unloading the van. Hastings, East Sussex.

Keith Moon's claim to have had twenty-three jobs in two years was of course an exaggeration, but not by much. Like many teenagers he spent his wages on records. According to his mother, Keith showed an immediate interest in music: 'From the age of three he would sit for hours beside an old gramophone player and play old 78 records of stars like Nat King Cole and Scots bandleader Jimmy Shand.'

London was a port and therefore one of the first places to receive goods from overseas. Often merchant seamen would bring back rock 'n' roll and rhythm and blues records from the US, either for their own listening or to sell on the dockside or to local record shops. It is no coincidence that the first wave of British rock 'n' roll bands all came from ports – The Beatles and others from Liverpool, The Animals from Newcastle and The Rolling Stones, The Small Faces, The Kinks and The Who from London.

After Elvis came Buddy Holly, Britain's own Cliff Richard and the skiffle artist Lonnie Donegan and a host of others. Of these by far the most important were Buddy Holly and Lonnie Donegan. Buddy Holly was an instant hit thanks to his easily imitated look, his guitar sound – noticeably rawer than Presley's – and the sheer simplicity of the songs. Pete's close friend Richard Evans remembers everyone hearing Buddy Holly and going out and buying a guitar.

> 'You could buy a guitar back then for next to nothing. They were horrible things to play, crude and ugly, but you could still learn how to play. If you wanted to play Buddy Holly songs you only needed three chords for most of his songs, A, D and E. If you were really ambitious you could learn C and F and that pretty much allowed you to play any rock 'n' roll song out there. The good thing about learning Buddy Holly stuff on a terrible guitar was that the moment you got hold of a decent guitar you actually sounded really good.'

Roger Daltrey, unhappy with the cheap instruments that were available in record stores, went and built his own guitar, hewn like John Entwistle's bass from a block of wood. His inspirations were Elvis (obviously), Buddy Holly, Chuck Berry, Little Richard and Lonnie Donegan. Donegan was a leading exponent of skiffle, a music so DIY that people would use washboards and other household implements as instruments. Roger explains:

> 'Lonnie Donegan was someone we could emulate. He very much showed me that it was possible to play music, to be known for playing music, to be successful in music with just the simplest things – you didn't need shed loads of money, just a decent voice and some like-minded mates.'

Roger Daltrey found what he was looking for when, in 1961, he formed the skiffle band The Detours.

Teddy Boys

More than seventy years after they first appeared on British streets, Teddy Boys remain one of the most notorious counter-cultural movements in the history of pop. They were the first defiantly working-class teenage movement and quickly became associated with violence and criminality. Now indelibly identified with the birth of rock 'n' roll, the Teddy Boy actually pre-dates modern popular music by more than six years. In retrospect it might have surprised Roger Daltrey to learn that the look he admired while growing up in the 1950s was the invention of Savile Row and Bond Street tailors, and was originally aimed at the British upper classes. After the war and the election of Clement Attlee's Labour government, and its implementation of a radically socialist agenda and extreme austerity measures, many in the British upper classes truly believed their days were numbered. They took solace in looking back to the Edwardian era, which had ended only forty years previously but represented a completely different Britain. Prior to two world wars the country had been powerful, rich and largely run by the landed gentry. Women had yet to be granted the vote (universal suffrage was introduced in 1918), the working class, as yet without unions or any significant parliamentary presence, were very much at the beck and call of the wealthy and the planet was coloured the pink of the British Empire.

Wealthy young men, particularly those in the Guards, adopted the look of the Edwardian era as a vivid way of illustrating their horror of a newly meritocratic Britain. In 1953 the *Daily Sketch* published a short article on the phenomenon:

'Originally, the Edwardian suit was introduced in 1948 by a group of Savile Row tailors who were attempting to initiate a new style. It was addressed, primarily, to the young aristocratic men about town. Essentially the dress consisted of a long narrow lapelled, waisted jacket, narrow trousers (but without being "drainpipes"), ordinary toe-capped shoes and a fancy waistcoat. Shirts were white with cut-away collars and ties were tied with a "Windsor" knot. Head-wear, if worn, was a trilby hat. The essential changes from conventional dress were the cut of the jacket and the dandy waistcoat. Additionally, barbers began offering individual styling, and hair-length was generally longer than conventional short back and sides.

'The style quickly spread to the upper-middle classes, and from there to the working classes. The Savile Row tailors who had so successfully pushed the look on the young Mayfair Bloods, the Guardees and the City Bankers became the victims of their own success as it swiftly became the uniform of the working-class

Pete That one year that Rog was older was so critical. He straddled the changing of the times from Rockabilly to R&B, and was the only proper Teddy Boy I ever met.

The Teddy Boys began as an upper-class rejection of post-war austerity and socialism. With uniquely British irony the look was appropriated by young working-class men, the very people the original purveyors of the Edwardian look wanted to distance themselves from. **ABOVE LEFT** Two Teds chatting outside the ABC cinema in Elephant & Castle. The Teds were originally a South and East London phenomenon. **ABOVE** A Ted shows off his drapes. **LEFT** A Ted having his DA done – so called because the back resembled a duck's arse.

Dance Hall Creepers. This, like so many working-class youth looks that followed, the Mod and football casual being two of the most obvious examples, was aspirational – the working class wanted to look wealthy. However, when the working classes appropriated the look, they gave it a newly aggressive edge. The press, which had liked the look, now began to describe it as spivish and delinquent. There was an element of truth to this. The working-class Teddy Boy made his first appearance in London's poorer South London neighbourhoods, notably Lambeth and the Elephant and Castle. He combined the upper-class Edwardian style with the zoot suits of the Peckham Market Spiv. As quickly as the working classes adopted it the upper classes dropped it.

'"It means that absolutely the whole of one's wardrobe immediately becomes unwearable," explained a disconsolate young ex-Guardee at the time. Those who now wore Edwardian dress were described in the papers as "creepers", "thugs", "yobs", "unfavourable social types", "zoot-suiters", "hooligans" and "spivs".'

In the summer of 1953 the Ploughboys, a South London gang, dressed in the Edwardian style, stabbed to death seventeen-year-old John Beckley on Clapham Common where a band had recently been playing the latest hits on the bandstand. The murder, brutal and seemingly pointless, caused widespread moral panic. Newspapers were fascinated by the look, as for the first time it was associated solely with an entirely new demographic: teenagers. And not just teenagers in general but those seemingly rebelling against the social order – of which Roger would soon be one.

In 1955 the new teen cult did much to live up to its fearsome reputation. When the movie *Blackboard Jungle* was shown in the Elephant and Castle it provoked riots, which would swiftly follow every showing of the film. It was the *Daily Express*, latching on to the Edwardian connection and shortening Edward to Teddy, that first called the rioters 'Teddy Boys'.

OPPOSITE ABOVE LEFT Teds in Notting Hill, London. Gangs of Teddy Boys would later be blamed for starting the Notting Hill riots after racist attacks on the newly arrived Afro-Caribbean community. **OPPOSITE ABOVE RIGHT** After the stabbing of seventeen-year-old John Beckley on Clapham Common by South London gang the Plough Boys, the Teds became public enemy number one, the subject of a media hysteria that would be repeated with the advent of every new youth subculture from Mod through punk to rap and rave. **OPPOSITE BELOW** Jinx, Rocky, Guff and Zak standing on the bonnet of their Tedmobile, Wales.

Picture Post, 29 M...

THE TRUTH ABOUT
THE 'TEDDY BOYS'
AND THE TEDDY GIRLS

The 'Edwardians,' or 'Teddy Boys,' have been branded as hooligans, juvenile gangsters and delinquents. They have also been called dandies and mother's darlings. It is a confusing picture of exaggeration and distortion. A PICTURE POST investigation seeks to bring it into focus. Our staff writer, HILDE MARCHANT, presents the facts. A PSYCHIATRIST of much experience with young people, interprets them. JOSEPH McKEOWN took the pictures

WE were in a dance-hall in Tottenham—a suburb of London—and the young men we wished to contact were distinctive and obvious. The floppy jackets hung to their knees, the poplin shirts were advertisement white, the trousers were ankle tight, the shoes were good black leather, and the ties were narrow bows. An ugly outfit? That is a matter of opinion; and we were not seeking opinion—only facts. To approach the facts meant we had first to approach the boys, talk to them, and challenge the honesty of their talk. And the first thing that struck me was that their clothes are deceptive. This Edwardian fashion gives a uniformity to a group of young people who are far from uniform. They are as varied, diverse and informal as any other group of human beings. They set a pattern in their velvet collars, dog-tooth checks and moccasin shoes. But there is no such standard pattern about their lives or behaviour.
But let them talk for themselves, for they are frank enough. What do they do during the day, or the week? One is a toy maker, one a glass cutter. Another is an engineer's apprentice, one a die cutter, another an electric welder and, surprisingly, another a National Serviceman on leave—back in his Teddy Boy civilian 'uniform.' (His hair was shorter than the others, but would still have horrified the Sergeant-major.) Their wages were good—ranging from the £4 17s. 6d. a week apprentice, to just over £12 a week for the skilled cabinet maker. Their suits cost between £17 and £20. All of them agreed that a good poplin shirt was just under £2 and that a pair of shoes was around the £3 mark. Most of them 'kept themselves'; which means they pay their parents something towards the rent and the household budget. Even so, pocket money was never less than £2 a week, and often double. They were not interested in drink—a beer, perhaps, but more likely a mineral water. They

THE SUIT THAT GRANDFATHER MIGHT HAVE WORN
The dance is contemporary jive. But the suit is an adaptation of the Edwardian 'masher's' outfit. It is also English in conception and, unlike recent men's fashions, owes nothing to Hollywood.

The label stuck. Rioting and violence got even worse when a year later the Bill Haley showcase *Rock Around the Clock* was released. It was at this point that the Teddy Boy began mixing Billy Haley's country look (bootlace tie, etc.) with the drape coats and drainpipe trousers. As the look grew in popularity, so did the Teds' reputation for indiscriminate violence. A group of racist West London Teds were said to have played a key role in the Notting Hill riots of 1955 when they began attacking Caribbean and Turkish shopkeepers in the area.

The jazz musician George Melly summed up the Teds' visceral revolt into style as an economic development from the thief, spiv and conman. 'They were not criminal in the old sense. They were not out for gain. On the whole, though, they were profoundly anti-social: the dark vein of pop culture, dedicated to violence, giggles and kicks.' Julien Temple, the director of the 1986 film *Absolute Beginners* (based on the novel about the Notting Hill riots) and *The Great Rock'n'Roll Swindle* of 1980, eulogised the Teds in *NME* as:

'the heirs to the spivs, an epic breed. Byronic in their scope. Most of all they frightened the establishment. They were much bigger and more dissenting than rock 'n' roll. They are a part of the despair of Britain after the hopes of the end of the war … They're like something out of the Wild West, they were villains, but really they were epic in that context.'

By the late 1950s, when Roger Daltrey was in his teens, Teddy Boys had come to be regarded as public enemy number one, a threat to the very fabric of British society. This is an irony that surely cannot have escaped the young aristocrats who adopted the look as a way of preserving all they believed to be good and wholesome about Great Britain. Neither would this be the first time working-class youth would appropriate and subvert a certain look.

1958 – 1964

3

Sparks

Pre-Who Beginnings

ABOVE Roger's band The Detours. Roger originally wanted to play guitar, but his day job as a sheet metal worker left his fingers in tatters, inadvertently turning him into a vocalist. OPPOSITE Pete, John and Roger in The Detours.

The life of a worker in a sheet metal factory in the 1950s was a hard one.

The work was monotonous, conditions were unpleasant and the hours long – a ten-hour day was not unusual, with maybe just half an hour at lunchtime to eat your sandwich. In the days before health and safety rules, sheet metal production was also not just hot, back-breaking work but often dangerous. Even a typical day could leave you with burnt and cut hands. In the evening, men would gather at the pub – often heading back there at the weekend too – and so it would go on. Their lives, like their marriages, tended to be short.

This, then, would have been Roger Daltrey's life had Elvis and Lonnie Donegan not intervened. Roger Daltrey was not the only teenager in Britain who saw in the new phenomenon of rock 'n' roll a way of escaping the daily drudgery of manual labour. According to Richard Evans, practically every kid who had seen *Rock Around the Clock* and fallen for Elvis and Buddy dreamed that rock 'n' roll would rescue them. As with so much that governed popular music back then (and for that matter still does), luck, timing and not what you know but who you know came into play.

In late 1957 the Congregational Church Hall in Churchfield Road, Acton, opened a youth club, which soon became known as the Congo Club. Here local kids were invited to take to the stage and play cover versions of tunes by Lonnie Donegan and jazz musician Acker Bilk. It was here that Pete Townshend and John Entwistle made their first public appearance playing in Pete's band, The Confederates. 'It was the only time I have ever felt nervous stepping on stage,' Pete recalls. 'I remember really blushing and there were only about five people in the audience.'

The Confederates, a trad jazz band very much in the mould of Pete's dad's band The Squadronaires, were known to be volatile, both musically and as people. John, by nature reserved, soon left and Pete was booted out after a violent confrontation with the drummer Chris Sherwin. Nonetheless Pete now had a real taste for music and performing. He also sensed, rightly, that trad jazz was on its way out. In 1958, Cliff Richard, the young British wannabe Elvis, had a huge hit with 'Move It'. It was the very first bona fide British rock 'n' roll song. What especially impressed Pete was Cliff's backing band The Shadows and their guitarist Hank Marvin. He gave up the banjo he had taught himself to play and got hold of an electric guitar that he began to teach himself.

At the same time John, who had played the clarinet, trumpet and guitar, decided to take up electric bass after hearing Duane Eddy's bass string solos. He would later tell the journalist Tony Jasper:

'I was playing the trumpet in a dance band. Playing interesting venues like Joe Lyons and social clubs. I was quite interested in playing guitar, but the guitarist kept breaking strings. I think, looking back, he must've tuned it up wrong. I had a guitar-playing friend who had an amp. He wanted me to play trumpet in his band, but when we got together he was way louder than me. So I decided to look into the guitar. It didn't work for me. The strings were too close together. The bass came much easier 'cos the strings were further apart. There were only two or three you could buy in England in those days. There was Tuxedo, Star and Lucky. They were way too expensive. I wanted a Fender, but you just couldn't get hold of them in those days. I think Jet Harris of The Shadows was the only person to have one in the whole of the UK.'

John decided to build his own bass, just as Roger had decided to build his own guitar. 'I had one made up. Same sort of shape as the Fender but not really very good at all. It had a great square back neck just glued onto the body. Quite often the glue would come unstuck and I'd end up with an instant harp.' John eventually replaced it with another cheaply made model that Pete remembers as sounding pretty good but John reckoned was 'diabolical'. Now on bass and with Pete on guitar the two played in various local bands. The most significant of these was The Scorpions, which Pete and John joined simply because the drummer Mick Brown owned a tape recorder. 'A tape recorder,' recalls Pete, 'was a very rare possession for such a young man. We used to use it for all sorts. We'd do little plays and comedies like we heard on the radio. One day Mick recorded me playing The Shadows' 'Man of Mystery' solo on an acoustic guitar. When he played it back it was the first time I had truly heard myself as a proper, real musician.'

The Scorpions rarely left the confines of Acton and so inevitably played the Congo Club. 'The Congo Club wasn't just a place where we'd go together to play and entertain,' Pete says. 'There was a lot of violence and sex and stuff going on too. We played Shadows numbers, which I know is a cliché, but that's just the way things were. There weren't really any other bands I liked. It was incredibly exciting appearing in front of an audience back then. People really did like us and that filled me with this new confidence. I got more and more into my guitar. It became truly obsessive.'

Roger Daltrey too was learning how to play his home-made guitar in his own band The Detours. And like Pete he had become obsessed with the instrument. Daltrey, inspired by skiffle and Elvis, was determined to make the band successful. He met John Entwistle carrying his home-made bass after he'd been rehearsing with The Scorpions. He invited him to a Detours rehearsal the following week. John felt very wary of Roger, who was cementing a reputation for being one of the toughest Teddy Boys in West London. Nevertheless he turned up. After John had watched the band play, Roger asked, in uncharacteristically humble fashion, 'Do you think we are any good?' John replied that he liked the band a lot, and there and then decided to leave The Scorpions and his best mate Pete.

By the beginning of 1962 The Detours comprised Roger, John, Harry Wilson and guitarists Roy Ellis and Peter James. After the band was rejected by the BBC Light Programme for 'insufficient experience', Peter James left. He was replaced by Reg Bowen, primarily because his parents allowed their house to be used as a rehearsal space. Roy Ellis had been another appointment of convenience. He was included in the band, despite his pretty terrible guitar playing, because he owned an amp. When, on 18 July 1962, Ellis drowned while swimming in the Thames, John put forward Pete as a replacement. Roger had already asked Pete to join when the two had bumped into one another on the stairs at school. Pete had been wary but keen. Like John, he was afraid of Roger, who had a reputation for fighting. In his book *Who I Am*, Pete recalled that first meeting:

'He simply informed me that John had told him I played guitar pretty well, and if an opportunity came up to join his band, was I interested? I was stunned … Judging by the faces of those around me, just the fact of Roger speaking to me meant that my life could very well change.

'As calmly as I could I told Roger I was interested. He nodded and walked away, but I wouldn't hear from him again until months later. By that time I had enrolled in Ealing Art College.'

ABOVE A very early line-up, with Roger still on guitar.

Two band impact!

TOWN HALL DANCE GALA SWINGS WITH NEW LOOK

SOFT lights, hot music, and big names brought about a "spectacular increase in attendance from the usual figure of a hundred-plus to more than 317" at the Gala Ball at the Town Hall on Saturday.

Glad to see so many stepping out on the first night of the new season was Mr. George Scott, Town Hall Entertainments Manager.

He put the success down to the two bands — the Ron Cavendish Orchestra and the "Detours" Jazz Group — which supplied music for all ages, the display by Peter Eggleton and Brenda Winslade, this year's international professional dancing champions, and the redecoration of the hall.

Licence

Six revolving lights, adding glamour to the scene in six colours, floral decorations for the stage, foyer and tables, and a licence, extending until 11.30, have all been added to ensure the success of the Council's Entertainment Committee's weekly dances and special Christmas and New Year Balls.

Attractions like Saturday's demonstration pair, who danced an encore, and the additional group which supplied the gist of the twist, are hoped to be included as often as possible.

The buffet, run by the Council Catering Committee, and the novelty and prize spots will be maintained.

The Chris Stone, Fred Hedley and Phill Spurr orchestras are among the attractions this side of Christmas.

Acton jazz and jive group, the "Detours," at last found their way to a local booking on Saturday when they were the second band at Saturday's Gala Ball at the Town Hall. Left to right : Roger Daltrey (18), Colin Dawson (19), Peter Townsend (17), Doug Sandon (18), and John Johns (17)

'I didn't learn much about art at art school, but I did learn a lot about playing guitar'

Art college was a revelation for Pete. At school he had been painfully introverted. Now he came out of his shell consciously and with a vengeance. British art schools would spawn a great many of the people behind what was initially known as 'the Beat boom'. Keith Richards, Ron Wood, David Bowie, Phil May, Ray Davies, Dick Taylor, Eric Clapton and John Lennon were all products of art school. Richards later summed up the spirit by saying, 'I didn't learn much about art at art school, but I did learn a lot about playing guitar.'

Pete also began learning about subversive forms of art. Ealing Art College often played host to controversial and subversive artists. Peter Blake, Larry Rivers, Robert Brownjohn, radical playwright David Mercer and Jasper Johns (whose pop art iconography of RAF targets and badges would later be employed by The Who to brilliant and lasting effect) all lectured there. Most significantly, in December 1962 Pete attended a lecture by the avant-garde Austrian artist Gustav Metzger entitled 'Auto-Destructive Art Auto-Creative Art', in which it was proposed that destruction, even violent destruction, can serve a high artistic purpose. A little later, at a similar event, Pete watched jazz bassist Malcolm Cecil saw a double bass to bits as part of a performance.

Pete This was a happy time for me. I was struggling at Ealing Art School with a terrible crush on a girl there, and on seeing this picture Roger's youngest sister Carol summoned me and we went out together for a while. This was the time I realised that Roger's older sister Gill and her boyfriend were proper Mods. So Roger was my first Ted, and his sister was my first Mod.

By now Pete had got in with a fellow student called Nick Bartlett who introduced him to Tom Wright and 'Cam' McLester, two Americans who were studying photography at Ealing. Tom and Cam shared a flat in Sunnyside Road and were well known for their enormous record collection, full of American R&B, jazz and blues, as well as for their fondness for marijuana. It was at Sunnyside Road that Pete first heard the blues of Lightnin' Hopkins, Howlin' Wolf, Little Walter, Jimmy Reed and the cool sounds of Mose Allison, Jimmy Smith, Julie London and Ray Charles. It was here too that Pete also heard Chuck Berry and, after Tom and Cam played him Booker T and the MGs' 'Green Onions', fell in love with Steve Cropper's way of playing lead guitar.

After Tom and Cam were deported for dealing pot, Pete and fellow art student Richard 'Barney' Barnes took over the flat in Sunnyside Road, and with it came Tom and Cam's entire record collection for their safekeeping.

At this time The Detours, whom he had just agreed to join after John had told him the band owned an amp (John: 'What I didn't tell him was that he would be sharing it with Roger'), were like a thousand other bands playing covers of Cliff Richard and The Shadows songs in matching suits. Pete had heard right – Roger did indeed 'rule the band with an iron hand'. This caused ructions within the group and frequent changes of personnel. Roger, still playing guitar, began to share the singing with Gabby Connelly, previously the bassist and singer of The Bel-Airs. However, as Daltrey's confidence grew, Gabby was eased out, even leaving his prized '61 Fender Precision to John Entwistle. John later told an interviewer, 'He [Gabby] kept the guitar hidden under his girlfriend's bed. He said I could have it if I paid off his fifty quid HP debt.' The Detours began to do rather well, getting some lucrative gigs and even opening for the likes of Screaming Lord Sutch, Cliff Bennett and Johnny Kidd & The Pirates.

Seeing Johnny Kidd & The Pirates had a huge impact on Pete. It was the first time he had ever seen or heard rhythm and blues first hand. Kidd, whose real name was Fred Heath, was Willesden born, a Londoner just like Pete, Roger, John and Keith. And yet he seemed to have an extraordinary understanding of American music. In pre-Beatles England he was, along with Cliff Richard and Lonnie Donegan, hugely important. Even now, thanks to hits like 'Shakin' All Over' and 'Please Don't Touch', he is regarded as a seminal figure.

Despite this the band stuck to their Shadows covers and, when The Beatles appeared, added their hits to their repertoire. It was around this time that Roger gave up the guitar entirely. His fingers almost permanently had cuts from the sheet metal work he did in the day, and handling the instrument became not just painful but impossible. This left Pete on guitar. For about six months the band carried on playing their Beatles covers, and building a large and loyal following. The decision to switch to rhythm and blues was Townshend's and it happened overnight.

The Detours agreed to a gig at The Oldfield, an R&B venue, as a favour to promoter Bob Druce. Roger later explained what happened to journalist Gary Herman. 'We lost all the fans we had at the time by playing blues. It took six months for them all to come back. But when they did there were twice as many of them.' By the end of 1963 The Detours were one of Bob Druce's most popular acts, playing up to five times a week and earning £12 a night. At the time this was seriously good money.

Then in December of that year The Detours supported The Rolling Stones at St Mary's Hall, Putney. The two bands were playing similar material, covering the likes of John Lee Hooker, Howlin' Wolf, Jimmy Reed and Muddy Waters. What took Pete's breath away was the way the Stones looked. They were a cocky, shambling, chicly dishevelled mess. 'I think I learned more about rock 'n' roll theatre that night than any other,' remembers Pete. 'Jagger walked on stage and was an instant star to me.' However, it was Keith Richards who would leave the most indelible impression on Pete. As the curtains were about to part for the Stones to take the stage, Pete noticed Richards stretch his arm high above his head and then swing it across his guitar as a limbering-up exercise. Pete knew instantly that this is the way he wanted to hit the strings. Very soon this exaggerated windmilling would earn him the nickname Birdman, which made a pleasant change from Nose on a Stick, which is what Roger had called him.

TO MARK RE-OPENING OF
ACTON TOWN HALL

A GALA BALL

will be held

SATURDAY NEXT. 1st SEPTEMBER
7.45 to 11.30 p.m.

THE RON CAVENDISH ORCHESTRA
and
THE DETOURS' JAZZ GROUP

Demonstration by

PETER EGGLETON and BRENDA WINSLADE

International Professional Champions 1962

Cathi Turner, who was at that St Mary's show and later followed both the Stones and The Who as a young Mod, remembers being blown away by both bands:

> 'Funny thing is,' she says, 'when you're a fan you see these bands as fully formed. That was the first time I had seen The Detours and I assumed they had always been an R&B band. As a fan you have no idea how much luck and timing come into it. Looking back, if Roger hadn't done that sheet metal job he would never have hurt his fingers, so he may never have given up the guitar, which means Pete would never have taken over. Without Pete, no R&B, no Who. You think they had it all planned, but actually they were making it up as they were going along.'

That whole generation were making it up as they went along. Inventing the look, the behaviour, the tropes, the sound and, above all, the rules of rock 'n' roll for all groups and singers for the decades that followed.

WANTED

PETE.   PETE   DOUG   ROGE   JOHN

THE
DETOURS

FOR

JIVING & TWISTING

2ᵈ REWARD!   AWAKE OR ASLEEP

WHITE HART HOTEL
ACTON
264, HIGH STREET, ACTON, W.3

JIVING & TWISTING
MONDAY
AND THURSDAY

ALSO

EXCLUSIVE SUNDAY CLUB

FEATURING

BEL-AIRS   RIVERSIDERS
FEDERALS   DETOURS   CORVETTES

7.30—11.0 p.m.   LICENSED BALLROOM BARS

Admission 3/6 (Members)   Girls 2/- before 8 p.m.

Enquiries: 3, Thorney Hedge Road, Chiswick W.4 (Taylor Entertainments)

FOX & GOOSE HOTEL
HANGER LANE, EALING. W.5
JIVING & TWISTING
FRIDAYS
FEATURING THE DYNAMIC
"DETOURS"

7.30—11.00 P.M.   4/- ADMISSION

LICENSED BALLROOM BAR

BUSES—83, 187 TO DOOR   112, 105 TWO MINUTES   TRAINS—HANGER LANE, PARK ROYAL

COMMENCING FRIDAY, 11TH JAN.

ALL The Detours pretty swiftly established themselves as a popular act in their native West London.

In the British seaside city of Brighton, the scene of so many pitched battles between Mods and Rockers, there is a pub called The Prince Albert. It's located on a narrow side street that was for many years popular with Rockers and bikers. Now it is mostly used by Brighton's large student population. Upstairs has been converted into a music venue that, though tiny, has showcased some very fine singers and bands. It is the outside of the pub that really grabs the attention. The famous British artist Banksy painted his notorious *Kissing Coppers* on this wall. Around that arresting image another artist has covered the whole side of the pub with a huge painting dedicated to rock 'n' roll's most enduring stars. Done in a style that recalls the dramatic political graffiti of terror-torn Belfast, it is a vividly colourful celebration of rock and pop's icons. Amy Winehouse, Kurt Cobain, Donna Summer, Syd Barrett, Jim Morrison, Johnny Cash, Frank Zappa, Jimi Hendrix, Dusty Springfield, Captain Beefheart, Frank Sidebottom, Sandy Denny, Joe Strummer, Ian Curtis, Bob Marley, John Peel, Mark Bolan, Michael Jackson, John Lennon, Brian Jones, Marvin Gaye, Phil Lynott, George Harrison, Elvis Presley, James Brown and Freddie Mercury stare down at you from The Albert's four-storey exterior wall.

But it's another face that your eyes are inevitably drawn to. Down on the bottom right of the mural, rising up from the pavement, is Keith Moon. It is a perfect place to put

Moon: he stands at ground level with his arms round his old drinking buddy Oliver Reed. It's quite common to see tourists leaning against the wall to have their picture taken with the infamous hell-raisers. Moon is dressed in his party attire – a black dinner jacket over a T-shirt. It's the Keith Moon of the 1970s – Moon the Loon, the Dear Boy who came single-handedly to define rock 'n' roll mayhem and who, at least for this particular graffiti artist, came to define The Who.

It's a good call. It's almost certain that, without Keith Moon, The Who would not have existed. However, at the beginning of the 1960s, the decade that would see The Beatles, The Rolling Stones and The Who dominate and redefine popular music and popular culture, Keith Moon's future did not look particularly rosy. In fact, the idea that his face would come to symbolise a band he did not found and who have outlived him by almost forty years would probably have struck him as thoroughly absurd (he did have a keen sense of the absurd). At school Moon had not just been a bad pupil, he had been laughably atrocious. If Roger Daltrey had allowed a certain very London sort of machismo to get in the way of what would have been a promising education, Moon was simply awful at studying. Harry Reed, his art teacher, wrote on his school report: 'Retarded artistically, idiotic in all other respects.' The same teacher would regularly break rulers and other pieces of art room equipment on Keith's arse in futile attempts to discipline him. And this was his art teacher. 'Comedy,' wrote his physical education teacher, 'comes before everything.' His history teacher awarded him a final year mark of five out of a hundred. Only his music teacher had anything good to say about him: 'Great ability.' But even this was qualified: 'Must guard against a tendency to show off.'

When Keith left school at fourteen he went from one dead-end job to another. He told people he was a drummer long before he owned a drum kit. He had been a bugle player in the Sea Cadets, but had moved on to the drums. But no one, including his own doting parents, believed he was any more serious about drumming than he was about any of his other whims. Nonetheless he did spend a lot of time listening and, just as importantly, watching drummers. He was especially enamoured of the flamboyant American jazz drummer Gene Krupa. Krupa, according to *Melody Maker* jazz writer and one-time percussionist Roy Carr, had turned the drums from the back line into a front-line instrument. 'When Gene played with Benny Goodman,' recalls Carr, 'people went along not so much to see Goodman as to see this matinee idol guy make the drums "talk". And that's what Moonie wanted to be – this great personality. And he achieved it.'

First, though, Keith needed a drum kit. He eventually got hold of one after meeting Gerry Evans, another working-class kid from North London who just happened to work in the drum department of Paramount music on Shaftesbury Avenue. The two boys quickly became friends, even though Gerry was aware that there was something not quite right about Moon. Gerry recalled how acutely embarrassing it was to travel to and from his North London home in the company of Keith, who would do anything to rile the respectable, besuited commuters. One particular trick of Keith's was to declare very loudly to a crowded commuter carriage that he felt sick, and then start making the most appalling guttural retching noises, sending his fellow passengers scattering as he produced a paper bag and faked vomiting into it. This was not a one-off thing – it happened every day, sometimes more than once. And yet Gerry liked Keith, who had a huge knowledge of drums and the nerdier aspects of drum kits. Eventually Gerry invited Keith to have a go on his own kit, as there was no way Paramount were going to allow this wayward boy anywhere near their stock. What he saw shocked him, as he would later tell Keith Moon's biographer Tony Fletcher:

> 'Keith … was like a madman let loose on a drum kit with no idea what he was doing. He was just hitting everything in sight, and making a load of noise. To me it was (a) the thing that you don't do, and (b) it sounded

like rubbish. It was like dealing with a madman. I was saying to him, "No, don't do all that, try and learn a paradiddle." And he wasn't having any of that. There was no way that this guy was going to be a professional drummer; it was impossible, because he didn't have a clue. He was like the worst drummer you'd ever seen in your life.'

Gerry was horrified, but he told Keith that if he was going to be a drummer he needed a kit. So with the help of his parents Keith bought a Pearl set of drums on hire purchase – a sort of rent-to-buy scheme that helped the less well-off get their hands on luxuries like television sets. The drums cost £75 and Alf Moon, Keith's dad, acted as guarantor on the HP papers. It was known as putting it on the 'never, never', since no one ever seemed to be able to pay their debt off.

A short time later a chance meeting with Carlo Little, the drummer with Wembley band The Savages, provided Keith with his first real opportunity to learn to play the instrument he'd been so long professing to love. Carlo remembers a slight boy with a cherubic face in a sharp Italian suit approach him after a gig and regale him with compliments and beg him for lessons. Carlo was initially reluctant to take Keith on, saying that not only was he not a teacher but he could probably do with some lessons himself. But Keith begged him and eventually Carlo relented. 'I can only teach you what I know,' he said by way of agreeing. 'Ten bob for thirty minutes. Wednesday at seven. Here's the address.'

Keith went for several lessons with Carlo, but as he would later tell his pal Gerry, the most important lesson he learned from The Savages' percussionist was how to deal with the bass drum. Carlo wouldn't tap the bass drum like the drummers of the time, he would hit it hard. Keith would hit it even harder. He didn't want to be The Shadows' drummer, like so many of his contemporaries. He wanted to be out front, extrovert and extreme. He wanted to emulate Carlo Little. And he was maybe the only person in the UK who wanted to emulate Carlo Little. Now all he needed was a band. The problem was that all the bands he joined were only semi-serious ventures. In 1963 he joined The Beachcombers and followed the same trail of pubs, clubs and dance-halls that were keeping The Detours (barely) afloat. The Beachcombers' other members always saw the band as an aside, a way of having fun, meeting girls and earning a few extra bob. Keith, who had spent his days in Soho with Gerry admiring gold lamé suits and talking about being a superstar, needed people more disciplined and committed than the guys he was used to playing with.

By 1964 The Detours were just such an act. They had fully committed themselves to R&B. Pete Townshend had pushed them in that direction. However, the Detours were still very much Roger's band. It was Roger who arranged the gigs, Roger who planned the act, Roger who drove the van. Roger essentially did everything. 'You gotta remember,' Daltrey would say years later, 'if Pete had been left to his own devices he would've laid in bed all day long when he was at art school. If we're honest he would've laid in bed with a joint and never made a gig. Someone had to go out and bang on the door and do all that bloody side of it, because it was unbelievable in those days. You could barely get them (the rest of the band) to carry an amplifier out. And there were no roadies, there was just me.'

Roger's drive and motivation was superficially similar to Keith Moon's: neither wanted to go from one dreary manual job to another. But, where Roger was a realist, Moon was a dreamer. Daltrey could at least hold down the job he despised. Keith could barely be bothered to turn up for the ones he so frequently left or was sacked from. He would often skip work to climb to the highest floor of the flats on Berwick Street in Soho so that he could look down over London,

picking out its landmarks, taking particular pleasure in pointing out to whoever he was with the famous London jazz club The Marquee, later to become one of London's and then the world's most famous rock 'n' roll venues. Moon would dream of playing there. Roger on the other hand actively worked to play there – and here and everywhere. 'I make no apologies for the fact that back then we wanted to be very rich and very famous.' The alternative was bleak. More hours slicing his fingers to ribbons in the sheet metal factory.

With Roger organising and Pete determined to push them creatively, The Detours were a pretty good R&B act. Which probably describes a thousand bands in London and across the UK at the time. At the beginning of 1964 a band called Johnny Devlin and The Detours appeared on the pop show

BELOW When Keith joined the band, his drumming would establish and differentiate their sound. The Mod look was the idea of Pete Meaden, an associate of The Rolling Stones manager Andrew Loog Oldham.

'What the fuck brought these four total individuals together in Greenford to play? What the fuck did that?'

Thank Your Lucky Stars, forcing John, Roger and Pete to think of a new name. It was Barney, Pete's flatmate, who came up with the name The Who, which was snappy, witty and neatly enigmatic. They had initially flirted with many names including The Hair, as the British popular press was obsessed with the length of teenagers' hair. The matter was settled the following morning when Roger came to pick Pete up and passing Barney on the stairs said, 'It's The Who, innit?'

Except it wasn't. Not quite yet. What they lacked was something to distinguish them from the crowd, from the Johnny Devlins and the Johnny-come-latelys in London's already crowded R&B scene, something that would turn them from the latest hot act (written about as 'maybe an alternative to The Beatles' in the *Acton Gazette*) into an incendiary force. What they lacked was Keith Moon. Looking back, Roger still seems surprised they ever found him. 'Whatever happened that day Keith Moon joined myself, John and Pete on stage? Something happened! There are billions of people on this planet. What the fuck brought these four total individuals together in Greenford to play? What the fuck did that?'

One of the things that helped was that The Who were forced to replace their original drummer, Doug Sandom. Dougie had been one of the reasons, maybe *the* reason that The Who had failed to impress Fontana Records when they auditioned for the label. Chris Parmeinter, Fontana's A&R man, told them that although he liked them very much he felt that with Doug being fifteen years older than the rest of the group he was far too old.

With this in mind, Pete thought it better that Doug stand down. Dougie was naturally upset by this, particularly in view of the fact that he had stuck up for Pete when at another audition the verdict had been that they should 'lose the gangly guitarist'. Roger, who was fond of Dougie, nonetheless made what was probably one of the smartest decisions he had ever made and stuck with Pete. Dougie played his last show for the band at the 100 Club on 13 April 1963. The Who then worked their way through a series of session musicians, none of whom felt right. Then, by a luck Roger considers almost cosmically ordained, Moon appeared.

Years later John Entwistle would recall how the final piece fell into place:

> 'We were playing Greenford one night with a session drummer and this bloke walks up to us and says, "My mate can play better than your drummer." So we said, "Well, let's hear him then. Bring him up." So he brought up this little ginger-bread man, and it was Keith with dyed ginger hair and a brown shirt, brown tie, brown suit, brown shoes. He got up on the kit and we said, "Can you play 'Roadrunner'?" So we played "Roadrunner" and he broke the [session] drummer's bass drum pedal and mucked up the hi-hat. And we thought, "Yeah, this is the fella."'

Keith Moon changed everything. 'From the moment we found Keith it was a complete turning point,' recalls Pete. 'He was so assertive and confident. Before then we'd just been fooling around.'

The Mods Revolt Into Style

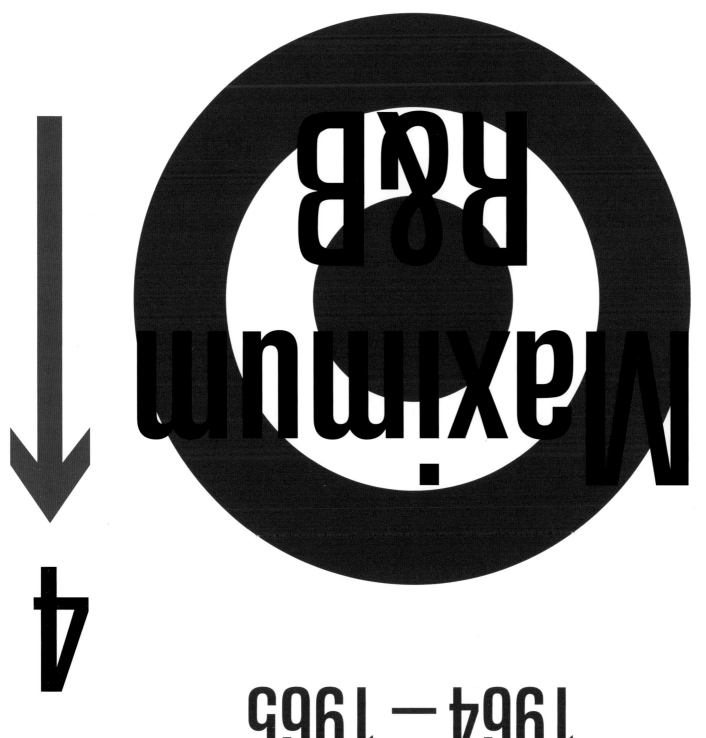

Maximum R&B

4

1964 – 1965

Finding Keith Moon had been, to paraphrase Roger, a one in a billion chance.

Now The Who would be picked up by one of rock 'n' roll's forgotten svengalis, Pete Meaden. Currently they were being managed by the well-meaning but ultimately hopeless Helmut Gordon, who referred to the band as 'my little diamonds' – 'Pete Meaden came in as their publicist. At just nineteen Meaden had helped Andrew Loog Oldham with The Rolling Stones' marketing; now he was after an act he could mould and call his own. Bright, tough and a natural-born hustler, Meaden had watched with interest as a Soho-based, highly elitist scene developed into a full-blown youth subculture. The Mods, originally The Modernists thanks to their love of American jazz and Italian suits, were by 1964 well on their way to becoming as notorious as the Teds. Mod had its own music (Tamla Motown, American R&B, West Indian Blue Beat), its own transport (Italian motor scooters), its own drugs (black bombers, purple hearts and any other amphetamine and derivative of Drinamyl that would facilitate a sleepless weekend of dancing) and its own look. If Teddy Boys had been flamboyant, Mods were at times flamboyant, at others coolly understated but always obsessive. Three years before his death in 1978 Pete Meaden gave an interview to Steve Turner of the *NME*, in which he delivered the near-legendary quote, 'Modism, Mod living, is an aphorism for clean living under difficult circumstances.' Mods, largely working class and originally from the poorer areas of London, dressed in Levis with a turn-up to show the red selvedge, Italian cycling shirts, British Fred Perry tennis shirts (the distinctive Laurel logo has become synonymous with the scene), sharp, tight, tailor-made suits, Madras cotton jackets, bowling shoes and expensive brogues. It was a scene devoted to detail and minutiae. As the journalist and chronicler of Mod Paolo Hewitt would say many years later, 'Anyone can wear a shirt, but deciding upon the right amount of buttons on the cuff and the height of the collar, that takes thought and style.' For the serious Mod, God and the Devil were all in the detail.

The look, highly idiosyncratic, sometimes androgynous (plenty of male Mods wore eyeliner, to the horror of their parents, teachers and workmates), clashed with the more reactionary style it superseded – that of the leather-clad Rocker still in thrall to Bill Haley, Elvis and Americana. Pretty soon a clash of styles turned into physical clashes as Mods and Rockers up and down the country used bank holiday weekends to beat merry hell out of one another on the beaches of Britain's seaside resorts. Tabloid headlines generated a moral panic that in turn generated more headlines. Holiday-makers' fears that their weekend would be disrupted by gangs became a self-fulfilling prophesy. To Pete Meaden all this was gold.

In 1974, ten years after Mods dominated the headlines, Meaden explained his logic to the journalist and publicist Barbara Charone. 'I had this dream of getting a group together that would be the focus, the entertainers for the Mods. They would be a group that would be the same people in the audience.' In 1971 Pete Townshend, by then in the grip of Eastern mysticism, acknowledged the impact the scene had on him.

'It was a great show of solidarity. You felt like you belonged to something. This was when I first became aware of the force of rock as a reflection of what was going on in the streets. But we, The Who, were never in any danger of getting obsessed with the Mod image, because we were not so much a part of it as a mirror. When we were on stage we reflected the mood of the kids and caught their frustration and aggression.'

ABOVE The Mod-thug look has never been bettered.

Roger Daltrey offers a more sanguine explanation. 'He [Meaden] didn't have to force his ideas on us very hard. He thought he could pick up on the Mod thing 'cos the Mods had no focal point at all. And The Who became that, even though we were a bit old.' Roger was just twenty, Pete and John were nineteen and Keith was seventeen. Entwistle, the least keen of The Who to embrace the new look, remembers Meaden taking them to have their hair cut, then dragging them round Carnaby Street kitting them out in skating jackets, tight T-shirts, Levis with huge selvedge-revealing turn-ups and boxing boots. 'I walked through a puddle in my boxing boots and the soles fell off. I think I only wore that bloody skating jacket once.' For all of John's reservations, the move was a smart one.

Meaden now decided the band needed to change their name. He wanted something that would represent the hedonism and aggression of the working-class Mod. 'We're all into pills, into a bit of pot, and we're hip and we dress hip,' he announced to the band, drunk on the image he was creating. 'We are going to be called The High Numbers.' At the time 'number' was slang for a regular working-class Mod. High was self-explanatory. The one and only record released by The High Numbers is the single 'Zoot Suit', with 'I'm the Face' on the B-side. Both songs were composed by Pete Meaden; 'Zoot Suit' borrowed heavily from 'Misery' by The Dynamics, and 'I'm the Face' was influenced by 'I Got Love If You Want It' by Slim Harpo. A Face on the Mod scene was a leader. Zoot suit referred to clothes (some) Mods wore. Meaden simply could not get enough of signposting the band's allegiance to the Mod subculture. He hustled features in *Record Mirror, Fabulous* and *Boyfriend,* in which Pete, Roger, John and Keith would appear in boating jackets, boxing boots and anything else that screamed MOD!

Despite all this effort, the single sold a dismal 500 copies, with one copy being bought by John Entwistle's gran and at least 10 per cent of the records being bought by Meaden himself in a crazy attempt to help the single into the charts. Meaden's blatant opportunism had been seen for exactly that. Mods liked subtlety and hidden signals. Meaden's bull-headed approach offered the exact opposite. The group, crestfallen after the humiliation of 'Zoot Suit', were on the verge of breaking up or going part-time. Nonetheless Meaden carried on pushing. He convinced Pete to drop some of the band's best-known numbers and replace them with covers of songs by Marvin Gaye, The Temptations, Martha and the Vandellas and The Miracles. Although it seems extraordinary now, Tamla Motown was not, outside of Mod circles, well known in the UK. The choice of music got the band a decent and growing crowd. Thanks to gigging, the band were known. In West London they had played The Railway Hotel, St Mary's Hall, The Oldfield and, most vitally, The Goldhawk Social Club, 205 Goldhawk Road, either as The Detours or The Who. The Social Club was a Mod mecca. Now what they needed was decent management.

ABOVE John and Pete rehearsing. **OPPOSITE** Pete Meaden believed that the Mod scene needed a band as a focal point, and to push the point home he changed The Who's name to The High Numbers, which is Mod street argot meaning both a top Mod and a Mod on amphetamines. The High Numbers' first single was 'I'm the Face', a Face being a known top Mod.

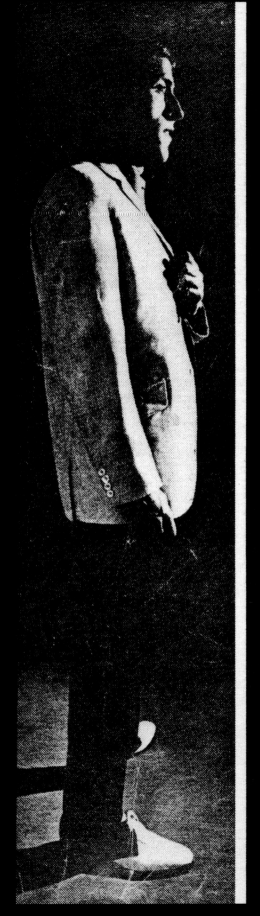

on their first disc outing,

four hip young men

from london say:

i'm the face

and wear:

zoot suit

(the first <u>authentic</u> mod record)

the four hip young men?

the high numbers

fontana t f 480
release date july 3rd 1964

LEFT John, Roger, Keith and Pete. An early publicity shot of a properly Modded-up Who back when they were still The High Numbers. **BELOW** Keith, double trouble.

On a hot July night, a twenty-nine-year-old film director called Christopher 'Kit' Lambert was driving past The Railway Hotel in Harrow, North London, where The High Numbers happened to be playing. He saw a large group of kids spilling out of the pub doors and sitting on scooters outside. He stopped his car and crossed the street to investigate. He would later tell the author George Tremlett that this was a Damascene moment. 'The atmosphere in there was fantastic. The room was black and hot. Steaming hot. And the audience seemed hypnotised by the wild music and the feedback Pete Townshend was already producing with his guitar and amplifier.' Lambert immediately rang his business partner Chris Stamp and told him he had at last found a band worthy of a film.

Mod had its uber-Mods, known as 'Faces'. These were the fellers with the best taste and the best looks. One such was Chris Stamp, the son of an East End barge owner and the younger brother of the actor Terence Stamp. Chris had for most of his teens been a street fighter until his brother managed to get him a job clearing scenery at the ballet – he

lured Chris in by promising that this would be the easiest way to meet pretty girls. Chris instantly fell in love with classical music. It was through this that he had met Kit Lambert.

Lambert could not have been any more different to Stamp. Rich and cultured – he was the son of the famous British composer Constant Lambert – he was also openly gay. In the documentary *Lambert and Stamp*, Chris Stamp tells the film-maker James D. Cooper that they were both outsiders. 'We both felt marginalised, me through my class, him through his gayness.'

The two outsiders were utterly convinced that the film industry would never have anything to do with them, and so they determined to make films of their own. Pop and Mod were news at the time – the biggest news. So for some time now the hugely posh Lambert and the Cockney barrow boy Chris Stamp had been looking for a group to make a documentary film about, but all the ones they'd liked were already too successful and therefore too costly.

The room was black and hot. Steaming hot. And the audience seemed hypnotised by the wild music

Currently creating a storm in London's "Scene" club on Wednesday nights are the HIGH NUMBERS, the first really mod group to hit the group scene. The boys have been the centre of interest for pressmen and agents for several weeks since their sensational debut at the "Scene" club, in Ham Yard off Great Windmill Street in the heart of London's Soho. The High Numbers have been signed up by Arthur Howes and Jimmy O'Day for a series of Sunday dates starting on August 9 at Brighton Hippodrome where they will be appearing with Gerry and The Pacemakers. Other dates so far negotiated include the Blackpool Opera House with the Beatles on August 16, and Kelvin Hall Glasgow with the Animals and the Yardbirds on September 4. An autumn tour for the boys is being planned but the High Numbers will be playing at the "Scene" on Wednesday nights for the next three months. Their disc "I'm The Face" was last week given a Top Fifty Tip by RM Pop Jury. (RM pic Bill Williams).

ALL The High Numbers quickly acquired the devoted Mod following Pete Meaden had hoped they would.

Even with a flop behind them The High Numbers were attracting crowds, thanks perhaps to their new repertoire of Tamla hits. And the right sort of crowds too – young, hip, druggy and dangerous. Stamp flew back from Ireland and went to see the band at Watford Trade Hall. Like Kit he was totally blown away. In 1966 he told *The Observer:* 'The first time I saw them I was knocked out. But the excitement I felt wasn't coming from the group. I couldn't get anywhere near them. The excitement was coming from the people blocking my way.' The High Numbers were now one of the best-known bands in West London.

Stamp and Lambert agreed that The High Numbers would be their first subject as film-makers. They would make a documentary about the band that would chart their progress from obscurity to success. But the more they thought about it, the more they were convinced they could actually help create that success. They consulted with The Beatles' lawyer David Jacobs, who told them that The High Numbers could break their contract if they personally approached him.

The violence struck genuine fear into the heart of Middle England

In August 1964, after some predictable legal wrangling, The High Numbers signed an agreement with Chris Stamp and Kit Lambert's New Action Management. Helmut Gorden fumed about losing his little diamonds' and even went on to sue the original solicitor who had drawn up the first contract. But for all his foot stamping he had lost the band. Kit and Chris, meanwhile, had never managed anyone in their lives. Nonetheless, this weird partnership between East End wide boy and urbane-public-school-educated English gent would prove invaluable when managing a band as volatile and as replete with huge and competing personalities as The High Numbers.

Pete, Roger, Keith and John had, in many ways, landed on their feet. However the deal they signed was, even by the rotten, rapacious standards of the time, astonishingly awful. Management got 40 per cent of all earnings, with the remaining 60 per cent split four ways. In addition they were paid the fixed sum of £1,000 a year each. But this almost didn't matter, because their new management really seemed to love and understand the band. Kit and Chris, soon to be joined by Chris's Mod mate Bill Curbishley, were true fans. The only thing they didn't like was the name, The High Numbers, which they regarded as crassly obvious and restrictive. Kit thought it sounded like a bingo hall. So for the third time that year the band were asked to change their name. They reverted to The Who. Now everything was in place.

Four months earlier, in April 1964, one of the most seismic events in British youth culture took place. On Whitsun bank holiday weekend, Mods clashed with Rockers on the streets and beaches of Brighton, Margate, Southend and indeed, practically every other British seaside resort. The incident was reported in every British newspaper and became one of the most notorious incidents of hooliganism in UK history. Named 'The Battle of Brighton' by the tabloids, the weekend was immortalised fifteen years later in the centrepiece to the movie *Quadrophenia*, which turned The Who's opera into a super-stylish, post-punk, kitchen-sink rock odyssey. At the time, though, it would be no exaggeration to say that the violence struck genuine fear into the heart of Middle England. The *Daily Mirror* reported it thus: 'The bank holiday began with tourists flocking to the coast but ended with them fleeing for their lives as Mods and Rockers turned beaches into battlefields.'

ABOVE Pete looking an awful lot like Jimmy, the Mod anti-hero he would create nearly ten years later and who would be immortalised by Phil Daniels in the film *Quadrophenia*. **OPPOSITE** In the wake of the Mod movement, riots swept across Britain's seaside resorts, as Mods and Rockers fought on beaches and in coffee bars and outside dance halls. **OVERLEAF LEFT** Brighton, 1965. **OVERLEAF RIGHT** Margate, 1964.

DAILY SKETCH

Monday, May 18, 1964   Price Threepence   ✦✦✦   WEATHER: Sunny and warm

'FOUR POLICEMEN INJURED AS 2,000 BOYS AND GIRLS BATTLE ALONG DREAMLAND RESORT'S MARINE PARADE

36 ARRESTS IN NEW MOD v ROCKER RIOT

Another sizzler today

3-11-6
15-0
16-6
10-0
5-0-8

KEEP your sun hats on today. It's going to be another scorcher.

Forecast for most areas: Mainly dry, with long periods of sunshine.

This follows the warmest Whit Sunday since 1960. South Coast resorts basked in the seventies, and in London it reached 72 degrees.

Bournemouth topped the resorts' sunshine league with 13.9 hours.

Packed

The sunshine brought out 9,000,000 vehicles — the AA said that roads in the South-East were like "seething car conveyor belts."

Crowded Southend turned away coachloads of trippers in the afternoons.

And Brighton was so packed that hundreds of visitors camped out last night in tents and cars in the roads and on roadside verges.

ROAD TOLL RISES—SEE BACK PAGE.

By JAMES LAING

TWO thousand teenage troublemakers turned the Dreamland seaside town of Margate, Kent, into a nightmare yesterday.

They fought police, smashed windows, overturned kiosks and hurled bottles and deckchairs in a Clacton-type invasion.

By midnight 36 had been arrested. Four policemen—two constables, an inspector and a sergeant—were injured in the fighting.

QUOTE by a police spokesman: "These youngsters are just being very stupid. And a big nuisance."

AT BRIGHTON rival teenage gangs fought on the seafront. Several youths were taken to hospital with cuts.

Back to Margate . . . and no day trippers left a fresh row flared.

BOTTLE THROWER

Teenagers moved along the front, shouting, hand-clapping and beating out a rhythm on litter bins with wood from hundreds of shattered deckchairs.

Police reinforcements broke up the mob.

One policeman grabbed a youth who had thrown a bottle at a police van and commandeered a taxi for his arrest.

Earlier I saw mothers lift babies from their prams to protect them.

Older children screamed as they became caught up in fights.

Extra police were rushed to Margate from all over East Kent.

FIRST CLASH . . .

Violence followed violence—and this was the time-table.

IN THE EARLY HOURS the teenagers arrived.

AT 7 a.m. fights began when the "Mods" descended on 100 "Rockers" on the beach.

The "Rockers" fled.

AT 10 a.m. came the first clash with police when the "Mods" tried to climb railings on to the mile-long Marine Parade.

Police ordered them back.

Stones and deckchairs were thrown—and it was **► Back Page**

Two girls fight on the ground as other teenagers watch, grinning. This was just one incident among many when the "Mods" clashed with the "Rockers" at Margate yesterday. It was a day of violence in the sun . . . and frightened day trippers went home early.

Fifty years later the *Mirror* revisited the day:

'In the spring of 1964, simmering rivalry between the groups reached a flashpoint as they clashed repeatedly on seaside piers and promenades across the country. But the worst of the violence was seen in Brighton, as families were trapped in a shocking showdown that sparked moral panic about the state of British youth. Tony Edwards was eighteen and one of the first band of Mods to arrive on the Sussex coast that day. He says: "The Rockers had outnumbered us for years but leading up to 1964 we'd grown in numbers – now it was payback time.

"When we arrived on the beach there were just a few Mods and a big group of Rockers in the middle. Within about 90 minutes the beach filled up with hundreds of Mods.

"Then someone on our side threw a pebble at them and within a few seconds they were just being blitzed. I saw one guy who'd been cut on the head with blood running down his face.

"In the end the police had to charge on to the beach and escort this group of Rockers off the seafront, which must have been humiliating. They were tough men and we were just little kids poncing around in fancy clothes.

"But we weren't going to take their crap any more. It was the holidaymakers I felt sorry for. They looked terrified."'

A month after the Battle of Brighton, Townshend did something at The Railway Hotel in Harrow that inadvertently captured the nihilistic spirit of the fights between the Mods and the Rockers, something that would become one of rock 'n' roll's most enduring tropes. The moment is so important that Pete begins his autobiography with a vivid recollection of the night it happened.

Pete Townshend opens his autobiography with a description of one of the most famous, some would say notorious, shows The Who have ever played. At The Railway Hotel in front of sweating gangs of pilled-up Mods they are playing a series of R&B classics – 'Smokestack Lightning', 'I'm a Man', 'Road Runner'. Pete is running his guitar up and down the mic stand producing wave after wave of feedback. Inadvertently, he thrusts the instrument into the low ceiling, ripping off its head. 'It is at this moment that I make a split-second decision – and in a mad frenzy I thrust the damaged guitar up into the ceiling over and over again. What had been a clean break becomes a splintered mess. I hold the guitar up to the crowd triumphantly. I haven't smashed it: I've sculpted it for them.'

It would be the first of many, many times The Who would smash their instruments. It was destruction as creation. 'That Tuesday night,' writes Pete, 'I stumbled upon something more powerful than words, far more emotive than my white-boy attempts to play the blues. And in response I received the full-throated salute of the crowd.' Whether it was a Dadaist statement or a tribute to Pete's art school hero Gustav Metzger, it was for the crowd unimportant. They loved the visceral nihilism, the anger, the musical expression of their frustrations. 'A week or so later, at the same venue, I ran out of guitars and toppled the stack of Marshall amplifiers. Not one to be upstaged, our drummer Keith Moon joined in by kicking over his drum kit. Roger started to scrape his microphone on Keith's cracked cymbals.' Destruction became The Who's signature. So much so that Pete was unbothered when some labelled it a gimmick. Pete knew he was sending out a message. The message made The Who instantly memorable, instantly infamous, instantly The Who.

ALL Pete smashing his guitar. For him it was an act both of defiance and artistic independence. For many onlookers it simply looked like yobbery and nihilism. The effect would be the same, turning The Who into one of the most notorious and feared rock 'n' roll acts in Britain.

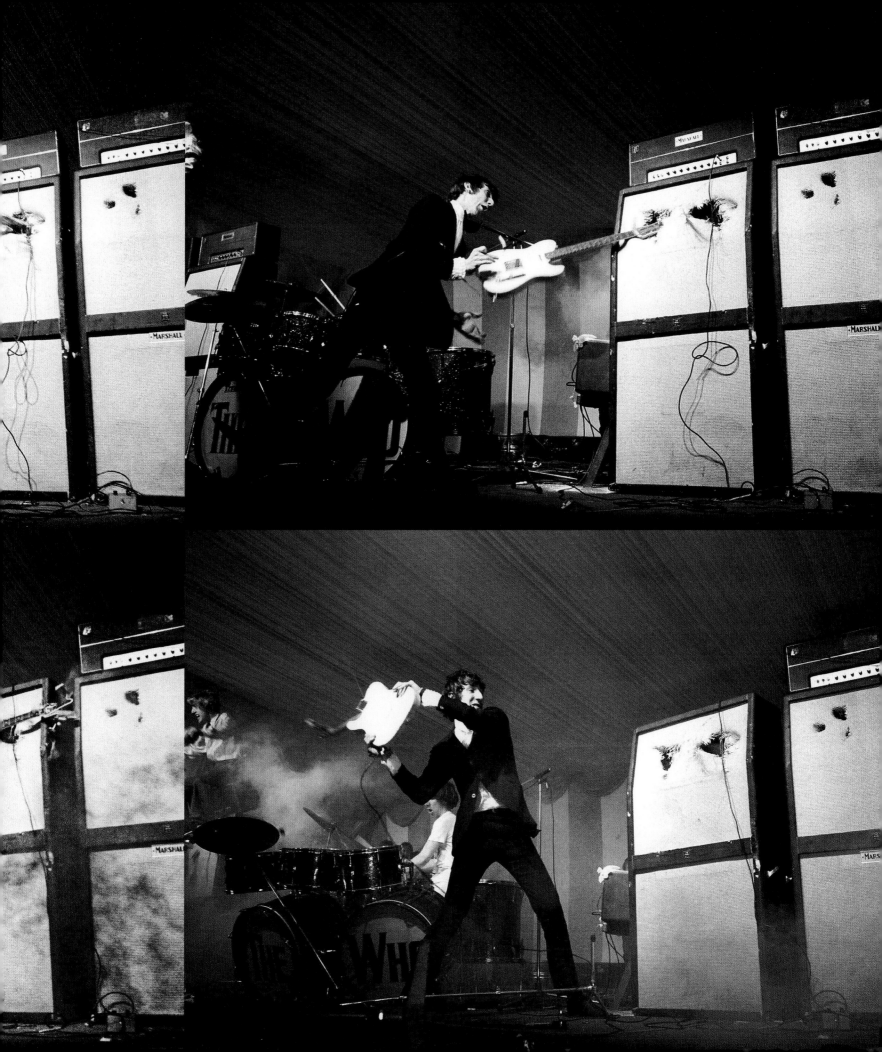

Witness to this was Kit Lambert. The sight of a young band destroying their equipment in front of gangs of sweating, pilled-up Mods would have shocked anyone. It would shock anyone now. In 1964 it didn't just look destructive – it looked suicidal. Kit was aghast. However, on the London Mod scene word spread fast that The Who ended shows by destroying their instruments. At The Who's next show a huge crowd turned up for a repeat performance. When Pete failed to oblige, the young Keith Moon wrecked his kit. Lambert's initial horror – aesthetic, moral and financial (how were they going to replace this stuff?) – was quite suddenly replaced by the realisation that there was a huge demand for destruction. Be it on the beaches of Brighton or in the venues of North London.

Kit and Chris Stamp set to work trying to sell the energy and dynamism of their band. They employed Brian Pike, an old advertising associate of Kit's. Pike came up with one of the most striking posters ever designed. The Maximum R&B poster was designed specifically for The Who's Tuesday night residency at The Marquee Club, which began in November 1964. A stark, high contrast black-and-white

photograph of the stick-thin Townshend, arm held aloft nanoseconds after hitting a power chord, was placed next to the band's name – and 'The Who' featured an arrow extending from the 'O' in imitation of the biological symbol for male. The poster was capped off by the slogan 'Maximum R&B', a phrase invented by Lambert. It is hard to think of any artwork before or after that so accurately and economically expresses the spirit of a band, and it has subsequently become one of the most iconic images in the history of rock 'n' roll.

ABOVE The Who would often play two shows a night. Here they are in Stevenage, 1966. **OPPOSITE** One of the most famous rock 'n' roll gig posters in history, printed to advertise The Who's residency at The Marquee Club.

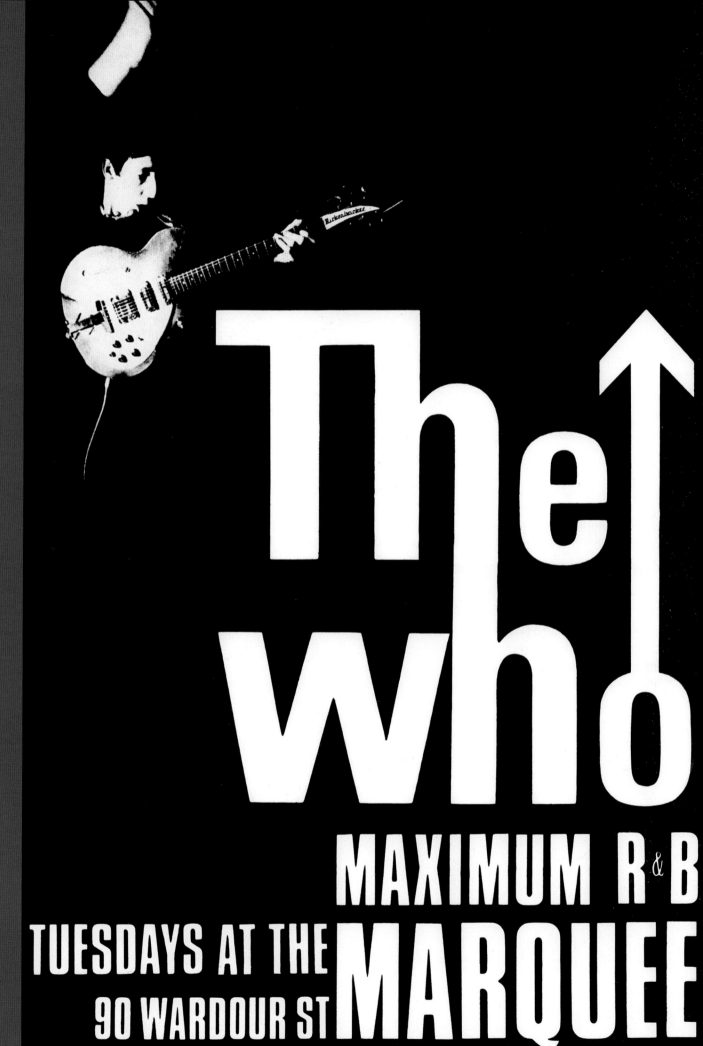

BELOW Chris Stamp (left), Kit Lambert (right). **OPPOSITE BELOW** The Who recruited many of their most fanatical followers from the Goldhawk Social Club. Many of the top Mods who would later crowd out their Marquee residency came from there.

Pete Very few pictures of Kit ... he was often laughing.

Pete Good photo of me. One of us looks like a Mod and it isn't any of the others.

Lambert and Stamp then spent £300 printing up 1,500 fly-posters and 2,500 handbills to be distributed around London pubs and clubs. They also set up a 'secret society' of One Hundred Faces (top-boy Mods), which they recruited from the band's hardcore Goldhawk Social Club following, with the most influential receiving free tickets and the others getting half-price admission. Within just three weeks the group's Tuesday night residency at The Marquee Club (then still nominally a jazz club, but thanks to The Who and the Stones it was to become a byword for ground-breaking rock 'n' roll) had broken all attendance records. The Who were getting bigger crowds than Manfred Mann and The Yardbirds. Lambert and Stamp also encouraged The Who into playing the Red Lion in Leytonstone, in London's East End. Mod was now a solidly working-class movement, and the solidly working-class East End practically ranked as a Mod ghetto. And yet The Who still didn't have a record deal.

At the tail-end of 1964 The Who recorded 'I Can't Explain' with producer Shel Talmy. Like so many debut records of the time there were a whole bunch of session musicians on hand, the assumption being that young bands simply didn't know how to play. Talmy says that having seen The Who play in Shepherd's Bush he wanted the band's studio sound to be as close as possible to their live sound.

When the band arrived at Pye Studios they were a little miffed to discover that Jimmy Page, later of Led Zeppelin, was there to play lead guitar. In 1971 Townshend said, 'He [Jimmy] nearly played the solo on the A-side, but it was so simple even I could play it.' The B-side, 'Bald Headed Woman', featured Page's fretwork after he refused to let Pete use his Roger Mayer-patented fuzz box. Things were in some ways even tougher for Roger. For some time he had been working his voice up to sound as soulful and raw as possible, imitating his heroes James Brown and Howlin' Wolf. In the studio he was asked to deliver a far poppier, less acerbic vocal. 'That was painful for me. It was a different style of singing and I had to entirely reinvent myself vocally.'

Kit Lambert and Chris Stamp knew they had one of the most volatile and unorthodox bands on their hands. As film-makers they also knew they had one of Britain's most visual acts. Their aim now was to get The Who on *Ready Steady Go!* Since its first screening in August 1963, *RSG!* had established a reputation as the smartest, most stylish and visually innovative pop show on TV. The spirit of *Ready Steady Go!* was embodied by its host, the young, beautiful and irrepressible Cathy McGowan. Two years older than Pete Townshend, and dubbed 'Queen of the Mods' by the press and 'the girl of the day' by The Animals' Eric Burdon, a good deal of McGowan's appeal lay in the fact that she was the age of *RSG!*'s viewers. Young girls loved her looks and saw her as a role model, and young boys fancied her.

Lesley Hornby, who a little later as Twiggy became arguably the world's first supermodel, saw McGowan as a trailblazer: 'I'd sit and drool over her clothes. She was a heroine to us because she was one of us.' Anna Wintour, the future editor of American *Vogue*, was, according to her biographer Jerry Oppenheimer, one of the thousands of teenagers whom the show introduced to fashion. *Ready Steady Go!* was the perfect fit for The Who, because just like Cathy McGowan the band were an idealised, hyper-real version of their fans, a posterised, cathode-ray distorting mirror that reflected back only what was young, rebellious, stylish and, to an appalled older generation, utterly incomprehensible.

Lambert knew *RSG!*'s producer, Robert Bickford, a former *Daily Mail* record reviewer. On 29 January 1965 The Who made their first appearance on the show. A few days earlier Lambert had scoured The Marquee Club for the best-looking Mods and most-devoted fans of the group. On the day of transmission the studio was swamped by Who fans. The effect was dramatic; The Who looked like they had their own Mod army. Kit now put all his efforts into getting The Who played on Radio Caroline, the offshore pirate station. Chris Stamp bombarded the station with calls. He knew the station's founder, Ronan O'Rahilly. Ronan also ran The Scene Club in Ham Yard, a popular Mod club where The Who often played. Chris Stamp, the London wide boy that he was, believed in 'having an in', and Ronan was his in. He demanded The Who be played. Finally 'I Can't Explain' broke into the UK top ten and by April of that year had made it to No. 8.

ABOVE The Who on the hugely innovative *Ready Steady Go!* – Britain's top pop show. **OPPOSITE** John and Pete with *Ready Steady Go!* presenter Cathy McGowan, also known as Queen of the Mods. **OVERLEAF** 'Arrived twenty-five minutes late … ponderous and unentertaining…' The BBC's very snooty, disapproving audition report on the behaviour of The Who. Not everyone at the Beeb was quite so negative, as one person wrote, 'The lead singer has personality', and another described them with the faintest of praise as 'reasonably efficient'.

Lambert and Stamp then spent £300 printing up 1,500 fly-posters and 2,500 handbills to be distributed around London pubs and clubs. They also set up a 'secret society' of One Hundred Faces (top-boy Mods), which they recruited from the band's hardcore Goldhawk Social Club following, with the most influential receiving free tickets and the others getting half-price admission. Within just three weeks the group's Tuesday night residency at The Marquee Club (then still nominally a jazz club, but thanks to The Who and the Stones it was to become a byword for ground-breaking rock 'n' roll) had broken all attendance records. The Who were getting bigger crowds than Manfred Mann and The Yardbirds. Lambert and Stamp also encouraged The Who into playing the Red Lion in Leytonstone, in London's East End. Mod was now a solidly working-class movement, and the solidly working-class East End practically ranked as a Mod ghetto. And yet The Who still didn't have a record deal.

At the tail-end of 1964 The Who recorded 'I Can't Explain' with producer Shel Talmy. Like so many debut records of the time there were a whole bunch of session musicians on hand, the assumption being that young bands simply didn't know how to play. Talmy says that having seen The Who play in Shepherd's Bush he wanted the band's studio sound to be as close as possible to their live sound.

When the band arrived at Pye Studios they were a little miffed to discover that Jimmy Page, later of Led Zeppelin, was there to play lead guitar. In 1971 Townshend said, 'He [Jimmy] nearly played the solo on the A-side, but it was so simple even I could play it.' The B-side, 'Bald Headed Woman', featured Page's fretwork after he refused to let Pete use his Roger Mayer-patented fuzz box. Things were in some ways even tougher for Roger. For some time he had been working his voice up to sound as soulful and raw as possible, imitating his heroes James Brown and Howlin' Wolf. In the studio he was asked to deliver a far poppier, less acerbic vocal. 'That was painful for me. It was a different style of singing and I had to entirely reinvent myself vocally.'

Pete I remember this. It was in a record store in Shepherd's Bush Market, our very first publicity shoot I think, organised by the record company.

Given the demands on Roger, and Pete's suspicion of the hired session musicians, it is amazing how staggeringly raw, self-assured and infectious 'I Can't Explain' is. The song's opening, brilliantly insistent riff, apparently an abortive attempt by Pete to rip off The Kinks' 'All Day and All of the Night', later inspired, among others, The Clash for their single 'Clash City Rockers'. 'I Can't Explain' remains one of the greatest and most imitated songs in pop history. The song is ranked No. 9 on *Pitchfork Media*'s list of the '200 Greatest Songs of the 1960s', No. 59 on *Spin*'s list of the '100 Greatest Singles of All Time' and No. 371 on *Rolling Stone*'s list of the '500 Greatest Songs of All Time'. Not bad for a record that took just over two hours to record.

Oddly, Pete seemed entirely unbothered by the notion that The Who were being fashioned into a pop band. 'From my point of view, when British kids who were in bands got into R&B, what they discovered was a new way to write pop songs that was entirely and purely British.' This has been true of so much British pop. Take an American idea, get it slightly wrong and sell it back to America. The Who and the Stones did this with R&B. The Sex Pistols and The Clash with punk rock. The Prodigy with house music. Pete Townshend, always participant, observer and chronicler, perhaps saw this more clearly than any of his contemporaries.

In December 1964 'I Can't Explain' was released on Decca Records in the US. A month later it came out in the UK on Brunswick Records thanks to deals hastily negotiated by Lambert and Stamp. In February the single charted in the UK at No. 45 and by April had broken into the top ten, getting as high as No. 8. In the US, where Decca remained alarmingly clueless about pop, R&B and rock 'n' roll, the single barely made the *Billboard* top 100, charting at No. 93.

'I Can't Explain' was to be the first of a string of UK pop hits for The Who, each more audacious than the last, each playing not just with sound but with the social dynamics of rock 'n' roll – its look, its power to rouse and offend, its ability to create schisms, even its ability to transcend the ephemeral, to aspire to the status of art. That, at the time, wasn't just audacious, it was positively insolent. But Pete the art school student, now teemed with the cerebral Kit Lambert, was already beginning to see things that way.

Each more audacious than the last, each playing not just with sound but with the social dynamics of rock 'n' roll

Kit Lambert and Chris Stamp knew they had one of the most volatile and unorthodox bands on their hands. As film-makers they also knew they had one of Britain's most visual acts. Their aim now was to get The Who on *Ready Steady Go!* Since its first screening in August 1963, *RSG!* had established a reputation as the smartest, most stylish and visually innovative pop show on TV. The spirit of *Ready Steady Go!* was embodied by its host, the young, beautiful and irrepressible Cathy McGowan. Two years older than Pete Townshend, and dubbed 'Queen of the Mods' by the press and 'the girl of the day' by The Animals' Eric Burdon, a good deal of McGowan's appeal lay in the fact that she was the age of *RSG!*'s viewers. Young girls loved her looks and saw her as a role model, and young boys fancied her.

Lesley Hornby, who a little later as Twiggy became arguably the world's first supermodel, saw McGowan as a trailblazer: 'I'd sit and drool over her clothes. She was a heroine to us because she was one of us.' Anna Wintour, the future editor of American *Vogue*, was, according to her biographer Jerry Oppenheimer, one of the thousands of teenagers whom the show introduced to fashion. *Ready Steady Go!* was the perfect fit for The Who, because just like Cathy McGowan the band were an idealised, hyper-real version of their fans, a posterised, cathode-ray distorting mirror that reflected back only what was young, rebellious, stylish and, to an appalled older generation, utterly incomprehensible.

Lambert knew *RSG!*'s producer, Robert Bickford, a former *Daily Mail* record reviewer. On 29 January 1965 The Who made their first appearance on the show. A few days earlier Lambert had scoured The Marquee Club for the best-looking Mods and most-devoted fans of the group. On the day of transmission the studio was swamped by Who fans. The effect was dramatic; The Who looked like they had their own Mod army. Kit now put all his efforts into getting The Who played on Radio Caroline, the offshore pirate station. Chris Stamp bombarded the station with calls. He knew the station's founder, Ronan O'Rahilly. Ronan also ran The Scene Club in Ham Yard, a popular Mod club where The Who often played. Chris Stamp, the London wide boy that he was, believed in 'having an in', and Ronan was his in. He demanded The Who be played. Finally 'I Can't Explain' broke into the UK top ten and by April of that year had made it to No. 8.

ABOVE The Who on the hugely innovative *Ready Steady Go!* – Britain's top pop show. **OPPOSITE** John and Pete with *Ready Steady Go!* presenter Cathy McGowan, also known as Queen of the Mods. **OVERLEAF** 'Arrived twenty-five minutes late … ponderous and unentertaining…' The BBC's very snooty, disapproving audition report on the behaviour of The Who. Not everyone at the Beeb was quite so negative, as one person wrote, 'The lead singer has personality', and another described them with the faintest of praise as 'reasonably efficient'.

BRIERS
FINANCIAL TIMES
PRESENT
VERY
COMIC
THE GUARDIAN
Directed by

RECORDED ON: FRIDAY, 12th FEBRUARY, 1965   Producer in Charge: ROGER PUSEY

HEARD BY TALENT SELECTION GROUP: MONDAY, 15th February, 1965

ITEMS: "Baby Don't You Do It Now"; "Luby Come Home"; "Shout and Shimmy".

INSTRUMENTATION: Lead Guitarist/Leader; Bass Guitar; Drums; Vocalist/Harmonica.

The first two members of this group arrived 25 minutes late.
Quite co-operative once started but not endowed with much sense
of urgency. A rather thumping R & B sound. The lead vocalist
seemed quite "with it" in the R&B field although the voice
quality was harsh and rather unpleasant. Backing not so good
although lead guitar seemed to be more sure of himself than the
rest. Overall not very original and below standard.

NO

The instrumental party of the group provides a good driving
sound. I think the lead voice is quite presentable but the
backing voices less good. In all a pleasant and commercial
sound, which with more rehearsal and experience would have my
YES.

YES

A slightly above average R & B group. Although not all that
outstanding, the vocalist was good for this type of material
with plenty of personality. Instrumentally they were all quite
adequate and with slightly more suitable material could be useful.
A border-line pass.

YES

A good R & B group, the lead singer has personality - the sort of
group that with the right material and production could very
easily make a hit, a well rehearsed competent group.

YES

Ponderous and unentertaining for me. Reasonably efficient, but
to the limit of their capabilities, which makes them not good
enough. Too many unpleasant sounds that lack atmosphere, despite
their enthusiasm.

NO

R & B group: rather boring exponents of 12 bar blues sequences: -
a very pronounced Isley Brothers influence. This is a group who
if they made a good record in this idiom would probably mean
something, but their repertoire for pre-recorded programmes, where
five or six numbers are required, would be extremely repetitive.

NO

An earthy driving R & B group - good lead voice and effective
backing voices. 2nd Number was rather long and tended to be
monotonous. Good uninhibited version of "Shout and Shimmy".

YES

YES - Confirmed by J.E.Grant 18.2.65

Comment: An earthy R&B group with a good lead voice.

The Who were now definitively on the map. The problem was that 'I Can't Explain' had made just £35,000. Ten grand went to the retailers, Decca Records took £16,000, another five grand went to the Inland Revenue, Pete and his publisher David Platz took £2,000 each in composing royalties, leaving nothing for the rest of the band, although somehow each of them came out of it with £250. Lambert and Stamp did some sums and realised that if every hit The Who had was going to cost them this sort of cash, their new company New Action would be a minimum of £60,000 in debt by the end of 1965.

Lambert had to hit upon another way of selling the band that wouldn't actually bankrupt them. Figuring that in the new racket of pop and R&B any publicity was good publicity, he decided to use The Who's appetite for destruction. Pete couldn't just smash guitars, he could talk like he wanted to tear down society, and British society in 1965 was in a state of violent flux. Lambert, like The Clash's Bernie Rhodes and Sex Pistols' Malcolm McLaren would do a decade later, set about using the tabloid and music papers to manufacture outrage. Pete, ridiculously bright, hugely well versed in college notions of conceptual and auto-destructive art and keenly aware of the impact of *Blackboard Jungle* and *Rock Around the Clock*, was only too eager to oblige. In 1972 he told *The Observer*, 'Kit [Lambert] used to brief us before we went into interviews about what we should say. He wanted us to be as objectionable, arrogant and nasty as possible.'

Thus in the space of a mere few weeks Pete would shock journalists appalled by the thought of the snotty, overreaching working classes by telling them he owned a small fleet of luxury cars. In reality he owned, in his own words, 'a beaten-up banger'. Jonathan Aitken, a columnist for the Conservative *Evening Standard* and later a disgraced Tory cabinet minister, was told by Pete that the band would spend £50 a week each on clothes, when actually thanks to New Action's disastrous accounts, they were having to borrow clobber for photo shoots.

LEFT The Who, like the Stones, would perfect a surly belligerence that everyone from The Clash through The Stone Roses to The Libertines have attempted to imitate.

THIS PAGE The Who on the BBC programme *A Whole Scene Going* in 1966.
OPPOSITE The US single cover for 'My Generation'.

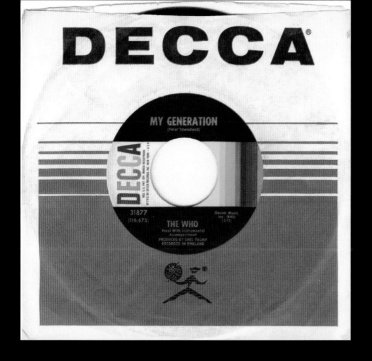

Recording for the song that would become one of the best known and most notorious in the history of popular music began on 13 October 1965. The song, which had initially been discarded as lightweight, went through several different changes. Kit Lambert would regularly sweep into Who rehearsals and demand that Pete, who he saw as his protégé, make some grand statement. 'We need something Wagnerian,' he would boom at the bewildered looking band. Chris Stamp thought that 'Generation', as it was known then, could be that grand statement. After Pete was pushed to keep the song and then urged to toughen it up, it became just about the grandest statement pop had ever made. The song is a snarling, three-chord attack that ends in walls of feedback and distortion, making it sound like The Who are actually in your house smashing up their instruments. It is a thoroughly modern slice of anarchy, perfectly in tune with Metzger's ideas on auto-destructive art. Just as important as the sound is Pete's lyric, a rallying cry for the disaffected that turns an angry explosive racket into something truly subversive. It is in fact the first truly subversive song in British rock 'n' roll.

It is perhaps appropriate that the recording of one of rock 'n' roll's most antagonistic anthems should have been, even by The Who's standards, an especially confrontational experience. At least that was the rumour. Both Roger and John said the sessions were unusually acrimonious and punctuated, according to Roger, by 'near punch-ups'. It is also apt that a song that acquired almost instantly legendary status has, since its release, been the subject of so many rumours, tales, lies and apocryphal stories.

The most fantastical of these is also the most compelling. In 1965 Pete Townshend owned a large and battered thirty-year-old Packard hearse he used to drive himself and The Who's gear around in. Pete claims that the Queen Mother had the

However, not everything said for effect was a lie. In the same interview with the *Standard* Townshend gave a still more shocking explanation as to why The Who would smash their instruments. The group, he tells Jonathan Aitken, are about 'tremendous fire energy. We don't want our instruments to stop us doing what we want … We smash our instruments, tear our clothes and wreck everything. The expense doesn't worry us, 'cos that would get between us and our music. If I stood about worrying about the price of a guitar, then I am not really playing music. I am getting involved in material values.' To an older generation who had come through the war and rationing, this mixture of sneering cockiness and wanton waste was utterly beyond the pale. Pete capped off the idea that The Who were public enemy number one by saying that the band were propelled by a 'built-in hate'. The Clash, Sex Pistols, Guns n' Roses, Manic Street Preachers, Nirvana, The Prodigy and every Gangsta rapper to have ever swaggered up the rock 'n' roll hall of fame learned lessons (wittingly or not) about the dynamics of subversion from those early Pete Townshend interviews.

Now what The Who needed was a song to match their onstage fury and snotty, nihilistic interviews. The single that followed 'I Can't Explain' was 'Anyway Anyhow Anywhere'. A jazz-inspired Mod classic with a blistering chorus, it captured something of what made The Who so brilliant, unsettling and dangerous. What followed next, though, wouldn't just help to define The Who, it would help to redefine rock 'n' roll. Because 'My Generation' wasn't just a song – it was a call to arms.

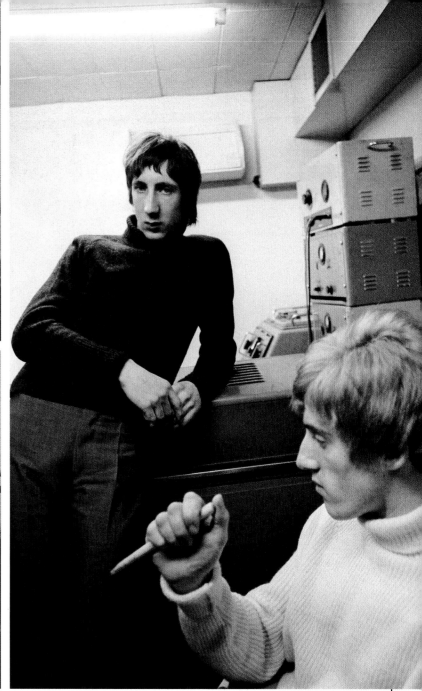

Pete I always thought Shel never let anyone but me into the IBC control room. Keith is there and so is Rog, so I must be wrong. Sorry, Shel.

THIS PAGE The Who recording *My Generation* with producer Shel Talmy. The deal they struck with him was so awful they are paying him royalties to this day, much to the chagrin of their managers Bill Curbishley and Robert Rosenberg. **OPPOSITE** Tape boxes from the *My Generation* album studio recording.

vehicle towed off the Belgravia street where he had it parked, Her Majesty saying that the sight of it ruined her daily drive through the neighbourhood. Pete certainly seemed to believe this had happened, and his revulsion at the incident magnified his disdain for the residents of Buckingham Palace.

The idea that 'My Generation' was not just an attack on the older generation but an attack on the very symbol of that generation – and that the attack was inspired not by some abstract political disagreement with the Monarchy but a personal slight – is so good it hardly seems worth debunking. Much more likely is that Pete was looking for a way to express the anger he had seen at gigs, and which seemed, in the form of the rioting Mod, to be sweeping the nation. '"My Generation", he told *Rolling Stone* magazine in 1985, 'was very much about trying to find a place in society.'

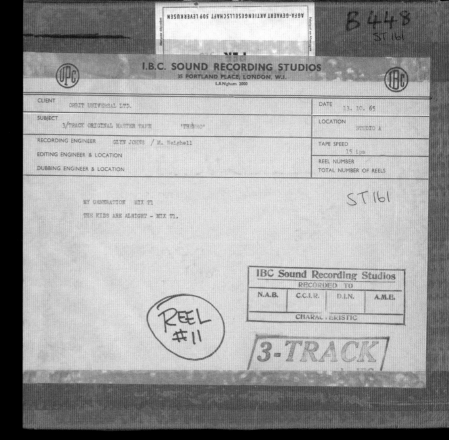

The two most infamous lines in the song are worth revisiting simply because even today, after more than fifty years, they have an audacity, anger and free-booting nihilism that still has the power to shock. 'Hope I die before I get old', spat out by Roger Daltrey, pretty much became the template for every youth rebellion that followed, and a clarion call for everyone from the French Marxists and Situationists of Paris 1968 and American anti-Vietnam war protesters to the British punk rock anarchists of the mid-seventies. In reality, that line along with the whole tone of the song is considered one of the most distilled statements of youthful rebellion in rock history, and it made the track an acknowledged forebear of the US and British punk movements.

Just as contentious as the actual words is Roger Daltrey's delivery – a manic, angry, frustrated stutter. This is at its most memorable when Roger sings the line, 'Why don't you all f-f-f-fade away.' Every Mod would shout 'fuck off' in place of 'fade away'. The line seems deliberately, playfully, designed to inspire just that reaction (the Mods in the movie *Quadrophenia* relish screaming 'fuck off' as they dance to the song at a party in a house they later trash). In fact it seems that the stutter was more of an accident, or at least not a deliberate attempt to flirt with 'fuck' and further rile an already riled older generation.

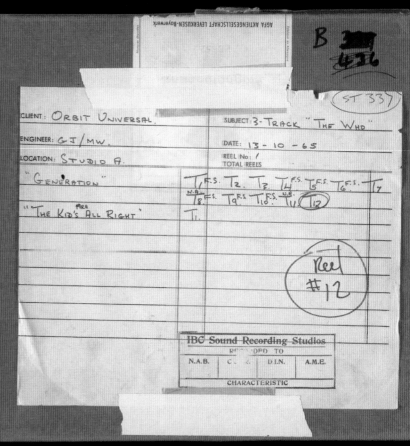

Pete has often claimed that 'My Generation' was his attempt at doing a 'talking' blues number. He has said it was initially written without the stutter, but after hearing John Lee Hooker's 'Stuttering Blues', he reworked the song into its present form. Pete has also claimed that the song began as a folk song and that it was his take on a Bob Dylan song, Dylan being a huge influence on him at the time. Roger Daltrey has

note again (something that at the time, given the lack of money and the volatility of the band's personalities, was a distinct possibility), 'My Generation' would have secured their place in rock 'n' roll history.

In December of that year The Who released their debut album, which was titled *My Generation* and perfectly embodied the raw savagery of the band live. However, the band had mentally moved on and felt the album said very little about who they were and what they had become. Roger blamed producer Shel Talmy. 'It was very scrappily done. It wasn't like it was recorded while we were on stage, that album was recorded very quickly and cheaply and it just wasn't what we were all about by then.' Pete went a whole lot further, actually writing a review of his own album in *Record Mirror*. Even now his frankness beggars belief. 'I hate it … It's rubbish … It's crap.' The record marked the end of The Who's Mod period. In 1972 Pete looked back at that

WHO WAX PROTEST

The Who have recorded a protest song written by group member Peter Townshend. Called "My Generation," it will be released on Brunswick on October 29.

Ballroom and club dates for the Who this month are Scunthorpe Baths Hall tomorrow (Saturday), Milford Haven Pill social centre (2nd), Bishop's Stortford Rhodes centre (23rd), Slough Carlton (24th), Watford Trade (25th), Swindon Locarno (28th), Wembley Starlite (29th) and Manchester University (30th).

said that the stutter was his attempt to sound like a British Mod on speed. However, producer Shel Talmy insisted it was simply 'one of those happy accidents' that they decided to leave in. Roger seemed to confirm this when he said that he had made no attempt to rehearse the song prior to the recording, was nervous and was unable to hear his own voice through the monitors. The stutter, he said, was his best shot at fitting the lyrics to the music. The BBC, who mostly still didn't get pop music and certainly didn't get youth rebellion, initially banned the song. Not because it didn't want to offend the older generation or the Queen Mum, but because they felt Roger's stuttering might offend people who stuttered. They pretty swiftly reversed their decision when they realised how hugely popular the song was on stations like Radio Caroline.

'My Generation' reached No. 2 in the British charts. It is the highest charting single The Who have ever had in the UK. It s safe to say that even had The Who never recorded another

ABOVE LEFT Carnaby Street, London, September 1965. Pop stars meet to create anti bowler hat group the Bowler Hat Brigade. Among the groups were The Animals, The Kinks, The Rolling Stones and The Who. **OPPOSITE** The Who playing up to their hooligan image, graffiti-ing a wall for a publicity shot.

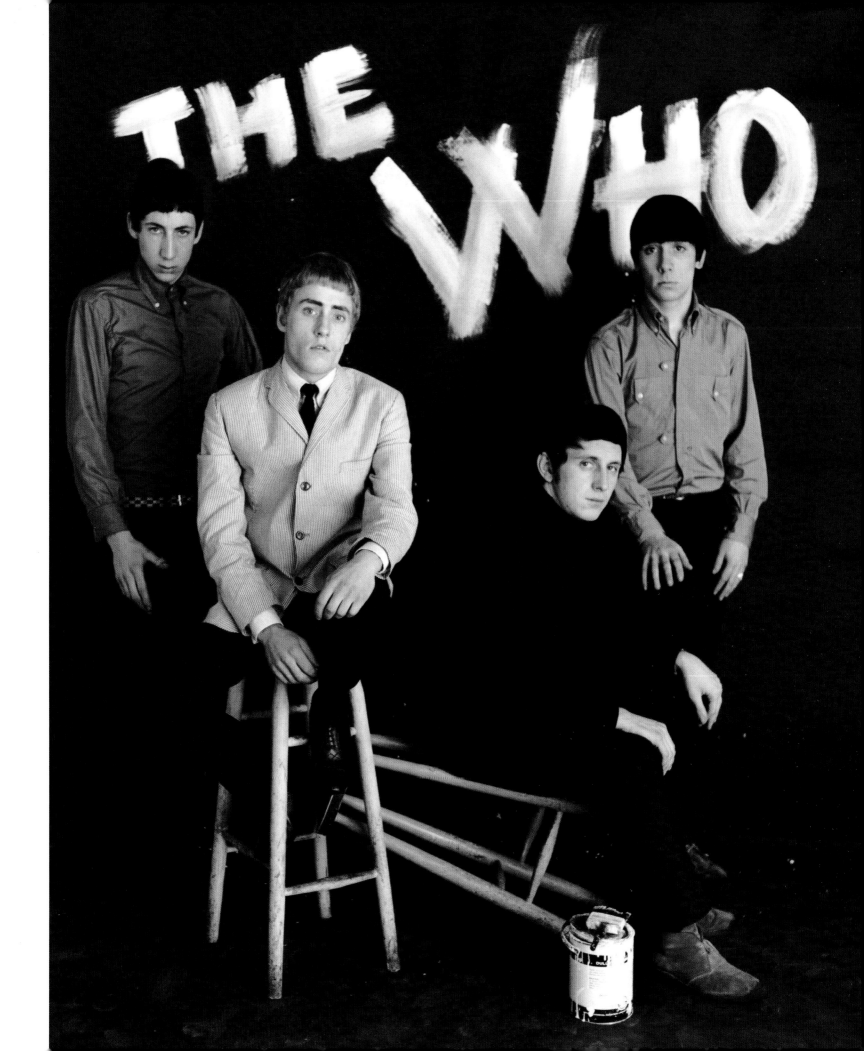

period with journalist Nick Logan and attempted to explain how he was able to so accurately reflect the feelings of teenage Who fans. 'I was able to achieve that by actually being involved. What was so great was the unanimity of it, the way I could blend in and be one of them. There was no class thing; the point was I was involved with it and I could write songs as a pilled-up Mod that were straight from the heart. Songs like "Can't Explain", "Anyway Anyhow Anywhere", "My Generation". But I think that's where they stopped.' Roger agreed: 'I think if he had stuck with writing songs for that group of kids in Shepherd's Bush, what would have been written after that? Pete was always thinking about bigger things, writing about bigger things. For me at least he wanted to be an interpreter of it all.'

The Who would now get more ambitious, more arty, more ferocious and more self-reflective. Pete had always been into music not just as a sound but as a concept. Thus The Who had always been both band and meta-band, able not just to write songs but write songs about songs. Pop art, the art movement of the day, a movement Pete had an academic and innate understanding of, became a way to explain their new phase. And their new look.

OPPOSITE The Who looking their most quintessentially British in a publicity shot for *My Generation*. **BELOW** The band posing in the West End, only a few minutes' walk from the Mod mecca, Carnaby Street.

Lambert and Stamp

2015 saw the release of the seminal documentary *Lambert and Stamp*, a film about The Who's mercurial managers Kit Lambert and Chris Stamp. Using archive footage of The Who and and new interviews with Pete Townshend, Roger Daltrey and Chris Stamp, the movie chronicles the strange, unique and wildly creative relationship the two managers had with the four members of The Who. Here, it's director James D. Cooper talks about his film – a tale of misfits brought together by the extraordinary circumstances of post-war Britain – and his friendship with Chris Stamp who died as the film was being completed.

'I see this film as a love story, essentially timeless and universal. What is at the core of the relationship between Kit and Chris is something that touches everybody. It's about two guys who felt and didn't feel certain things about their place in the world, and who formed a relationship in order for the world to make a little more sense to them. They were two guys who felt marginalised and who took action in the hope of finding their place in the world. In doing so they found something bigger than themselves.

'If there is a threat we seek unity, and for Kit and Chris part of that notion of threat had come about because of the Second World War.

'It is certainly something that Chris Stamp talked about. He came from the poorest of poor backgrounds in London's East End. This was a neighbourhood that had been brutally and continuously bombed, a place where you had to rely upon one another just out of a primal sense of survival.

'I did not have the good fortune of knowing Kit Lambert, but I did know Chris Stamp and what drew me to this story was Chris's mind. He had this incredible mind, a truly transcendent mind that he obviously formed early on, and Chris like Kit was a war baby, a war child. You have to have an incredible sense of self in order to give up what you are and become what you imagine you could be. Being a very young child during the war and in the immediate years afterwards in the part of London he was from gave Chris an immense sense of survival, and a huge sense of adventure. Chris never played it safe.

'Chris, by engaging with Kit Lambert and making the decisions that he made to move forward with that relationship, showed something enormously brave and unique. This is a young working-class kid who was a member of a gang, surrounded by similarly tough kids. In the gang world Chris was from he was rising fast. And yet he chose to risk all of that to befriend an openly gay man, from a completely different class and different educational background. And this is at a time where it is illegal to be gay, where it is an imprisonable offence. He knew that this could cause him a lot of problems and difficulties in the world he came from. He made this decision, having no real clue where it might lead him, or what it might cost him. That uncertainty, for a born survivor, made his decision all the more momentous.

'Chris really was able to transcend boundaries, first his class and later, with The Who, what constituted art. His brother, the actor Terence Stamp, helped enormously in this. Terence helps to get Chris out of the East End via the ballet, of all things. But after that Chris carries on transcending. By the time he meets The Who Chris has a great career going. He is working in the British film industry and he has a flat in Chelsea; he is listening to jazz, he is smoking weed, he is reading books, he is driving a flash car. He has clothes, he has girls, he has all the things he had ever thought he wanted. He is drenching his mind in knowledge that simply wasn't available to him in the East End only a very short time before. In the film he describes this very idyllic life and then he says, 'I just felt dissatisfied.'

'When he said that to me I was amazed. Chris, you grew up with bombs falling, you have gotten yourself out of poverty and gangs and a life of crime and God knows what else. You are now living in West London and working in film, you are leading a life you could not even have dreamt of only a few years earlier and yet it's not quite doing it for you?

'There is something about the sort of mind he had that simply refuses to believe that this is all there is, no matter how obviously awful, seemingly inescapable or apparently great 'THIS' is. Chris just always felt there was something else. Something deeper.

'The circumstances of the relationship between Chris and Kit are extraordinary. Two minds that are constantly seeking to transcend. To be more and more of something, to get beyond whatever world they had built for themselves, no matter how comfortable that world. I think what they saw in The Who, or recognised in The Who, was the idea of kindred spirits, of people equally as restless and energetic and curious. I think it was love at first sight. I think they saw an opportunity not only in Pete Townshend but in the four guys to truly live out some of their wildest and most ambitious artistic ideas. I think they also saw the band's relationship somehow reflecting the dynamic of their own — the love, the beauty, the complexity. I really believe that they felt they could better articulate their own artistic relationship through these other, equally complex, equally brilliant people.

'Early on in the film Chris explains how he and Kit both felt marginalised. He because of his class, Kit because of his gayness. Kit may have come from the best of the best, so to speak, but he had a very daunting legacy thrust upon him. Combine that with his sexuality and you begin to understand why not only did he not feel he belonged but why he didn't want to belong. He was as much of an outcast from the system as Chris was. I think when you find someone who understands you that well, who shares that sense of the outsider with you, I think you want to expand

Pete Lovely Kit Lambert with lovely me.

it, you want to share it. As Chris says in the film after he'd made the decision to fully embrace Kit Lambert and what was to become their seemingly invincible alliance, 'Hey, my mind wasn't that sophisticated back then, but I knew something.'

'What becomes interesting with The Who is that it develops into a family, a family of misfits but a family nonetheless. Kit and Chris as the figurative mother and father are able to create this sense of safety and security within which Pete, Roger, John and Keith can work and invent and be artists. Chris told me that when he met The Who he and Kit decided that in order to do what they wanted to do they first had to make the guys feel safe. They wanted to make an environment in which each of the guys could feel as though their individuality, their identity, their aspirations could be expressed, where the very conservative judgements of society of the time would be allowed to inhibit the creative process. The Who were in a sense a tangible expression of Kit and Chris's own relationship. It is a fascinating thing.

'Chris and Kit are film-makers, they are storytellers. In The Who, some huge personas, they see love and conflict and danger and a narrative. There is also an element of casting. If you are making a movie or a theatre piece you need characters, and The Who provided character and conflict. The shrewd side of it was also to see that here was a band thanks to all that and also to Pete's art school background who would be responsive to their more ambitious ideas and concepts. I think Kit really felt that he could shape Pete because Pete was so bright, so receptive, so enthusiastic. He was the perfect vessel, not because he was empty but because he was brimming. Roger's arc in the film is also fascinating. He was initially a misfit in The Who and struggled to find a place. He was tough, volatile and made very hard choices that were probably against his nature for the greater good of The Who. In the process he transformed himself from a misfit into a star and a legend. Kit Lambert and Chris Stamp provided the structure and inspired transcendence within it, not only for themselves but for all four members of The Who to reach beyond their own personal limitations.

'I am honoured to have known Chris Stamp. I am also honoured to have made this film along with the participation of surviving members of The Who Pete Townshend and Roger Daltrey, to get a sense of intimacy as to how all of this worked.

'So this is a love story. It is about Chris and Kit, and Roger and Pete, and John and Keith. But it is also about my love of Chris Stamp, and I hope that comes through as well.'

OPPOSITE TOP Keith, Pete and Kit in a break from recording *Tommy*.
OPPOSITE BELOW LEFT Chris Stamp and Kit Lambert outside 6 Chesterfield Gardens in Mayfair, London. They set up Track Records in 1966. **ABOVE** Ace Face Chris Stamp with Pete. **LEFT** A moody looking Kit stares into camera as Roger ponders taking on the character of Tommy.

Who are the Mods?

There is perhaps no subcultural look more quintessentially British than that of the Mod. A young man pouting, suited and booted, hair immaculately styled and leaning on a scooter, practically demands that your mind drop a Union Jack in the background to complete the picture. And yet Mod began as a tribute to French and Italian movie stars and African-American jazz artists. It was if anything a rejection of British culture, or at any rate a rejection of the drab, rationed, stuffy, morally and socially conservative post-war years. The Eton-educated Conservative politician Harold Macmillan was the incarnation of all that Mods regarded as hopelessly drab and passé. In fact, his tenure as Prime Minister from 1957 to 1963 began at the same time Mods first started appearing in London's West End and ended a year before the Battle of Brighton, when Mod went mainstream.

Where the Teddy Boys had been a strange collision of upper- and working-class culture, with the working class eventually appropriating the looks of those who regarded them as social inferiors, Mods had more complex origins. The writer Simon Frith says that Mods emerged out of the London Beatnik scene that grew up around Soho's coffee bars, which often hosted folk singers and poetry readings. Coffee bars certainly acquired a notoriety around that time. According to then art school student John Mothersole (an early devotee of the Italian style that would later become a part of the Mod look), when his girlfriend's parents discovered he had taken her to a coffee bar off the Charing Cross Road they were furious. 'For a moment back then coffee was subversive. It's 'cos these places were full of art school students reading Jack Kerouac and listening to what the *Daily Mail* referred to as 'Negro Music', and I think in everyone's mind they couldn't believe we were going there just to drink coffee and chat. They assumed that we were plotting some sort of socialist revolution or something. But we were basically going there 'cos pubs were terrible back then. Pubs were where your dad went. I think after the *Daily Mail* wrote their umpteenth headline about Beatniks and coffee bars, maybe some people did start plotting revolution. But me, I was just taking my girlfriend out.'

It is certainly true that the early Modernists were so called because of their enthusiasm for the new, whether that was jazz, pop art, beat novels and poetry or technology. The early Mod look does at times appear to emulate the style of Blue Note artists like Kenny Dorham, Herbie Nichols and John Coltrane that were so popular with the Soho Beatniks. West Indian music, most particularly ska and rocksteady, was also quickly adopted by these early Mods, some of whom would later borrow from the Jamaican Rude Boy look, wearing pork pie and trilby hats on top of their sharply cut, too-tight-to-sit-in suits. But Mod's true distinction, what marked it from what had gone before, was that it managed, like punk a generation later, to be both cerebral and visceral, gritty and arty.

The jazz singer and writer George Melly, while acknowledging Mod's roots in the post-war jazz boom, saw the subculture as an entirely working-class phenomenon that very swiftly became ruthlessly focused on clothes. These young men, according to Melly, had money to spend

and challenged class strictures through dressing, dancing and having more fun than their elders and betters – as though style itself were a passport to upward mobility. They called themselves 'faces'. This chimes with social historian Mary Anne Long's claim that the 'first-hand accounts and contemporary theorists point to the Jewish upper-working or lower-middle class of London's East End and suburbs' as being the originators of Mod. These Jewish teenagers, often the sons of tailors or with connections in the rag trade, had suits made up to imitate the French and Italian movie stars they so admired and who represented a glamour and exoticism absent in ration-card UK. Jean-Paul Belmondo was considered the epitome of continental cool. Many of these early Mods smoked French and Italian cigarettes, such was their devotion to all things continental. The designer Johnny Moke, an early Mod, remembers a fellow 'face', Les, habitually sporting a striped jumper and beret. 'We saw him once sitting in Aldgate Wimpy holding up a copy of *Le Soir*. When we went in and joined him we saw that he was really reading the *Sunday Pictorial*, which he had concealed in the middle pages.' Italy and France were everything. Many early Mods affected the 'French crew' haircut, a fringe and bouffant confection, and the slackened lower lip modelled by the movie star Jean-Paul Belmondo. This gloriously effeminate pout was known to Mods as 'throwing a noodle'. Posing, pretending was what it was all about. The very same tailors who had supplied the Teddy Boys with their zoot suits and drape coats were now cutting cloth in a neat, tight, thin-lapelled tribute to Marcello Mastroianni and Federico Fellini's *La Dolce Vita*.

By the early 1960s the individualism of the Mod had somewhat given way to a much more defined look. Nonetheless the famous fastidiousness of the Mod was more pronounced than ever. The rock journalist Nik Cohn, a friend of Pete Townshend and an early and astute observer of British youth culture and style, recounted the story of one Thomas Baines, whose teenage dedication to sartorial exactitude was such that he 'refused to have sex at parties unless there was a shoe tree available and a press for his trousers'.

This quasi-religious fervour about clothes found its polar opposite in the leather, grease and grubbiness of the Rocker look. Essentially the Rockers were what remained of the Teddy Boys. Older, burlier and not remotely interested in French New Wave cinema or Italian neo-realism, the Rockers' unwavering dedication to rock 'n' roll and Americana made them look hugely reactionary and old-fashioned despite the fact that they preceded the Mods by only a few years. Clashes between Mods and Rockers were both inevitable and, by the time The Who came to Mod, were happening regularly and with increasing bitterness and violence.

Ironically, in 1964, just as Mod reached its height, it seemed to dissipate. Being a Mod was now less about being an individual and more about being part of a wider movement and to a pretty alarming extent conforming to its norms. The character Jimmy in *Quadrophenia* illustrates the dichotomy of being a Mod in the mid-sixties. Jimmy wants to be someone, an individual, someone who stands out from the

TOP Dressing up for a Saturday night out. **ABOVE** Pete and Keith getting fitted for suits at a London tailors. **OPPOSITE ABOVE** The Who standing beneath Nelson's Column. Nelson practically looks like a fifth member of the band. Despite the fact that Mods were inspired by the look of American jazz singers, listened to Caribbean music and drove Italian scooters, they somehow created a uniquely British look. This may in part be down to the promo shots for *My Generation*, which took place against various London landmarks. **OPPOSITE BELOW** Roger straightening his hair. Mods did not have curly hair.

crowd, yet he's part of a gang that has adopted a uniform style of dress. The terrace chant, 'We are the Mods', sung by tens of thousands of identically dressed teenagers on the beaches of Brighton, Southend and Margate, was in its robotic, tedious intensity the very antithesis of Mod's original spirit.

By now Mods were mainly working-class teenagers. The school leaving age was fifteen. The British economy, after almost a decade of austerity, was booming and many young men and women had no responsibilities and plenty of cash. They saw little value in saving for the future, and in the short years between leaving school and getting married spent their cash on clothes and drugs – speed being a favourite since it allowed them to dance all weekend. Some of the original Mods, put off by the uniformity of the scene and imbued with a genuine desire to distance themselves from the fighting, now preferred to call themselves Individualists or Stylists. Pete Townshend seems to have genuinely understood both aspects of the scene. He is widely credited with making the look much more adventurous, introducing Union Jacks, RAF targets and slogans (here his art school background played a huge part), which would eventually see the rise of the psychedelic Mod that very swiftly gave way to the hippie. Equally, though, Townshend is someone who thanks to his working-class roots had a genuine understanding and empathy for the broader and more brutal movement, and *Quadrophenia* lays its anger and contradictions bare.

By 1966 working-class Mods had been renamed Hard Mods. Still smart, they wore their hair shorter and had replaced the winkle-pickers and brogues with working boots, normally Doc Martens, which were comfortable and enormously hard-wearing. This group would later be known as Suede Heads and, later and most notoriously, as the look became ever more paramilitary, skinheads.

However, this did not mean Mod was dead. In his superb book, *Mods – A Very British Style*, the writer Richard Weight argues that in its concerns Mod has pretty much influenced every youth cult since. Certainly by the mid-sixties, 'Mod' had become an all-purpose adjective applied to anything young or fresh or stylish or simply unconventional – Mary Quant, Biba, The Beatles, Terence Conran and Habitat were all labelled Mod at some point. Carnaby Street is still seen by many as the home of Mod. The whole 'Swinging London' cliché owes much to Mod, as can be seen even when it's mocked. Mike Myers' affectionate Austin Powers movies owe as much to Mod as does the original Swinging London movie *Blow-Up*, which Myers parodies so well. This is all fairly obvious. What Richard Weight makes such a convincing case for is that Mod is the DNA of youth culture, the place from which every youth movement – punk, Two-Tone and rave – has grown.

Of course specific elements have been recycled countless times. Punk and New Wave took heavily from Mod. Nick Lowe, the artist who helped to make Stiff Records so successful, says that punk was just the reincarnation of Mod. 'I was like a lot of people, an ex-Mod who had got conned by the whole hippie horseshit. Punk brought back the

RIGHT A Who badge employing the Union Jack. The Who invested heavily in iconography of Empire, often ironically. **BELOW** Flyer for The Who's Marquee residency. **OPPOSITE** Mods with their beloved scooters.

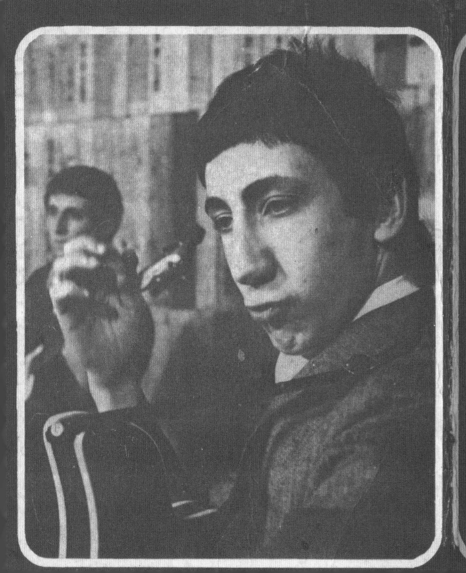

MAXIMUM R&B
THE WHO
MARQUEE
90 Wardour Street
EVERY TUESDAY
Admission 5/-
2/6 ONLY
with this ticket

straightforwardness and modernity of Mod.' Look at a picture of the The Clash almost forty years after they made their debut and they look very Mod. Clash contemporaries and fellow punks The Jam looked exactly like Mods because they were Mods and they certainly helped to fully revive what Richard Weight refers to slightly dismissively as the off-the-peg 'Mod revival' of the late seventies – a process carried along by Madness, The Specials and Two-Tone music – which reached its apotheosis with the release of *Quadrophenia* the movie in 1979.

Since then Mod has reappeared in the clothes and style of both Blur and Oasis and even in bands like The Horrors. Where the spirit of Mod – innovative, showy, witty and adventurous – seems to have survived best, though, is in Britain's football stadiums. Football Casuals, as these smartly dressed, working-class supporters later became known, appeared suddenly at the height of the early eighties Mod revival. Grant Flemming, a teenage East End Mod at the time, recalls how swiftly the Casuals appeared on the streets of London. 'I went on holiday with my mum and dad to Tenerife for a fortnight and all my mates were Mods. I get back and every one of them is a Casual, or what we called Soul Boy back then. And it was brutal, you had to become a Casual. It was like the Turkish-enforced conversions to Islam. Convert or die. I converted.'

From Liverpool to London, football Casuals like their Mod antecedents looked to the Continent for inspiration, most particularly Italy with its famously expensive sports labels like Fila and Tacchini. In Liverpool and Manchester kids started wearing Lois jeans, Italian anoraks and Fred Perry tops, earning them the nickname Perrys in Manchester. In the North they listened to Joy Division and Echo & The Bunnymen. In the South they were into David Bowie, jazz funk and soul. The look, like the music, varied wildly from region to region, although the floppy, neo-public school fringe known as the wedge was something worn throughout the UK. Manny from The Stone Roses, a one-time Mod who also converted to Casual, says the haircut is what made the look so deceptive and scary. 'The wedge would drop into your eyes, meaning you kept having to flick your head to one side. It was a very effeminate look. I was always playing with my hair, combing it, flicking it. We looked like choirboys, like Aled Jones with Stanley blades.'

The Mod spirit still exists in the football Casual movement, although there is no longer a look, more a desire to impress and surprise. Gaudy logos swiftly gave way to hidden signals as the Casuals started wearing clothes that, though hugely expensive, had either no label or one that could be easily removed. For this, and for their excellent tailoring, Stone Island and C.P. Company have remained two favourites on Britain's terraces. Elsewhere, most particularly at Paul Weller concerts, you see Mods slavishly recreating what has gone before. This certainly proves the enduring appeal of the 1964/1979 look. In the video to John Newman's hit 'Love Me Again', any one of the dancers could easily have stepped out of footage from an early Who gig. The spirit, however, as Richard Weight explains, is to be found elsewhere, in the savage rhythms of grime music or at a West Ham home game.

1965 — 1969

5

The Who's Pop Art Years

Pop art was colourful, subversive and hugely self-aware.

The pop art look, one we now most readily associate with Mod, was in fact Pete soaking up the ideas of Pete Meaden and the kids who came to their shows, and combining them with lessons learned at art school. Pop art was, at least to begin with, a British artistic movement that had emerged at roughly the same time as rock 'n' roll. This made it contemporaneous with Pete's interest in music. Most interestingly, like The Who themselves, it was a British take on American culture. It parodied, celebrated and referenced the artefacts of mass culture. In many ways, by repeating images, quoting comic books and elevating common objects to the status of art, it was post-modernism before that term had been invented. For Pete it was certainly post-Mod. 'We stand for pop art clothes, pop art music and pop art behaviour. This is what everyone seems to forget. We don't change off stage, we live pop art.' If the early Mods had been immaculate understatement, Pete's post-Mod, pop art style was about manic overstatement.

He took to wearing medals and had a Union Jack fashioned into a jacket, not as some patriotic statement (as later came to be believed) but as a way of making people see this symbol of empire in an entirely new way. It was a form of desecration, just like wearing World War medals that hadn't been earned. This violation of the British national flag was most obvious when Pete started draping a Union Jack over his speaker cabinet, which he would symbolically spear with his guitar at the end of the show.

Most famously Pete adapted the RAF red, white and blue target, a symbol hitherto associated with victory in the Battle of Britain, into a T-shirt. Military historians will remind you that the RAF red, white and blue symbol is a roundel rather than a target, but for The Who and all their followers, it was a symbol, something to be aimed for, something that said you had arrived, a mark of success. For them it was a target, a bullseye. The rest of the band took to these ideas with just as much enthusiasm as Pete. Roger would use black adhesive tape to create designs on jumpers. Keith wore the target T-shirt with the words POW printed comic book style on them. Another slogan beloved of Keith was 'Elvis For Everyone'. Pete's understanding of the commodification of pop was startling given just how young the medium was. The Rolling Stones' Brian Jones was so impressed by the band he went around telling journalists that The Who occupied the position the Stones once had (and this was 1965). 'They are the only young group doing something new both visually and musically, and originality normally means success,' said Jones. Keith Moon, meanwhile, had befriended The Beatles. Paul McCartney called The Who 'the best thing to happen on the 1965 scene'.

OPPOSITE For the New Year's Eve 1965 episode of *Ready Steady Go!*, *The New Year Starts Here!*, The Who, now well on their way to mega stardom, performed alongside the other big faces of the day, including The Animals, Tom Jones, The Kinks, Lulu, Dusty Springfield and The Rolling Stones, among others. They performed 'I Can't Explain' and 'My Generation'.

However, despite the attention of rock 'n' roll royalty, regular appearances on *Ready Steady Go!* and endless touring (sometimes playing two or three shows a night), The Who still weren't making any proper money. Roger, always the most forcefully ambitious of the band, felt uncomfortably close to the sheet metal factory. The problem was partly the lousy deal they had signed with producer Shel Talmy, who Pete would later tell *Zigzag Magazine* 'had to be got rid of'. A legal fight that would dominate most of 1966 got underway when 'Circles', the song Talmy intended to be the follow-up to 'My Generation', was rejected by The Who in favour of 'Substitute'. By now The Who had left Talmy's Brunswick Records and signed to Robert Stigwood's Reaction label where they released 'Substitute'. To Talmy, having his song replaced was bad enough; to have it substituted by a song called 'Substitute' infuriated him. The move caused instant ructions, with Talmy filing a suit in the High Court claiming copyright infringement. The flip side of the record featured a song called 'Instant Party', which was actually just a version of 'Circles'. The Who had to withdraw the record. Amazingly, 'Substitute' was released three times, its third release featuring the B-side 'Waltz For A Pig', a jazz instrumental credited on the label to The Who Orchestra. The Who Orchestra were actually the Graham Bond Organisation. On this track they were Graham Bond, Dick Heckstall-Smith, Mike Falana and Ginger Baker. The track was written by Ginger Baker under the pseudonym Harry Butcher and was directed at Shel Talmy.

'Substitute' came out in March 1966 and can be regarded as the first salvo in Pete Townshend's pop art campaign. The song was intended to be a deliberate pastiche of the Stones. (In early demos Pete affects a strutting, Jagger-like vocal.) With Pete now in the producer's chair, it marries a beautifully memorable tune to Keith and John's revved-up rhythms (Pete's idea) and a lyric that stoners still ponder over to this day. It was undoubtedly Pete's cleverest lyric yet – the story of a man who is not remotely as he seems. Maybe he is lying to a girl, maybe he is lying to the world, quite possibly he isn't even of this world.

The lyrics, lent by Roger's delivery a sense of menace as palpable as that of 'My Generation', is a hall of mirrors, a tale of deception and consumerism, a plea for understanding that seethes with resentment and revels in its own fakery. Like a repetitive Andy Warhol silk-screen print, 'Substitute' demands you engage with an image that becomes less clear the more familiar you are with it. The song's protagonist tells you he is a liar, tells you who he is not and where he doesn't come from. It charted at No. 5 in the UK but failed to make the *Billboard* top 100 in the US. However, it remains one of The Who's most popular songs, in no small part because of that head-spinning lyric.

Relations with Talmy now in tatters, The Who needed a way out. It came at a price. Shel Talmy was finally bought out by Stamp and Lambert promising him 5 per cent on all Who recordings for the next five years. At the time, with The Who being as combustible as they were, this seemed like a pretty good deal. In fact it turned out to be a huge windfall for Talmy. Meanwhile, Decca in the US renewed The Who's deal and advanced Stamp and Lambert £25,000. In the UK the band signed with Polydor for an advance of £50,000.

Pressure was now on The Who to get new records out. 'Substitute' had been a ground-breaking single. Between March and December 1966, The Who had released 'Substitute', 'I'm A Boy' and 'Happy Jack', and also the EP *Ready Steady Who* on the Reaction label. Sadly, these original releases were accompanied by 'Legal Matter' and 'The Kids Are Alright', neither new, both culled from the previous year's *My Generation* album and released by Shel Talmy without the band's permission on Brunswick. Talmy, much to the fury

of the band, would later that year also release 'La-La-La-Lies' from *My Generation*. The exploitation of the band's first album perhaps explains why The Who's Mod period seems to have lasted at least a year longer than it actually did. With hindsight it did them no harm. 'Legal Matter', which, given Talmy's court battles with the band, he must have relished releasing, is a great pop song about being young, bored and no longer in love, and 'The Kids Are Alright' is a great love song that has become a Mod anthem.

At the time, though, Pete's songs were becoming lyrically and structurally bolder by the day and he didn't much want anyone's mind confused by material he felt he had thoroughly left behind. This is why in the same period that Shel Talmy was, in Pete's view, flogging a dead horse, The Who were releasing some of the most adventurous work of the period. 'I'm a Boy', 'Happy Jack' and 'Pictures of Lily' are respectively a song about a male child treated as a girl by his domineering mother, a song about a disabled man and a song about teenage masturbation. The novelist Pete Haynes, who under the name Esso once drummed for the seminal punk rock outfit The Lurkers (West London's answer to The Ramones), regards this period of The Who as the most revelatory:

> 'For me it's the most fascinating, since it involves strange subjects and a new looseness that truly allowed Keith Moon to express himself. You have this very young man, Townshend, writing about a disabled man, about sexual confusion, about wanking. This is a bloke barely out of his teens. And essentially you are seeing that he is no longer working on pop songs as such, he is trying to tell stories. So the lyrics demand a much looser structure to the songs, which of course frees Keith up even more; Keith can suddenly come centre stage. To me Townshend at this time is really writing theatre, although it's not RADA, it's the fucking Lavender Hill Mob. And that makes sense 'cos think about his parents, they both belonged to a music hall tradition, and that again is about telling stories.'

This notion of Townshend being something more than just a simple writer of pop songs became very obvious in the recording of their second album, *A Quick One*. Pete remembers the recording as essentially silly, but hugely creative. 'Basically it was a scream from start to finish,' he told Alan di Perna. 'Running around the studio hitting bass drums and playing penny whistles, going out in the street and coming back in with the poor engineer trying to follow us with a microphone. It was a good, good period for The Who. That was when we realised studios were the greatest places.'

ABOVE The Who taking a break from filming on London's Kings Road. Note that the hair is getting longer and the trousers slightly wider.

Pete Because of Kit Lambert's Parisian connections we were immediately taken up by a cool crowd when we first played there in 1965.

In the final days of recording, The Who realised they were ten minutes short of completing the record. Kit Lambert, with typically crazy ambition, suggested Pete knit together several different stories 'in the form of an opera'. Pete initially thought the idea was ridiculous. But Lambert practically turned the concept into a dare and any initial doubts Pete had were buried by the notion of living up to the challenge.

A Quick One, While He's Away took six different themes ('Her Man's Been Gone', 'Crying Town', 'We Have a Remedy', 'Ivor the Engine Driver', 'Soon Be Home' and 'You Are Forgiven') to tell a story of infidelity, forgiveness and redemption.' Pete and Kit even talked about putting the album out with a libretto, but the idea was rejected as too expensive. *A Quick One*, with its referencing of boutique culture and cover designed by the artist Alan Aldridge, seemed in many ways to sum up Swinging London. More importantly, though, it hinted at Pete's ambition. The Who were very much a part of British rock 'n' roll's top tier, perpetually mentioned alongside The Rolling Stones and The Beatles.

In the US, however, The Who were still virtually unknown. In December 1966 Chris Stamp rectified this by insisting that Decca Records employ three 'switched on' marketing men who would henceforth devote themselves full time to promoting The Who. He also got them a deal with Premier Talent, the most important booking agents in America. A scammer to the bone, Stamp achieved this latter deal largely by subterfuge. The company's CEO, Frank Barsalona, had already turned down The Who earlier that year and developed quite a dislike for the band. Stamp waited until Barsalona had gone on a lengthy business trip and approached his partner Dick Friedberg, subjecting him to a hard sell worthy of any Cockney barrow boy. When Barsalona returned, The Who had signed with Premier and Stamp was back in the UK. Barsalona spent days fuming over what the company had lumbered themselves with.

Meanwhile, back in Britain, Stamp and Lambert were already plotting The Who's American invasion.

1967 is arguably one of the greatest years in the history of popular music. Jimi Hendrix, The Doors and The Velvet Underground all released their debut albums; The Beatles put out the seminal *Sgt. Pepper's Lonely Hearts Club Band*, and Van Morrison released his first solo album, *Blowin' Your Mind*. For The Who the period that began in early 1966 with 'Substitute' reached its climax in December '67 with the album *The Who Sell Out*. Described by *Rolling Stone* magazine's editor Jann Wenner as 'fantastic', the album mixed songs with advertising jingles (both real and fake) in a brilliantly ambivalent, witty critique of consumerism.

OPPOSITE The Who playing on French TV. The symbols and geometric patterns now associated with the heyday of Mod actually had more to do with a post-Mod look. The flags as a backdrop would later be appropriated by punk rockers The Clash on their 1978 Sort It Out tour. **ABOVE** The Who messing about on a photo shoot.

TOP LEFT Pete in the studio. **TOP RIGHT** Pete with The Who's sound engineer Bob Pridden, usurping Keith's position on the drums. Didn't last long. **ABOVE** The Who visiting Battersea Dogs Home in 1965 in order to find a guard dog to mind their gear, which was continually being robbed. While they were looking for the right dog their van was stolen with five grand's worth of gear in the back.

Pete This is my studio in Soho. A large room right at the top of a building. I demo'd 'Sparks', 'Happy Jack' and 'A Quick One, While He's Away' here. Later, the place became the base for the first dedicated Meher Baba Association headquarters in London.

1967 was also the year that the counter-culture, now dominated by the hippies, truly came to be regarded as a threat to the status quo. That summer Detroit exploded into five days of riots and looting. The rioters played Motown R&B artist Martha Reeves' 1964 hit, 'Dancing in the Street'. That same summer saw more than a 100,000 young people come together on the streets of Haight-Ashbury, San Francisco, lending first the event and then the whole year the moniker 'Summer of Love'. Across the US and Europe demonstrations against the Vietnam War, which US President Lyndon B. Johnson had massively escalated, became more persistent and more violent. For many in the establishment, groups like The Beatles and most particularly The Rolling Stones were seen not just as cheerleaders for an insurrection but as instigators. And The Who would by the end of the year throw their weight behind the movement.

The Who began that year realising (for the umpteenth time) that they were almost bankrupt. This ugly fact did not stop Chris Stamp and Kit Lambert from deciding that now would be the perfect time to found their own record label. Lambert saw this as a way of circumventing the big labels. It was indie before indie. He told *Disc* magazine, 'I have always dreamed of having my own label. I would like to turn it into a hip EMI. I've spent my life having rows with record companies and the only solution is to have one of my own.'

Track Records' first signing was an unknown American guitarist and singer called Jimi Hendrix. Hendrix had moved to the UK from his native Seattle, and according to Chas Chandler, the original bass player with The Animals who became co-manager of Hendrix in 1968, 'Kit had knocked over tables wanting Jimi to be on the new label he was launching'. For Pete Townshend, though, Hendrix, who employed feedback and wielded his guitar like a weapon, seemed almost too close to the bone. 'He was the first man to walk all over my territory and I felt genuinely intimidated by that.'

In April that year The Who put out their first single for the new label. Titled 'Pictures of Lily', it was a none-too-subtle celebration of boyish teenage fantasies and masturbation. Pete called it 'merely a ditty about masturbation and its importance to a young man'. As with all the singles that had come before it, the fact that the subject matter was contentious didn't in the least detract from its qualities as a pop song. Quite the reverse. While Jimi Hendrix and many other artists had pretty swiftly come to regard the pop single as trivial and almost beneath them, Pete Townshend and The Who loved the pop single. Indeed, in their hands it became a uniquely subversive vehicle. 'Pictures of Lily' made the top five in the UK but failed once again to even penetrate the top 50 in the US.

ABOVE October 1967. The year of psychedelia. Keith in ever-mocking mood is dressed as a court jester.

Pete Tom Wright took this photo. We were in Florida in the woods around his stepfather's house. We had some sun on our faces, and a lot of the pictures are some of the best ever taken. We appear to have succumbed – briefly – to hippydom. My lovely pink coat was made by my girlfriend Karen.

OPPOSITE Roger Daltrey, the pugnacious Shepherd's Bush Mod, giving flower power a go. **ABOVE** The Who may have worn the uniform of the hippie for a time, but they were never in any sense hippies. **RIGHT** Artist and long-time Who collaborator Mike McInnerney's seminal psychedelic poster artwork. Along with Nigel Waymouth and Michael English, he gave British psychedelia its distinctive look.

THE WHO

PRINTED BY T.S.R. ENGLAND © OSIRIS VISIONS LTD. 10 WESTBOURNE TERRACE W.2 0A123 HAPSHASH AND THE COLOURED COAT.

Pop Festival, regarded as the forerunner to all of today's music festivals (it was in fact the second ever music festival, the first having occurred just one week earlier in Marin County), turned California from a state into a place synonymous with hippie counter-culture, and San Francisco was now the undisputed capital of counter-culture, which London had been only a year earlier. Looking back it is also no exaggeration to say that Monterey was the high point for the Summer of Love, before exploitation, bad acid and disillusionment kicked in. The Who as headliners had come *from* the right place to be *in* the right place. Monterey propelled them into the US mainstream at exactly the right time.

The band, however, did not enjoy playing the show. Kit Lambert had refused to pay for their regular equipment to be shipped out, so they used rented Vox amps. Both John Entwistle and Pete would later complain that this robbed them of the deafening volume that had become their signature. The audience were none the wiser. At the end of a frenzied performance of 'My Generation' the crowd were stunned when Pete destroyed his guitar, Keith Moon kicked his drum kit across the stage and smoke bombs exploded behind the PA.

The Who were followed by their label-mate Jimi Hendrix. Pete had tossed a coin with him to see who would be the final act. Hendrix ended his Monterey show with a feedback-drenched version of The Troggs' 'Wild Thing', which he capped by kneeling over his guitar, pouring lighter fluid over it, setting it on fire and then smashing it into the stage seven times before throwing its remains into the audience. To the stunned crowd, The Who and Hendrix looked to be reinventing rock 'n' roll before their very eyes. Pete felt Hendrix had upstaged The Who. The music critic Robert Christgau, reviewing the two bands in *The Village Voice*, called it a spectacular draw, writing:

'Music was a given for a Hendrix stuck with topping the Who's guitar-smashing tour de force. It's great sport to watch this outrageous scene-stealer wiggle his tongue, pick with his teeth and set his axe on fire, but the show-boating does distract from the history made that night – the dawning of an instrumental technique so effortlessly fecund and febrile that rock has yet to equal it, though hundreds of metal bands have gotten rich trying. Admittedly, nowhere else will you witness a Hendrix still uncertain of his divinity.'

The Who, Hendrix and Stamp and Lambert's Track Records had well and truly arrived.

The Who, a little like The Kinks, had almost come to consider themselves to be too English for America. However, all that was about to change. In the spring of '67 The Who embarked on their very first US mini-tour. In New York The Who came as a genuine shock. The band's auto-destructive art was something the UK had become used to. Americans had never seen anything like it. In just seven days the band bashed, smashed, kicked, crushed and destroyed twenty-two microphones, four speaker cabinets, five guitars and a ten-piece Pearl drum kit. NYC was smitten.

That summer the band returned to the US to play the Monterey International Pop Festival as part of a legendary line-up that included The Mamas and the Papas, Jefferson Airplane, Otis Redding, Janis Joplin and Jimi Hendrix. The Monterey

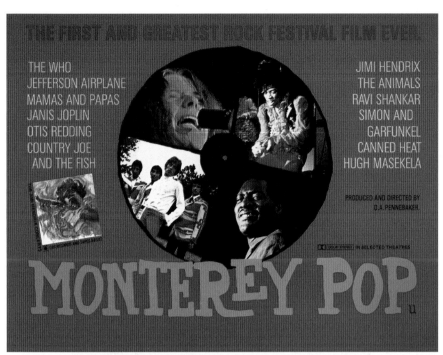

THE FIRST AND GREATEST ROCK FESTIVAL FILM EVER.

THE WHO
JEFFERSON AIRPLANE
MAMAS AND PAPAS
JANIS JOPLIN
OTIS REDDING
COUNTRY JOE
AND THE FISH

JIMI HENDRIX
THE ANIMALS
RAVI SHANKAR
SIMON AND
GARFUNKEL
CANNED HEAT
HUGH MASEKELA

PRODUCED AND DIRECTED BY
D.A. PENNEBAKER.

IN SELECTED THEATRES

MONTEREY POP

OPPOSITE & LEFT The Monterey Pop Festival, 1967. **BELOW** John Entwistle backstage at Monterey with the Jimi Hendrix Experience. **OVERLEAF** The Who live at Monterey.

If Monterey had been one of the high points of the year, The Who returned to the UK to be greeted by one of the low points. Mick Jagger and Keith Richards, along with several of their friends, had all been arrested in a drugs bust at Keith's Redlands home in Sussex. The trial was ongoing as The Who came back to the UK. The two Rolling Stones, who pleaded not guilty, were found guilty in a jury trial. Jagger was sentenced to three months in prison for possession of four amphetamine pills, and Richards was sentenced to twelve months in prison for allowing his home to be used for smoking cannabis. The sentences, considered unusually, punitively long, became a *cause célèbre* in the UK. To the surprise of some, *The Times* editor William Rees-Mogg came to the defence of the Stones, writing his famous 'butterfly on a wheel' editorial. The Who, in an expression of solidarity with Jagger and Richards, hastily recorded two Rolling Stones hits, 'The Last Time' and 'Under My Thumb', which they rush released.

In fact, thanks to both public pressure and the Stones' excellent lawyers, Jagger and Richards would spend less than two days in prison for those convictions before their prison sentences were quickly thrown out on appeal. (The legal repercussions of being convicted of drug-related crimes would still haunt the Stones for years, with Jagger and Richards having difficulties obtaining visas or entry into certain countries.) The incident, however, seemed to confirm in Pete's mind that the counter-culture that had so embraced him and his band had a dark side. Pete, who was always a mix of child-like idealism and scepticism that bordered on the plain cynical, didn't just see this darkness coming from how the hippies were reacting to the establishment, he saw it as inherent in the movement itself.

On the flight back from Monterey Pete had dropped acid for the first time. To say it had been a bad trip would be to sorely understate matters. However, the drug had given him a taste for the transcendental. He found this after reading the works of the Indian guru Meher Baba, which had been given to him by his friend Mike McInnerney. In several interviews towards the end of 1967 Pete talks of a new inner peace. He even at one point claimed that all the band were disciples of Meher Baba. 'Baba is the avatar of the age, the messiah. He can't do anything but good. He has completely and utterly changed my whole life and through me the group as a whole.' The rest of the band had no real interest in Baba.

LEFT Left to right: Roger, Pete, Jimi Hendrix, John and Keith. Jimi signed to The Who's Track Records label in 1966.

If Monterey had been one of the high points of the year, The Who returned to the UK to be greeted by one of the low points

OPPOSITE The medals and target badges have been replaced by a picture of Pete's guru Meher Baba, the inspiration behind the *Tommy* and *Lifehouse* albums.

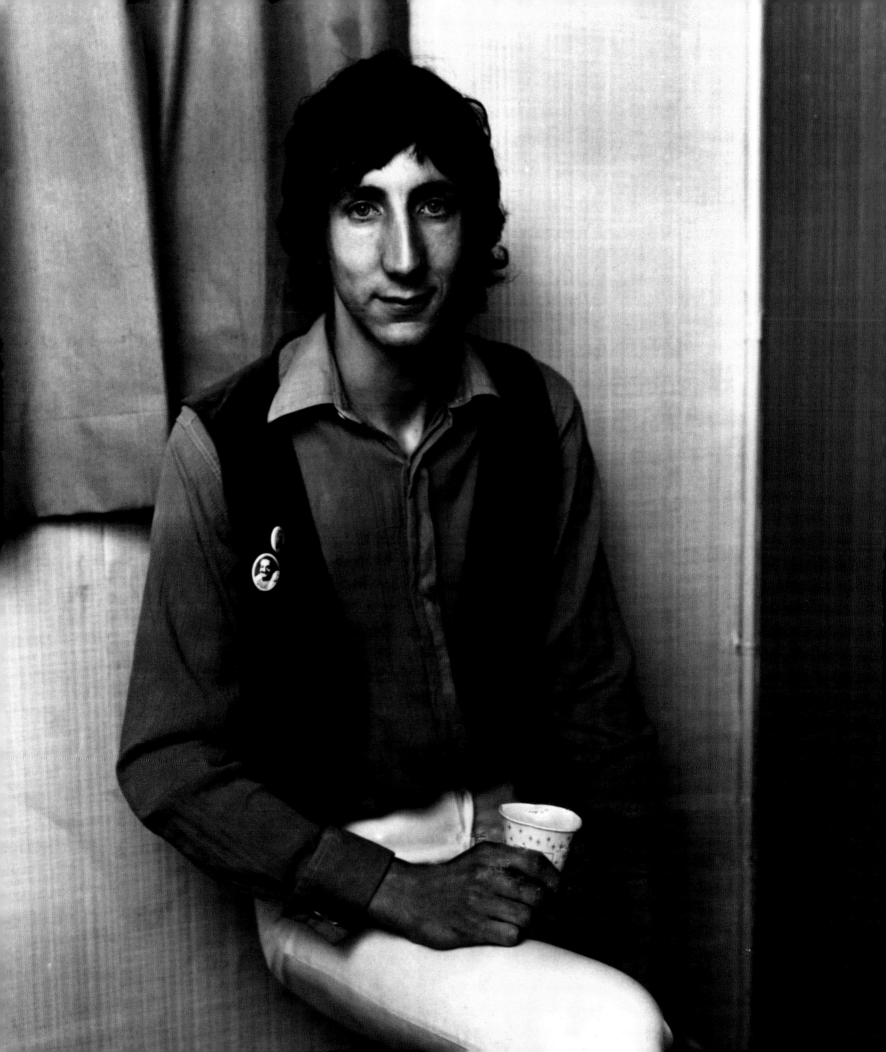

his new-found idealism would not find its way onto record for some time. Instead, for their third album The Who decided to parody, deride and celebrate the consumerism of a generation that the author Tom Wolfe would dub the Me Generation. It all started with "Jaguar",' Pete told *Melody Maker*:

'The number was a really powerful and loose thing. Something like "The Ox" from our first album, with Keith thrashing away like hell and us all pumping out "JA-GU-AR" like the Batman theme. At the time we were working on new ideas for the album and all I could see was that we had an album of fairly good songs but there was nothing to differentiate it from our last LP. It needed something to make it stand out. We thought of using a powerful instrumental number we had done for Coca-Cola, and then I linked it up with the number "Jaguar". And then of course we thought, why not do a whole side of adverts? As things progressed we realised we could do a whole album that could be built around this aspect of commercial advertising.'

The result was *The Who Sell Out*, which was to be the crepuscular zenith of The Who's pop art period. On that record was a song Pete Townshend had written one year earlier. He believed it was so good that he had been saving it, hoping that if he ran out of ideas this would be the song to rescue a whole album. He called it his 'ace in the hole'. As far as Pete was concerned, 'I Can See for Miles' was the best song The Who had ever written, the song he had spent a lifetime working up to. When it was released as a single in the US it reached No. 9 in the *Billboard* charts, an extraordinary achievement for a band who had only a few months earlier been virtually unknown. It went to No. 10 in the UK. Pete had fully expected it to be The Who's first UK No. 1. Its failure (if you can call getting into the top ten a failure) left Pete shocked and appalled. And it changed everything. 'The day I saw it go down without reaching any higher I spat on the British record buyer. To me this was the ultimate Who record and it didn't sell.'

Pop art, Mod, even rock 'n' roll and R&B as the group had understood them – it all ended that day. The magnificent 'I Can See for Miles' was, as it turns out, a swansong for 'The Who Mark I'.

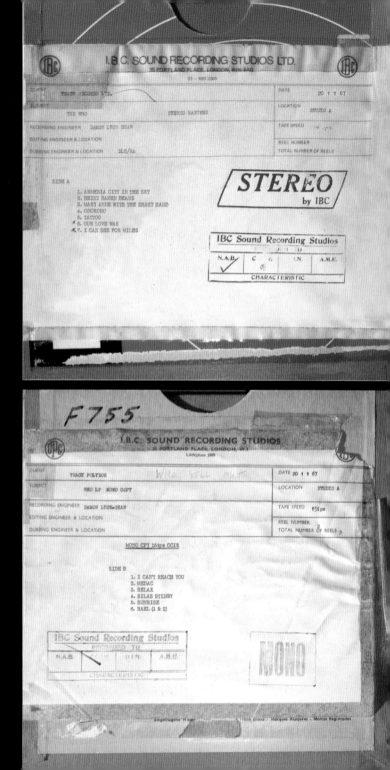

RIGHT Tape boxes for *The Who Sell Out* album. **OPPOSITE** *The Who Sell Out* parodied the rampant consumerism of the late sixties. Roger spent so long lying in a bath full of freezing naked beans that he contracted pneumonia.

OPPOSITE Roger, now looking every inch the angelic sixties flower child; Pete, still much more moody and attached to his Mod roots. The artwork and look were about as psychedelic as The Who. **FOLLOWING PAGES** Newly discovered backstage shots taken by fans on the 1968 US tour and in 1969 where The Who premiered *Tommy* at one of the world's foremost opera houses, the Concertgebouw in Amsterdam.

Pop Goes Art

The prediction business (2)

When we think about pop art nowadays we think about the work of Andy Warhol, Roy Lichtenstein, James Rosenquist, Claes Oldenburg and other mostly New York-based artists. However, pop art was an international phenomenon and one that actually began in the UK – remarkably, since Britain, while famous for its literature, architecture and popular music, had been less renowned for its painters. British artists made almost no notable contribution to Modernism, the movement that immediately preceded pop art, and one most graphically and beautifully expressed by the American Abstract Expressionists like Jackson Pollock, Franz Kline and Willem de Kooning. For these artists the notion of representational painting was dead.

The Renaissance precepts set out in fifteenth-century Italy, that it was the job of nature to imitate God and the job of art to imitate nature, had by the end of the nineteenth century been challenged by science and philosophy, most notably in the forms of Charles Darwin and Friedrich Nietzsche. Art became inward looking, searching for a new purpose: what, after all, was the point of being part of an equation if the most important figure in that equation, God, was non-existent or indifferent? Abstract art, and art about art, became the best and most obvious way for artists to examine their and art's purpose. The Swiss Dada movement of the early twentieth century was so contrarian it actually went so far as to declare all art dead. So intent were members of Dada on opposing all the norms of bourgeois culture that the group was barely in favour of itself: 'Dada is anti-Dada,' they often cried.

If Dada had in part been a reaction to the horrors of the First World War, Abstract Expressionism was a reaction to the next, but a narcissistic one, expressing the artist's inner turmoil. It was certainly a huge performance, as anyone who has ever seen film of Jackson Pollock painting will testify. The art critic Harold Rosenberg put it brilliantly when he wrote: 'At a certain moment the canvas began to appear to one American painter after another as an arena in which to act. What was to go on the canvas was not a picture but an event.' By the early 1950s, with the US richer that it had ever been and people already calling the twentieth

What we now most commonly associate with Mod is often a reflection of The Who's pop art period. Artists such as Peter Blake in the UK, and Roy Lichtenstein in the US, helped to inspire not just painters but rock 'n' roll artists. **OPPOSITE ABOVE** Peter Blake with The Who in the 1980s, when he oversaw the artwork to *Face Dances*. **OPPOSITE MIDDLE** Keith wearing a Lichtenstein-inspired top.

century 'the American century', the American visual arts, from cinema to painting, advertising to package design, were entirely dominant.

British pop art was a direct and emphatic response to this. It rejected the abstractions of the American Modernists by the reintroduction of identifiable imagery. A group of London-based artists, known as the Independent Group, was formed, and at their first meeting in 1952 the artists discussed the cultural implications of mass advertising, movies, product design, comic strips, science fiction and technology. The co-founder of the group, the sculptor Eduardo Paolozzi, dazzled his fellow artists with a collage he had made five years earlier, titled *I was a Rich Man's Plaything*. The collage, which looks very much like the kitch, hypersexualised covers of American comic books, includes the first use in art of the word 'pop', appearing in a cloud of smoke emerging from a revolver. The group determined that they would work around 'found objects' – things like advertising, comic book characters, magazine covers and various mass-produced graphics that mostly represented American popular culture. Pop art, then, embraced the representational and therefore rejected America's most prominent art movement, but embraced American pop culture. It was high art as low art. You can see exactly why this concept would have appealed to the young Pete Townshend. Like The Who, pop art was British, and just as pop art looked to the US for inspiration, so too did The Who. Most importantly, pop art intentionally elevated the commercial and the mundane. The Who, with a former art student as songwriter and with Kit Lambert as manager, had a lofty, near evangelical belief in rock 'n' roll as art. The movement and the band were a perfect fit.

By the mid-sixties artists such as Andy Warhol in the US and Peter Blake in the UK had completely altered notions of what could and couldn't be considered art. Warhol would later go on to work with The Velvet Underground and Blake with The Beatles, famously designing the sleeve to the *Sgt. Pepper* album. The Who borrowed their target T-shirts from Jasper John's target paintings and Peter Blake's famous 1961 painting *The Real Target*, and went about as far as any band has in understanding and promulgating pop art with the album *The Who Sell Out*. Like Blake and Warhol, Townshend's attitude to commercialism, mass media and manufacturing is ambivalent. Some critics have cited the pop art choice of imagery as an enthusiastic endorsement of capitalism, while others have noted an element of cultural critique in the pop artists' elevation of the everyday to high art. There is probably a bit of truth to both. For instance, Andy Warhol, by painting a can of soup and displaying that painting in an art gallery, was not just emphasising that commodity, but making the point that art itself is, at base, merely another commodity.

Ironically for The Who, striving for a seamless merging of the realms of high art and popular culture, real commercial success would come not with the obviously pop art album *The Who Sell Out* but with *Tommy*, the one that Pete Townshend said was a conscious effort to leave pop, though certainly not art, behind.

1969–1974

6

Tommy Can You Hear Me?

The Invention of the Rock Opera

In the year between the release of 'I Can See for Miles' and the recording of *Tommy*, The Who released just three singles.

These were 'Call Me Lightning', 'Dogs' (a song about the White City greyhound track in West London) and 'Magic Bus', which had been written at the same time as 'My Generation' but mothballed because it didn't seem to quite fit the times. Now, with hippies doing Route 66, or packing off to Afghanistan in VW camper vans, it was released. There was also a compilation album, *Magic Bus,* released only in the US and a clear attempt by the record company to cash in on the whole hippie phenomenon.

The endless touring, really the only thing that had kept the dogs from the door, became slightly less hectic, as money began to flow their way. In May of that year Pete married his girlfriend Karen Astley and the couple moved into a large Georgian property in Twickenham, West London. John Entwistle, who had written The Who's live favourite 'Boris the Spider', was encouraged by Kit Lambert to do a whole album's worth of children's songs. Keith moved into a place in Highgate village with his wife Kim and their two-year-old child Mandy. He made a half-hearted go at domesticity, but often found himself so bored he would wander his home with a shotgun, randomly firing at windows. So, just as he had as a boy, he gravitated towards the West End and the endless booze and parties.

It was Roger who had undergone the biggest transformation. A self-confessed fighter, he had calmed down so much that the band nicknamed him 'Peaceful Perce', in honour of his humble upbringing on Percy Road. Roger attributed much of this to his change in lifestyle. The other band members, particularly John and Keith, were still doing very much what the rest of Britain's rock 'n' roll aristocracy were doing and turning life on its head by sleeping all day and partying all night. Roger, who had once spent his spare time tear-arsing it into London in his Corvette, was now happily settled with his American model girlfriend Heather Taylor in a fifteenth-century cottage in Berkshire. True to his aspirational working-class background, he spent weekends renovating the place. The work ethic ran so deep in him he simply, like so many of his class, could not take time off.

OPPOSITE ABOVE Pete marries Karen Astley on 20 May 1968. **OPPOSITE BELOW** 'Magic Bus' publicity shot. Keith is stroking the baby elephant. **LEFT** Pete has always had a fascination with greyhound racing. This is him and the band with the world's fastest greyhound, Yellow Printer, and the animal's trainer. The dog is mentioned in The Who's single 'Dogs', released in 1968. **OVERLEAF** The Who live at the Isle of Wight Festival, 30 August 1969. Roger is wearing his infamous spaghetti suit. A little less than two weeks earlier they had played their seismic Woodstock show.

Relationships between band members were better than they had ever been. Roger credits that to America, which they toured in June of that year. 'I think America really brought us together. It was just the four of us and two tour managers, so we had to come together 'cos there was nobody else.' In San Francisco they learned that *Rolling Stone*'s editor Jann Wenner, who had at one point called them 'almost too English', had nominated them Band of the Year, a massive accolade from the world's hippest and most important music and counter-cultural magazine. On that tour Pete was interviewed by Wenner. It was a long, self-effacing interview. It was one of many he would give that would mix fierce ambition with rigorous self-analysis and would establish him as perhaps the most articulate and intelligent songwriter of his generation. Pete's ability to shock had not left him,

but unlike in the early Mod days when he lied to shock and played to the gallery, his interviews were now bruisingly sincere. It was with Jann Wenner that Pete first spoke of what would become The Who's most ambitious project to date. Pete, now utterly enthralled to the teachings of Meher Baba, had decided to write an album almost entirely inspired by his writings. The album would be called *Tommy*, and its sleeve would eventually be designed by Mike McInnerney, who had leant Pete those books.

In the sleeve notes to the 2013 edition of *Tommy*, written by Pete's mate Richard 'Barney' Barnes, sleeve designer Mike McInnerney attempts to explain the meaning of the album:

'The idea might initially have been about vibrations, but when Baba came along he [Pete] became very

interested in illusion and what we make of this world through our senses. He moved on from earlier ideas to this idea of a character who would have no functioning senses and was only able to be inside his imagination. So, perhaps, he was working from the idea from Baba that life is an illusion, and that all the senses we use just lock us into that illusion, they enhance that illusion … It became much more a metaphor for the way we live in the world. We think we're in the world in a real way because we taste, we feel, we touch; that's part of what reinforces the illusion and locks us into the illusion we are living.

'Pete's focusing on this Tommy character. Trying to understand this post-war baby who grows up and is attempting to come to terms with the world and make some kind of sense of it. I mean, it collapses in the end, but it's a kind of noble story. It's an attempt by an individual to try to make some sort of sense of the kind of complicated world in which they're in, at a time that was optimistic, about what a human being could do.'

Pete told Jann Wenner:

'The album will open as Charlie and Elsie Snerd give birth to a boy called Tommy who is born blind, deaf and dumb. The mother and the father and the family and everybody is very fucked up 'cos they've given birth to a deaf, dumb and blind kid. And he [the boy] doesn't know this. All he gets is feeling, this thing which we as musicians are giving him.'

Pete It must have been hard for Kit when I denied him the opportunity to add orchestral elements to *Tommy*. Instead he had to make do with me noodling about on a Lowrey Lincolnwood organ, still learning to play at the age of twenty-four (I only started playing keyboards in 1967).

Pete This is a good photo of Keith in 'orchestral percussionist' mode. But even when he was sitting at a drum kit he played more like an orchestral drummer than most rock drummers.

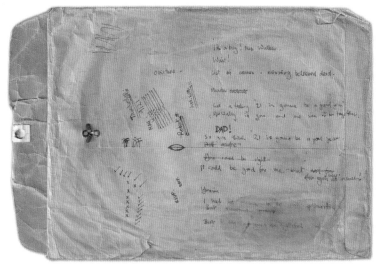

OPPOSITE ABOVE Kit Lambert in the studio recording *Tommy*. Kit decided to place Roger's vocals and the band's backing vocals high in the mix to emphasise that this was indeed an opera.

It wasn't the first time Pete Townshend had talked about doing a conceptual work. It wasn't even the first time they had attempted it, as the album *A Quick One* testifies. However, before *Tommy*, Townshend had always envisaged such a project as a series of singles. Pete after all had been a big believer in the pop single, even when his peers were losing faith in it. In the preceding years he had aired ideas about a large conceptual piece that would be made up of three-minute pop vignettes with interlinking storylines that could either be listened to as a whole or as individual singles. What he was describing sounds far closer in spirit to The Beatles' *Abbey Road* than it does to *Tommy*, but the two aren't as far apart as they might appear.

Under the tutelage of Kit Lambert, Pete Townshend had been encouraged to believe that pop was not some passing fad (this had pretty much been the mantra about Bill Haley, Elvis Presley and all the first generation rock 'n' rollers) but was capable, in the right hands, of attaining the status of high art. This appealed to Pete's intelligence and imagination, but it also tapped into something he genuinely believed, not just for himself and The Who but for all of rock 'n' roll. Great pop music was great art. Pete had never once thought that what he doing was churning out ephemera. He had listened to and fallen in love with enough music and seen enough of his own fans and the fans of others to realise pop could be redemptive, transformative, truly extraordinary. So Kit didn't have much convincing to do. One also suspects that Lambert was as keen to convince himself of these lofty notions as he was Pete. After all, so far as his father – a classical composer – was concerned, Kit was merely slumming it with a bunch of West London yobbos. What better way to flip the bird than to convince the world that today's rock 'n' rollers were tomorrow's Wagners, Mozarts and Puccinis!

It was megalomaniacal in the extreme, but it was also very much in keeping with the spirit of the times

With the comparative failure of 'I Can See for Miles', Pete was now of the belief that the pop single, at least for The Who, was in the past. So, with the encouragement of his mentor and muse Kit Lambert, Pete's notion of a series of themed singles gave way to the infinitely more ambitious, theatrical idea of a full-blown opera. It was megalomaniacal in the extreme, but it was also very much in keeping with the spirit of the times. In 1968 the Paris students who almost brought about a second French Revolution held up banners with the Situationist slogan 'Be Reasonable, Demand the Impossible'. In 1967 The Beatles made their psychedelic masterpiece *Sgt. Pepper*, a record that only a year or two earlier would have seemed unthinkable; The Small Faces were writing the weirded-out *Odgens' Nut Gone Flake* and The Kinks were recording the *Village Green Preservation Society* album. Anything seemed possible, so why not go one step further and make rock 'n' roll's first opera?

Initial reactions from the British press were not positive. No one accused Townshend of being pretentious (that would come later); what everyone seemed concerned about was the subject matter. It was labelled 'sick'. Pete reacted with understandable defiance and bewilderment. 'I don't consider it sick at all,' he told *Disc* magazine. 'What I was out to show is that someone who suffers terribly at the hands of society has the ability to turn all those experiences into a tremendous musical awareness. Sickness is in the mind of the listener.

And I don't give a damn what anyone thinks.' The album had yet to appear. It was initially intended as a single album, but The Who kept scrapping songs while sticking with the concept. It is testimony to how well they were all getting along that they simply allowed Pete to get on with it and chop and change as much as he deemed necessary.

With *Tommy* still no more than an idea, albeit a hugely well-publicised one, The Who ended 1968 by appearing as guests on *The Rolling Stones Rock and Roll Circus*, an ambitious TV Christmas special that would not see the light of day until almost thirty years later. The Who played 'A Quick One'. It was a tour de force performance that easily eclipsed the Stones, whose heroin-addicted guitarist Brian Jones looked like he was dying on stage. The rumour is that Jagger and the Stones' management had the film canned because The Who looked so good. Maybe, but watching *Circus* now it comes across as one of the last great examples of sixties rock 'n' roll camaraderie, evidence of an ambitious, young, beautiful group of artists all pulling in the same slightly bananas direction.

Pete I may be wrong, but I think the bust of Mozart may have been given to me by our gardener Mac. He was very old, and played the violin, and helped me set up several violins of my own.

Pete This was a good day for me. I loved the Stones, had the hots for Marianne Faithfull, loved Eric Clapton and Taj Mahal and even adored the mad Yoko Ono. I got a bit drunk with the sheer thrill of it all.

ALL *The Rolling Stones Rock and Roll Circus* was intended by Mick Jagger, Ronnie Lane and Pete Townshend to be an end-of-year psychedelic celebration of the best of sixties music. It wasn't screened until 1996, apparently because The Who blew the Stones off stage.

Although the recording of *Tommy* had begun in September 1968, The Who broke it off to tour. The album eventually took more than six months to complete (although Roger Daltrey claims that if you added up the time actually spent recording as opposed to discussing it, the album took more like eight weeks). The story of Tommy draws, in part, from Pete's memories of post-war London (although in the case of the rock opera it is the First and not the Second World War) and also from his experiences as a rock 'n' roll star and his observations about sixties counter-culture, drugs and the search for spiritual enlightenment. It follows Tommy from boyhood and utter sensory deprivation through to young adulthood, popular, Messianic adulation and finally rejection by his disciples.

The first part of the opera concentrates on its hero's plight. Tommy Walker is born in the First World War, his pilot father is declared missing in action and his mother takes a lover. Tommy's father, who was not dead, returns home to find his wife in the arms of another man. Mad with jealousy, Captain Walker kills the lover. The murder is witnessed, reflected in a mirror, by the toddler Tommy. His parents tell him, 'You didn't hear it, you didn't see it, you won't say nothing to no one.' Tommy, traumatised, sinks into himself and to all intents and purposes becomes deaf, dumb and blind. During the course of his parents' increasingly desperate attempts to cure him, Tommy is beaten up ('Cousin Kevin'), raped by his uncle ('Fiddle About'), exposed to drugs and taken to a female prostitute ('Acid Queen'). A doctor notices that Tommy appears to be communicating, at least with himself, via the mirror in which he witnessed the murder. His mother, utterly frustrated, smashes the mirror, awakening the boy from his catatonic reverie.

Part two of *Tommy* sees the hero turned into a messiah as the story of his miracle cure hits the tabloids. Tommy founds his own religion and becomes the object of blind devotion. The mercenary rapist Uncle Ernie sets up 'Tommy's Holiday Camp' to exploit those desperate to reach the same level of spiritual awareness that Tommy has achieved. Irritated by his fans, Tommy moves the goalposts, making any short cut to nirvana almost impossible. His followers rise up and reject him ('We're Not Gonna Take It'). Tommy is abandoned by everyone; isolated but utterly self-aware, he finds himself in much the same place as he was right at the beginning.

Initially Pete wanted Tommy to find himself through rock 'n' roll. However, in what must rank as one of the most bizarre and successful concessions to music criticism in the history of popular music, he changed his mind after speaking to his mate Nik Cohn, the *Guardian* and *The New York Times* music columnist. Pete played some demos to Nik and asked him what sort of review he would give it. Nik said that in its present state it only merited four out of five stars. Knowing how much Nik loved pinball, Pete asked him if he would get a five-star review if Tommy was a pinball player rather than a messianic rock star. That clinched it and the next day Pete wrote one of The Who's most famous and best-loved numbers, 'Pinball Wizard'.

When he was writing the song Pete thought of a teenage pinball champion known as Arfur who frequented the amusement arcades of Soho and was a friend of Nik Cohn.

Cohn was writing a fantasy book based around her called *Arfur – Teenage Pinball Queen*. The dedication reads: 'Live clean, Think clean, Shoot clean pinball'. An aphorism uber-Mod Pete Meaden would have been proud of. Pete has

Coded Pips. (To coincide with pictu...)
Deliberate Mistake
Mean Pin Ball

Since I was sixteen
I been attracted by silver balls
Used to go to the fairgrounds
Straight to the Slot machine halls
Ive pretty good

Ive played all the tables

Ever since I was a young boy
Ive played the silver ball
From Soho down to Brighton
I must have played 'em All
But Ive never seen anything like it
In any amusement Hall
That little deaf dumb + blind kid
Plays a mean pin ball

The Pin Ball Wizard
There has to be twist
The Pin Ball Wizard   out
Such a supple wrist !!

Pete In Soho while I was working on *Tommy* Nik Cohn introduced me to a real girl he called Arfur, and she actually played pinball.

ARFUR
A NOVEL BY NIK COHN

TEENAGE PINBALL QUEEN

OPPOSITE *Tommy* artwork showing a pinball machine. **ABOVE** The lyrics to 'Pinball Wizard'. The song was written in haste, after Pete's friend Nik Cohn said that the only way he would give *Tommy* a five-star review was if its eponymous hero played pinball.

said that one day Nik introduced him to the real Arfur and the two of them played pinball in the arcades in Old Compton Street near the Track Records' offices. Introducing a game as basic as pinball meant that the character of Tommy could in some way communicate via vibrations. The effect was to make the opera even more preposterous and therefore even more operatic. The day after his meeting with Nik Cohn Pete listened back to 'Pinball Wizard' and was so unsure of the song he thought twice about playing it to the rest of the band. When they heard it they were blown away. Managers Stamp and Lambert agreed it was to be the single.

Not all of Tommy came so easily. The album is often written about as if it were virtually a Pete Townshend solo effort. In fact, it was probably one of the most collaborative records The Who had ever made. Two songs that are central to Tommy's journey into hell (and out of it) were given to John Entwistle to write: 'Cousin Kevin', which is about bullying, and 'Fiddle About', which concerns the boy's rape at the hands of his uncle. Entwistle lends them an almost circus-like quality, which renders both very creepy indeed. Keith Moon came up with the idea of the base for Tommy's religion being a Butlin's-type holiday camp, inadvertently recalling the long summers Pete had spent with his folks at British seaside resorts. Roger himself says that he would spend 'literally hours' discussing the ideas behind the songs and their arrangements. Arguably it was Roger who was most affected by the album. During recording he came to Pete and asked, 'Can I be Tommy?' What he wanted was to 'method act' the part – become the deaf, dumb, blind boy and then the messiah. Pete agreed. In an interview for a documentary about the making of the album Pete remembers it like this: 'In The Who there was Keith. A genius. There was John. A genius. There was me, pretty close to genius. And then there was Roger. What was Roger? A singer. Just a singer. But Tommy transformed him.'

The album would end up costing £36,000 to record, a fortune at the time, meaning The Who were gigging at weekends to pay for it. Quite a few times during the course of recording Pete would ask himself if he had gone mad, bitten off more than he could chew. He would occasionally ask Kit if the plot was getting too silly. Kit would reply that opera would not be opera without a daft, utterly over-the-top, elephantine plot. The fact is, though, that in its themes of isolation, abuse, the pressures of stardom, the elevation and rejection, Pete was, like so many composers before him, telling a highly personal story.

If Kit was an evangelist for the project, Track Records' US and UK distributors, still very conservative, were less sure. With them Pete showed no shred of doubt. 'We told them they were going to have a five-million-copy album on their hands. I mean I was going up to people and shaking them by the lapels and saying, "Look, this album is going to sell more than any other album in the history of the fucking universe, so get your fucking brains together."' They got their fucking brains

together when they heard 'Pinball Wizard'. It really was the song that changed everything.

The album that went on to sell in excess of 20 million copies was showcased at Ronnie Scott's Jazz Club in London's West End. The reception The Who got was incredible and the press raved about it. 'Twenty-four hours after the event my ears were still singing. There were moments during *Tommy* when I had to clutch the table for support. I felt my stomach contracting and my head spinning, but we wanted more,' wrote Chris Welch in *Melody Maker*.

OPPOSITE Pete was interviewed in the *International Times*, a famously subversive publication that formed a part of the so-called underground press, mixing music, insurrectionist politics and the arts. **ABOVE** The Who showcased the album *Tommy* at Ronnie Scott's Jazz Club in 1969. The reaction from the assembled critics, artists and fans was rapturous.

The US, initially in the form of underground FM radio, couldn't get enough of it. Within just a fortnight *Tommy* had sold more than 200,000 copies, gaining the band their first US gold disc for selling a million dollars' worth of records.

That August, thanks to *Tommy*'s success, The Who returned to America to play a show at Tanglewood Music Center, Massachusetts, and another at the Woodstock festival. It's safe to say that their appearance at the Woodstock Music & Art Fair in Bethel, upstate New York, was one of the most important gigs, perhaps the most important, the band had ever played. With Monterey already under their belts The Who seemed to be festival stalwarts. Woodstock would become the most famous rock 'n' roll show ever, a model for everything from Glastonbury to Burning Man, and a byword for festivals and the love generation's wide-eyed idealism.

The Who hated every second of it. The band's tight, blistering performance was bizarrely at odds with the loping, drug-induced self-indulgence of many of the acts. Pete made his contempt for the event clear when he banned photographers from the stage, including Michael Wadleigh and his film crew who were documenting the event for Warner Brothers. Halfway through the gig, famous sixties politico Abbie Hoffman elected to march onstage and start ranting about fellow activist John Sinclair's arrest and imprisonment. Pete totally lost it, screaming, 'Fuck off off my fucking stage,' then smashed Hoffman into the photo pit with his Gibson SG.

As The Who reached the end of their set with the mellifluous and ethereal 'See Me, Feel Me', the sun rose over the festival, bathing Daltrey in dawn light. As John Entwistle would observe later, 'God was our lighting man.' Even Pete admitted that the finale could not have gone any better. 'It was incredible. I really felt we didn't deserve it in a way. We put out such bad vibes.' However, even God's intervention couldn't quite redeem the gig in the eyes of Daltrey, who still calls it 'one of The Who's worst shows'. For Townshend it was the excess and visible squalor that got to him. 'Listen!' he said, speaking to journalist Dave Schulps, 'this is the fucking American dream? It's not my dream. I don't want to spend the rest of my life in fucking mud, smoking fucking marijuana. If that's the American dream, let's have our money and piss off back to Shepherd's Bush where people are people.' So maybe the London Mod in Pete wasn't quite dead?

Mud and dope aside, Woodstock turned the band into superstars. And *Tommy* just kept on selling and selling. There are three famous versions of the album. The first, produced by Kit Lambert, is by far the best. Daltrey's vocals

As they ended their set with the ethereal 'See Me, Feel Me', the sun rose over the festival, bathing Daltrey in dawn light

OPPOSITE Pete's typewritten lyrics to 'Sally Simpson'. The song is in many ways about how rock 'n' roll and rock stars, especially when treated as messiahs, let you down. The inspiration came from an incident at the Singer Bowl in Queens, New York in 1968 when The Who played on a double bill with The Doors. A teenage fan was injured as she tried to touch Jim Morrison's face and was thrown off stage by security. **THIS PAGE AND OVERLEAF** On 17 August 1969 The Who played Woodstock. They hated every minute of it, despite the fact that the critics regarded them as the best act of the festival. The performance would turn them into superstars in America.

Hippies

A significant proportion of the Wandervögel moved to the United States in the first few decades of the twentieth century and settled in Southern California. Some opened the first health food stores. One group, known as the Nature Boys, settled in the desert outside LA and grew organic food and espoused a clean-living, back-to-nature lifestyle. A song celebrating the Nature Boys, and called 'Nature Boy', was performed by Nat King Cole and reached No. 1 in 1948, staying at the top of the charts for a full eight weeks. It was written by Eden Ahbez, a proto-hippie born in 1908 who grew his hair and beard long, wore white robes, lived on vegetables and nuts and promoted what he called 'Oriental mysticism', a grab bag of half-understood philosophies and religions that included elements of Islam, Buddhism, Hinduism and anything else that took his fancy. He was for instance an early advocate of yoga.

The hippy movement began to emerge at around the time Eden Ahbez had his No. 1 hit. The word 'hippie' or 'hippy' is an abbreviation of the beatnik word 'hipster', which was most likely borrowed from African-American slang 'hep'. Like the Mods and Teddy Boys, the hippies were a product, or at any rate a side effect, of the Second World War. The Baby Boom of the 1940s, to which The Who belonged, generated an unprecedented number of potentially disaffected young people. It is perhaps not coincidental that the counter-cultural movements became politically significant as the Baby Boomers came of age, and America lost its innocence. Several historians write that the counter-culture began in earnest with the assassination of US President John F. Kennedy. The Presidency of Lyndon B. Johnson brought an escalation of the Vietnam War and mass conscription, known as the draft, where these same young people suddenly found themselves fighting in the jungles of South-East Asia.

War, rock 'n' roll and an affluence that made anti-materialism easy all combined to create the hippie movement. A desire to drop out of mainstream society quickly turned into a desire for the transcendent. Drugs had always been a part of underground culture; the hippies, or at least some, claimed they were a necessity, a way of lending destiny a leg-up on the journey to transcendence. The two drugs most commonly and rightly associated with the hippie movement were marijuana and the hardcore hallucinogenic LSD, known simply as acid. Casual use of the drug evolved and expanded into a subculture that extolled the mystical and quasi-religious virtues of tripping. LSD was advocated as a way of raising consciousness. The novelist and pioneer of New Journalism Tom Wolfe wrote a widely read account of these early days of LSD's move from the university research lab onto the streets. In 'The Electric Cool Aid Acid Test' he documents the cross-country, acid-fuelled voyage of hippie guru Ken Kesey and the Merry Pranksters on their psychedelic bus. That journey would later be exploited by The Who's record company when they released 'Magic Bus' as a single.

Rock 'n' rollers were often not just users of LSD but enthusiastic proponents. The Doors, the Grateful Dead, Janis Joplin, Jefferson Airplane, Jimi Hendrix, The Beach Boys and The Beatles all became associated with LSD and undoubtedly helped widen its appeal. These

Dating the birth of the hippie is tough. A 1968 article in *Time* magazine, written a year after the Summer of Love, claims that hippie philosophy has its roots in Ancient Greece. More convincingly, other writers point to the Wandervögel, a German youth movement whose name means 'birds of passage' and that promoted anti-urbanism, paganism, folk music, hiking, rambling, communal living and 'creative dress'. These young people were inspired by the writings of Friedrich Nietzsche, Goethe, Herman Hesse and Eduard Baltzer, and would later become associated with the much more sinister *völkisch* movement. Though the word *volk* corresponds to 'folk' in English, in German it has connotations of 'people-powered'. The historian James Webb says that the word also has overtones of 'nation', 'race' and 'tribe'. The Nazis would recruit heavily from the *völkisch* movement. In his documentary about National Socialist architecture *Jerry Building*, Jonathan Meades talks extensively about the *fin de siècle* back-to-the-landers and proto-environmentalists, concluding that 'anti-urbanism is at best crankish and at worst a springboard to horror'. In the same documentary Meades calls the Nazis 'hippies in jackboots', while the Nazis liked to be known as 'armed bohemians'.

bands also helped to bring the Nature Boy Eden Ahbez out of retirement. The singer-songwriter Grace Slick (known as The Acid Queen) recorded one of Ahbez's songs, Donovan sought out Ahbez in Palm Springs and later claimed to have had a 'telepathic conversation' with him, and The Beach Boys' Brian Wilson is photographed sitting next to him during the recording of the *Smile* album. Hippiedom had well and truly arrived. At its height in 1969 hippies were estimated to constitute 2 per cent of the US population. That is a truly significant minority. The press called these kids the Flower Children.

The Beatles' seminal psychedelic album *Sgt. Pepper's Lonely Hearts Club Band*, released in 1967 at the height of the Summer of Love, was replete with references to LSD, the most obvious being the song 'Lucy in the Sky with Diamonds'. Just as importantly, these drug references were consciously interlaced with allusions to Hinduism, Buddhism and the Hare Krishna religious movement. A year after *Sgt. Pepper* the band travelled to Northern India to attend an advanced Transcendental Meditation training session at the ashram of the Maharishi Mahesh Yogi. Other attendees included Donovan and The Beach Boys' Mike Love. It was at the ashram that The Beatles wrote much of their classic 'White Album', *The Beatles*. The trip was widely reported, thus making drug use and the quest for spiritual enlightenment pretty much synonymous with one another. It is noteworthy that Pete Townshend fell for Meher Baba, an Indian guru who was unequivocally anti-drugs. Townshend himself hated LSD and was deeply suspicious of the whole of sixties counter-culture.

If the high points of the hippie movement had been the Monterey Pop Festival, the 100,000 gathering in San Francisco, Woodstock, The Doors' debut album, The Beach Boys' *Pet Sounds* and The Who's *Tommy*, the low points would mark the movement's death. *Tommy* stands out here because it in many ways predicts the hippies' naïve, credulous proclivity for false prophets.

In July 1969 the young pregnant actress Sharon Tate and four other people were butchered in her LA home. The following night Leno and Rosemary LaBianca were killed in a similarly sadistic fashion. Both homes were daubed with slogans written in the victims' blood. The

Pete Mike McInnerney, to the right of me here – we are looking at each other – was probably more important in the structuring of the story and shape of *Tommy* than any of The Who members. He did all the artwork. As a follower of Meher Baba he understood that I was doubling the duty of The Who's future work, from songs about the troubles of youth to a future of music with a spiritual function. We never tried to shove Meher Baba down anyone's throats. I was nudged into writing about Meher Baba, or talking about him, and I regretted it and still do. He himself said he didn't want his followers proselytising on his behalf.

savagery of the attacks shocked America. The shock was even greater when in December that year police arrested a group of young hippies and their guru Charles Manson, a failed songwriter and former con. Manson, claiming to have been inspired by messages hidden in The Beatles' White Album (he was on acid, remember), had hoped the killings would inspire a global race war between blacks and whites.

When pictures of him and his so-called Family emerged, they looked like poster kids for the Flower Generation. That they spoke of love – 'Charlie [Manson] is love' – listened to The Beatles, had hung out with The Beach Boys' Dennis Wilson and spent their days in the desert, high on acid and communing with nature, somehow made the crimes all the more horrific. The arrest of Manson and the young people he had ordered to commit the murders happened just two years after the Summer of Love and just days before The Rolling Stones organised what is remembered as the most notorious music festival of all time.

The Stones, still furious with themselves for not having played Woodstock, organised the Altamont Speedway Free Festival. As Jagger remembers, 'It was supposed to be a West Coast Woodstock.' On paper, to have a huge festival in California, the birthplace of the hippie, the centre for the anti-war movement and the home of so many of America's most important bands, was an inspired idea.

Taking the advice of the Grateful Dead and Jefferson Airplane, the Stones decided to employ Hells Angels as security. To be sure the animosity between the Hippies (particularly those of San Francisco's Haight-Ashbury) and the police was intense. The Stones did what so many of their generation would do and assumed that because the Hells Angels were also being treated as outlaws (for far better reasons as it happens) and because they too also wore their hair long and spoke in the same loose, California street argot, they somehow shared the ethos of the hippie movement.

They could not have been more wrong. The festival was flooded with bad acid, and the Hells Angels seemed to despise the flower-waving hippies. According to Grace Slick, 'The vibes were bad. Something was very peculiar, not particularly bad, just real peculiar. It was that kind of hazy, abrasive and unsure day. I had expected the loving vibes of Woodstock, but that wasn't coming at me. This was a whole different thing.' By the end of the day four people had died – three accidentally and another stabbed to death by one of the Angels as The Rolling Stones played. His death is captured on film in the documentary *Gimme Shelter*. Just four months after Woodstock, the hippie dream was dead.

Pete My very own geodesic dome. I love Bucky Fuller, and the *Whole Earth Catalog*. Sadly, I hired an alcoholic gardener who drove a mower right through the middle of it.

On the face of it both, Altamont and the Manson/Tate/LaBianca murders look like some squalid inversion of the hippie dream. In many ways that is true. However, the naïvity that lead The Beatles to India and saw men like Ken Kesey and Abbie Hoffman deified is not that different to the wide-eyed credulity that allowed Jagger to believe Hells Angels would make good security guards, or lead middle-class teenage girls to treat a manipulative, racist thug like Charles Manson as a latterday Christ, prophet and guru. During his trial Manson and his followers shaved their heads and tattooed swastikas between their eyes, seemingly affirming Meades' view about hippies and jackboots. Just as alarmingly, a hatred for the establishment had become so ingrained that even when Manson was revealed to be little more than an old-fashioned prison racist (nowadays men like Manson join the Aryan Brotherhood), a certain underground hippie magazine still chose to name him Man of the Year. It shows just how far into unreason parts of the hippie movement had sunk.

The sixties made fools out of an awful lot of people; a tiny minority it turned into killers. It also allowed for the rise of the modern-day bullshitter and charlatan. We surely owe nonsense such as life coaches, crystals and aromatherapy to the sixties. It is to the credit of Pete Townshend and The Who that they were able to see this when so many of their peers completely missed it.

After Manson and Altamont the counter-culture became far more focused and political. With most of the pretence about peace and love dissipated, it now centred in both the US and the UK around the anti-Vietnam War movement. Protests came to a head in 1970, when the National Guard shot live rounds into crowds of unarmed students at Kent State University, Ohio, killing four and wounding a further nine. The event inspired Neil Young to write the brilliant 'Ohio', later covered to heart-rending effect by the Isley Brothers.

If the counter-culture that produced the hippies had begun with the assassination of President Kennedy, it ended with the termination of US military involvement in Vietnam in August 1973 and ultimately with the resignation of the disgraced President Richard Nixon the following year. Not coincidentally, the years between 1963 and 1974 are arguably the most important in the history of popular music.

Pete This pair of hippies is Janet Street-Porter (now a journalist and broadcaster) and Billy Nicholls, who worked with The Who at times on vocals and as resident MD. This was at a party to raise funds for a London Meher Baba centre.

1971 – 1975

7

From Wagnerian Uber-concept to Kitchen-sink Drama

The Who's ability to be both visceral and cerebral had turned them into one of rock 'n' roll's three most important bands.

Which makes it surprising that the next three years appear to be so unproductive. Between *Tommy* (1969) and *Who's Next* (1971), the band's only new song would be the single 'The Seeker', a classic pop song about the futility of looking to leaders for salvation and youth's frustrated quest for identity and answers. However, 1970 did see the band make one of the greatest and certainly the best-known live album of that decade, *Live at Leeds*. The Who had made their bones on the live circuit, when for years gigging was the only thing keeping the bailiffs from the door. This was not helped by virtue of the fact that Kit and Chris had made such a bad deal with Shel Talmy, whereby The Who were still forced to pay him royalties on everything they recorded. After the release of *Tommy* they were cited by many as the best live rock 'n' roll act on the planet. Who biographer Chris Charlesworth wrote that when they played live 'a sixth sense seemed to take over', leading them to 'a kind of rock nirvana that most bands can only dream about'.

After *Tommy*, Pete was coming to realise that The Who's live performances were at least as important as their studio work. With that in mind, the band decided to record and release a live record. Initially the idea was to cherry-pick the

best recordings from their recent American tour. However, once Pete was back in the UK he baulked at the prospect of listening to all the hundreds of hours of recordings and told his engineer Bob Pridden to burn the tapes, which Pridden duly did. It was typical Pete – uncompromising, destructive, but drastically effective.

With nothing to release, the band decided to schedule two UK dates to play, record and release. The first was at the University of Leeds, and the second was in nearby Hull. Both shows were booked with the express purpose of recording and releasing a live album. The shows were performed on 14 and 15 February 1970 at Leeds and Hull, respectively. However, the Hull recordings were found to be all but useless when the band listened to them and realised that John Entwistle's bass guitar was inaudible on several of the tracks. It was decided that the Leeds show only would be released.

Even at the time this was highly unusual, as it was a relatively simple matter to take the best from several shows and string them seamlessly together in an album format. *Live At Leeds*, then, really was what it claimed to be, a show captured as brutally and honestly as is possible. The sense of immediacy and rawness was reflected in the packaging. Designed by Graphbreaks with the stamp lettering created by Beadrall Sutcliffe, the cover is intended to look like an illegal bootleg recording. The cover is brown cardboard with 'The Who Live at Leeds' printed on it in plain blue, black or red block letters as if hand-stamped with ink. It was a dramatic contrast to the *Tommy* sleeve, which had been designed by the psychedelic artist Mike McInnerney and featured the dystopian blue cross-hatching over a dead black void. The Live at Leeds cover, though, for all its minimalism, was no less imaginative. The original 1970 sleeve was a

gatefold with a pocket on either side of the interior – on one side the actual record in a paper sleeve and on the other, twelve facsimiles of various bits of memorabilia, including a photo of the band from the 1965 *My Generation* photo-shoot, handwritten lyrics to the 'Listening to You' chorus from *Tommy*, and the typewritten lyrics to 'My Generation', with handwritten notes. There was also a receipt for smoke bombs, a rejection letter from EMI and the early classic black-and-white 'Maximum R&B' poster showing Pete windmilling his Rickenbacker. The album even included the contract The Who signed to play the Woodstock festival. Like The Who themselves, the sleeve and the record were meticulously planned chaos.

When it was released, *The New York Times* called it 'the definitive hard rock holocaust' and 'the best live rock album ever made'. Jonathan Eisen of *Circus* magazine wrote that it flowed even better than *Tommy* and that not since that album had there been one 'quite so incredibly heavy, so inspired with the kind of kinetic energy that The Who have managed to harness'.

For all its critical and commercial success, *Live at Leeds* did nothing to dim the extraordinary light shone by *Tommy*. This is understandable. Made in the last year of rock 'n' roll's most important decade, *Tommy* was in many ways the sum total of all that had been right and wrong about the sixties. Insanely ambitious, it also nailed some of the daftest aspects of the hippies, the deification of rock 'n' roll stars, the fickleness of fandom and the contradictions of stardom – to be worshipped one minute and despised the next. It is hard for most people to realise what decade they are living in. Something now seen as all-defining can at the time seem like just another passing fad. Movements only become

movements with the benefit of hindsight. Pete's skill was to realise exactly what time he was living in; while peers like the Stones' Mick Jagger and The Beatles' George Harrison seemed to unquestioningly embrace all that the sixties were about, Pete – as *Tommy* makes clear – was both attracted and repelled by the decade.

What *Tommy* did reflect and imply was that millions of young people were in search of some kind of enlightenment and a better world. Whether this was a chimeric utopia that mostly found its form in drug-addled mass gatherings like the despised Woodstock didn't actually matter. While Pete had no patience with the counter-culture's narcoleptic decline into cliché and soulless repetition, he did empathise with its higher goals. Much of this can be attributed to Pete's devotion to the Indian spiritual guru, and self-proclaimed Avatar, or god in human form, Meher Baba.

Meher Baba's philosophies are not easily summed up. He was anti-drugs, even involving himself in long correspondences with American academic and hippie guru Timothy Leary (who coined the slogan 'Turn on, tune in, drop out'). Meher Baba questioned Leary's promotion of LSD and objected to its widespread use, calling the psychedelic 'a false god in a pill'. He believed in reincarnation. He taught that the Universe is imagination, that God is all that really exists and that each soul is really God just passing through imagination to realise individually His own divinity. In addition he gave practical advice for the aspirant who wishes to attain self-realisation and thereby escape the wheel of births and deaths. Most interestingly, in 1925 he swore a vow of silence that he kept until his death in 1969. *Tommy*, which explored the idea that complete sensory isolation could lead to enlightenment, had certainly touched on some of Meher Baba's methods. Now Pete wanted to produce a piece of work that would not just describe but aid the path to the enlightenment promised in the guru's writings.

Tommy hadn't just paved the way creatively, it had provided The Who with the sort of money and kudos that buys bands complete artistic freedom. As John Entwistle would later say:

'With *Tommy* we finally found out there was a lot of money coming in and we thought, "Whooah, I guess we've made it." You see, we always had this idea that *Tommy* was going to mean something. We liked the album, we knew it was gonna be important. But we didn't understand how big it would become. Every time we did a tour we would have to play bigger and bigger places.'

'I am not bored playing it, I am bored fucking talking about it'

Tommy had been a huge gamble. The Who and managers Kit Lambert and Chris Stamp had bet everything on it succeeding. Now it had turned into something of a monster. In their excellent book Anyway Anyhow Anywhere, Andy Neill and Matt Kent write that the veneration of the album had become distressingly cult-like. 'There were worrying signs that its significance was being taken out of all proportion by the new audiences it was attracting.' The band were perpetually questioned about the album's meaning, by journalists and by spaced-out fans. As Keith Moon said at the time, 'I am not bored playing it, I am bored fucking talking about it.'

Pete explained it this way, 'We were going down the drain, we needed something challenging after putting out corny singles like "Dogs" and "Magic Bus". Making Tommy really united the group, and that was the good thing about it. The problem is that it elevated The Who to heights they hadn't attained. It was highly overrated because it was rated where it shouldn't have been.' What he meant was that Tommy was highly misunderstood, treated almost as a gospel rather than a record. It got to the point where the album had almost succeeded in eclipsing the band. For Pete the job now became to complete a project that would eclipse Tommy.

'How could I make a record that went beyond Tommy?' he said to the director of The Who: The Making of Tommy, 'I want the story to be about music. I want it to be about the future. I want it to be about hope and vision, but it has got to be rooted in reality. How could I effectively make my new character deaf, dumb and blind without doing it again? And I thought, I know what I'll do. I will make him live in the future and I'll put him in a suit and he'll be in the suit and he won't live real life. He'll live pretend life, he'll live spoon-fed life, he'll live couch potato life, he'll live the life that film-makers, storytellers, advertisers, political manipulators and brainwashers want him to live. And thus he will be effectively deaf, dumb and blind.'

Pete made his announcement about the new project in the second of his monthly columns for Melody Maker. He wrote:

'It's not often that I get the chance, the chance to use an audience, or in this case a readership, to get feedback around an idea. I am not expecting to get letters or reactions or question timer buzzes or anything like that. I do the talking and I also do the feeding back on your behalf … Here's the idea. There's a note, a musical note, that builds the basis of existence somehow. Mystics would agree, saying that of course it is OM. But I am talking about a MUSICAL note. There is air that we breathe, we swim in it all our lives. We love it and our physical being, and we watch it sustain the world around us. We seem adaptable and receptive to all it produces, but most of all, and this has little to do with the essence of survival, most of us enjoy music.'

He titled the project Lifehouse, and he spent much of his time explaining the idea to his fellow band members and management in the way he had done to Melody Maker's befuddled readership. Stripped down, however, Lifehouse is fairly easy to get your head around. Especially now. The setting was Great Britain sometime in the immediate future. The country has been devastated by some terrible disaster, perhaps ecological, perhaps nuclear. All pleasures, most notably music, are prohibited by government diktat. The population live in mega-cites, wearing 'experience suits'. These suits are all linked to a central point, known as The Grid, from which Government pipes in experiences, or rather the illusion of experience. However, a young dissident called Bobby hijacks The Grid and starts using it to play liberating rock 'n' roll. Through music the people are able to divest themselves of their experience suits and in doing so reach a higher plain.

Looking back at the plot, it is easy to see where Meher Baba's idea of life being a sort of dream comes into play. What is far more interesting is how so many of Townshend's ideas for Lifehouse would be realised either in science fiction movies like The Matrix or in the reality of the internet and the virtual

relationships of social media. The fact that the project would involve the very new technology of synthesisers, and would take the form of live performances and audience participation (there were some very interesting ideas about playing weekly at the Young Vic, where audience and band would develop *Lifehouse*'s characters), as well as a motion picture, meant that had *Lifehouse* ever been made it could justifiably have called itself the world's first multimedia project. Forty years on, *Lifehouse* is both conceptually and plot-wise easy to understand.

According to Chris Stamp, however, the idea didn't grab either band or management at the time. 'It wasn't an idea

where I clearly remember everyone thinking "YEAH" about. But at the same time no one had thought that way about *Tommy*. We just began working on it. So we thought we would begin the process, because this whole Who thing was very much how ideas grew. So we thought we would begin the process.'

Roger Daltrey also remembers being sceptical but willing to give it a go. 'Pete came up with a basic script, which was like a film script that didn't make any sense. None of us could grasp it, but it had some good ideas in it. The one idea I really liked was that if we ever do find the meaning of life it will be a musical note. And I thought, yeah, that, in itself, that is a great idea.'

In Pete's book about the project, *Lifehouse Chronicles*, written in 2000, he reckons the problem he had in getting his band-mates to understand the idea was down to him over-rather than under-explaining it. 'I blamed the frustration *Lifehouse* caused me on its innate simplicity and my innate verbosity. One cancelled the other out.' A little later, in a slightly less conciliatory mood, he said, 'I was at my most brilliant and I was at my most effective, and when people say I didn't know what the fuck I was talking about what they are actually doing is revealing their own complete idiocy, because the idea was so fucking simple.'

Pete Me with my broken Rickenbackers in 1967. The photographer was Colin Jones, who became a really good friend to me, and to my future wife Karen, and who saved our marriage when he urged me to go back and apologise after we'd had a row. (The guitars went with one of our road crew to Liverpool for repair and have never been seen again. They will reappear …)

What would come about from others' failures to understand this 'fucking simple' concept would be, at least in the minds of the critics, The Who's greatest album, *Who's Next*. The irony is that, for Pete, *Who's Next* would always be testament to a failure, or at least a cruel reminder of what could have been.

Pete's ambition for *Lifehouse* was all the more pronounced given that the pressure to exceed *Tommy* was both internal and external. The Beatles had split in 1970, and the Stones had a terrible shadow cast over them by the events at the Altamont rock festival in which four people had died. Critics and public alike were looking to The Who to carry the legacy of the sixties into the seventies. So it is understandable that Pete was thinking big. Very, very big.

However, from the very off the Young Vic experiments in audience and group bonding didn't go as well as anyone had hoped. John Entwistle says that the point, as far as he could remember, was for band and audience to live together in the theatre. 'But in practice it didn't work 'cos they all had to go home for their tea.' Frank Dunlop, artistic director of the Young Vic at the time, and a hugely enthusiastic advocate of *Lifehouse*, blames its failure on the cynicism of Pete's fellow band members. 'I think what happened was that his co-workers did not think it was getting anywhere and so I think Pete lost heart.'

Pete would later confirm this in a short film The Who made about *Lifehouse*. 'When I tried to articulate things to people about what may happen, about what was going on, it probably sounded very confused. A lot of people became very concerned for me and eventually that concern turned out to be justified 'cos eventually I did start to come apart at the seams. I suddenly understood that there were very few people around me who understood what was going on. And there was a lack of conviction. Even within the band.'

Kit Lambert, as The Who's producer, decided that the only way to jump-start the project would be to move it from the uncertainty of the Young Vic to the Record Plant studios in New York, at the time the world's most sophisticated and hi-tec studio. However, even this went disastrously wrong when Pete and the band discovered that Lambert was in a very bad way.

'We had to stop because it turned out that Kit Lambert was doing smack. I was very, very straight at the time. I used to drink a bit, but I hadn't used drugs since 1967, and I certainly hadn't used narcotics. And I was very, very worried 'cos it looked to me like Keith was getting involved with it. And I was desperately worried Keith might become a junkie.'

Chris Stamp agreed that New York, with hindsight, was not the best place for a band as wayward as The Who to record.

'New York is the hedonistic town. So everyone was getting loaded. The more halcyon hallucinogenic days had given way to the more neurotic, narcotic days. And there's the night-life of New York, the after-hours bars, the clubs, the sex, the everything. It was just not the right place for sitting down and getting creative. So the recording didn't really work at the Record Plant, so what happened was Pete and the group just felt uncomfortable and went home.'

OPPOSITE The Who getting to grips with *Lifehouse* at the Young Vic. **ABOVE**
5 October 1972 at the Europa Hotel, Grosvenor Square. Pete and Keith were
at a press party to launch a Who-sponsored Ford Escort rally car. Keith arrived
dressed as a bear, led by Viv Stanshall from the Bonzo Dog Doo-Dah Band.
Viv was dressed as a vicar. Pete promptly nicked Keith's bear head.

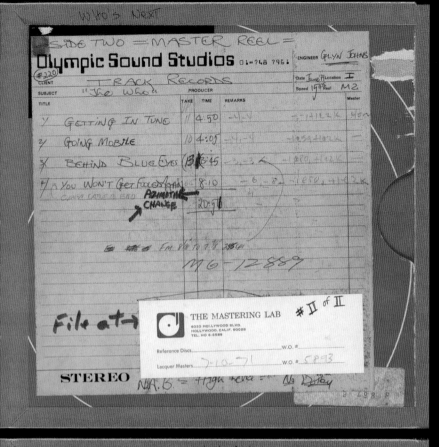

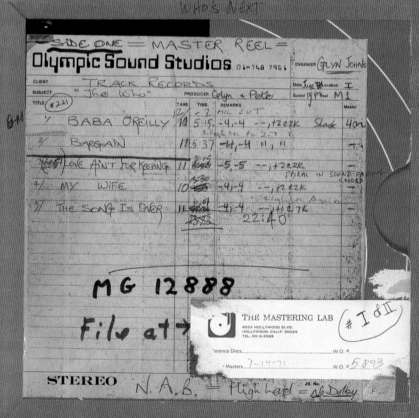

Back in London and without his estranged muse Kit, Pete gave the job of remixing the tapes to producer Glyn Johns. Johns suggested the band start from scratch, and they began recording and rehearsing at Stargroves, Mick Jagger's country mansion. Glyn then moved recording to Olympic Studios in Barnes, south-West London. Kit meanwhile, although drugged up and mostly absent, did still wield considerable influence over the band. Despite his deteriorating relationship with Pete he was the one to finally convince him to give up on *Lifehouse*. 'Pete,' he said, 'just let it go, it's not going to work. Just take the best songs and put it out as a single album.'

Pete, who would later say *Lifehouse* had caused him to have a nervous breakdown, no longer had the energy to fight. In the documentary *The Who, The Mods and The Quadrophenia Connection*, Richard Barnes, one of Pete's oldest friends, put it like this: 'There were two groups of people – people who understood *Lifehouse* and people who didn't. The people who understood *Lifehouse* included one, Pete Townshend. The people who didn't was everybody else he ever tried to explain it to and the whole rest of the human race, which was about four billion at the time.' It is small wonder that Pete eventually came to feel he was on a hiding to nothing. *Lifehouse* as a concept was dropped entirely. Glyn pared the songs down to form a single album, *Who's Next*, which Pete would later call 'the best non-concept album based on a concept The Who ever made'.

What remained of *Lifehouse* were the references to Meher Baba, and these Pete veiled by alluding to the minimalist artist and composer Terry Riley in 'Baba O'Riley'. 'Behind Blue Eyes' was to have been sung from the point of view of *Lifehouse*'s villain Brick, but is now widely read as Townshend at his most angry and introspective. 'Won't Get Fooled Again' was a song about revolution and terror. As Pete explained, 'in a revolution a lot of people get hurt'.

LEFT The master tapes for *Who's Next*.

Pete I never really liked the idea of The Who taking a piss against a *2001*-esque obelisk. It made more of *2001: A Space Odyssey* than my own *Lifehouse* story, which in a sense grew out of sci-fi stories like *2001* and *Fahrenheit 451*.

For many it is simply the best album The Who ever made. Certainly from the hypnotic, pre-rave synth of its opener 'Baba O'Riley', through 'The Song Is Over' and 'Behind Blue Eyes' to 'Won't Get Fooled Again', the album boasts some of Pete's best-known songs and shows Roger's voice at its absolute best. The scream towards the end of 'Won't Get Fooled Again' is the spirit of rock 'n' roll distilled. Both that song and 'Baba O'Riley' were also a radical departure from all that had gone before. As Richie Unterberger writes in his book *Won't Get Fooled Again*, 'it is hard to think of [it] as avant-garde now that it's been a hot single and played to death on classic radio, becoming one of the most famous of all rock anthems, but building any rock track – let alone a hit single – so heavily around extended passages of unaccompanied synthesiser in 1971 was radical.'

Glyn Johns, whose mastery of the new equipment proved so rewarding, also saw The Who's use of computers and synths as dramatically ahead of its time. '"Baba O'Riley" used synthesisers in a completely different way than anyone had ever used one before, where it actually provides the rhythm. It's not just a sound but it's the rhythm as well.'

Upon its release *The Village Voice* called *Who's Next* 'the best hard rock album in years'. In *Sounds*, Billy Walker wrote: 'After the unique brilliance of *Tommy* something special had to be thought out and the fact that they settled for a straightforward album rather than an extension of their rock opera says much for their courage and inventiveness.' An irony that surely could not have escaped Pete Townshend. The view that *Lifehouse* was a bullet dodged rather than a lost opportunity has hardened over the years. In a retrospective review for *All Music*, Stephen Erlewine concluded that the album was more honest than *Tommy* or the aborted *Lifehouse* project because 'those were art — *Who's Next*, even with its pretensions, is rock 'n' roll.'

Just as *Live at Leeds* had come along to remind people that The Who were not some art-house experiment, so the *Lifehouse* project, replete with ideas that still seem futuristic in the twenty-first century, was followed by *Quadrophenia*, a kitchen-sink drama about Jimmy, an angry, frustrated working-class Mod. There have been numerous attempts to revive *Lifehouse*, all of them coming to naught. A film was always, according to Pete, central to its success. *Quadrophenia* actually became better known as a film, and in many ways involved its audience far more than the strange and ultimately useless experiments at the Young Vic. However, both *Lifehouse* – in the form of *Who's Next* – and *Quadrophenia* reveal Pete Townshend as the consummate rock 'n' roll auteur.

ABOVE It's Chris Stamp in the pink jacket and Keith Moon wearing the white corset. The pictures were used as a regrettable press ad for the single 'Won't Get Fooled Again'.

Pete Townshend shares the novelist's and playwright's ability to be before, behind, without and within his characters. Even before his invention of the rock opera Pete was a master of effortless motion between third and first person. With *Tommy, Lifehouse/Who's Next* and *Quadrophenia* he could go from the metaphorically dense to the demotic, from specific detail to wide generalisation, from the actual to the numinous, from the scary to the comic. In this sense he resembles a novelist rather than a songwriter. And this is especially true of *Quadrophenia*, the only Who album written entirely by Pete Townshend.

Perhaps because Pete had no formal instruction in songwriting, he devised for himself a style of narration, an intense, present tense, 'free indirect' style that can leap up, whenever it wants, to a God's-eye view of Tommy or Jimmy, or life seen from the point of view of Tommy's put-upon mother, or the besotted rock 'n' roll fan or the credulous, violent revolutionary. He is all of these things and none of them. *Quadrophenia* is Pete Townshend at his most novelistic. Initially, however, when he explained the idea to people, it sounded only slightly clearer than that *Melody Maker* column about *Lifehouse* had done.

In August of 1972 Pete told *Sounds* that The Who had been working on an album but that he had lost interest. 'I said, look Glyn [producer Glyn Johns], I don't think I can stand this another moment longer. I've got to write another opera.'

The subject of this opera would (at this stage) be the four members of The Who. 'I thought a nice way of doing it was to have a hero who, instead of being schizophrenic, has got a split personality four ways and each side of this is represented by a particular theme and a particular type of song.' Thus Pete would be the good guy, a decent

underachiever who is violated; Roger would be a thug, smashing up the homes of innocents, stealing cars 'and such like'; John would be a lover; and Keith would be a dangerously out-of-control practical joker. This idea is visible and audible in *Quadrophenia*. 'Helpless Dancer' is Roger's theme, 'Bell Boy' is Keith's theme, 'Doctor Jimmy' is John's theme and 'Love Reign O'er Me' is Pete's theme. But the split-personality idea is not nearly as important as the title or Pete's early interviews about the album suggest it is.

Intentionally or not, however, it was a clever way to garner publicity for the band. In a 2009 interview for *Clash* magazine Pete would reveal that 'it was a sop to the band and their US fans to base Jimmy on the four members of The Who. It helped us all get inside it. In reality I believe we in the band worked the other way round: each of us in The Who based ourselves on characters, sometimes groups of characters, we had observed in the early days in our audience.'

This certainly sounds more plausible. *Quadrophenia*, which looks back at the early, often violent Mod years, sounds gruesomely authentic, in a way only someone who had been there could make it sound. The story centres around a young working-class Mod called Jimmy. He likes taking speed, fighting and sex. Jimmy's parents regard him as a freak, and he in turn sees his parents as dull and overbearing. He

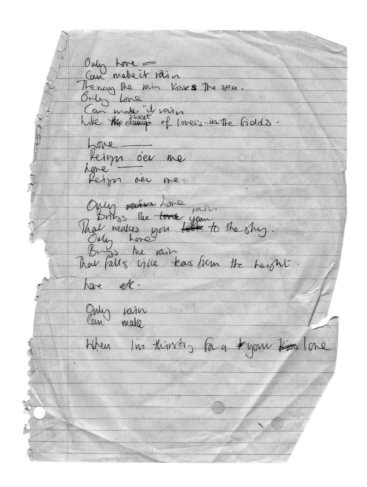

goes through dead-end jobs and even sees a psychiatrist. Perpetually doubting his own self-worth, he finds some kind of meaning in life as a Mod. However, even his Mod pals let him down, and his girlfriend leaves him for his best mate.

After destroying his scooter and contemplating suicide, he decides to take a train to Brighton, where he had enjoyed earlier experiences with fellow Mods. However, he discovers that the Ace Face, who had led the gang, now has a menial job as a bell boy in a hotel. He walks out onto a rock overlooking the sea, and contemplates his life. The ending is left ambiguous as to what happens to Jimmy on the rock.

If the central character in *Lifehouse* had been trapped in dream, Jimmy is a dreamer trapped by grinding reality. And if *Lifehouse* was overly complicated, then *Quadrophenia* is drastically simple and Jimmy is entirely credible. Poorly educated, but poetically wistful, desperate to present himself as an individual, but slavishly devoted to a cult, Jimmy's world view is further limited by a range of prejudices and a stubborn, combative spirit. Yet he is the vehicle for a drama about post-war British anxiety, failure and prosperity, about youth and thwarted aspirations. In many ways *Tommy* had been an album about being a rock 'n' roll star, whereas *Quadrophenia* is an album about being a rock 'n' roll fan. It was The Who as meta-band again. Not just writing rock 'n' roll but writing about the dynamics of rock 'n' roll.

The journalist and broadcaster Simon Price, who as a biographer of the Manic Street Preachers knows a fair bit about the art of being in a meta-band, says this about *Quadrophenia* and Jimmy:

> 'The important part of the opera isn't the fighting on the beaches, but when Jimmy goes back to Brighton and sees the Ace Face working as a bell boy in the Grand. The Ace Face, the Mod supreme, who had been so

cocky in court, is now so servile. A cap-doffing lackey. *Quadrophenia* is ostensibly about Mod culture but really could be about any counter-cultural movement and the way all youth cults eventually let you down. Work means nothing to Jimmy, his family really aren't there for him, so Mod becomes his family. His tribe becomes his family, his way of trying to find some identity. So when he sees the leader of that tribe sucking up to holidaymakers, the whole edifice comes crumbling down. He's left with nothing, but somehow he is more free than he has ever been. A bit like the end of *Tommy* really.'

If the *Lifehouse* sessions and the recording of *Who's Next* had strained the relationship between Pete and the increasingly erratic and addicted Kit Lambert, *Quadrophenia* brought things to a painful breaking point. He had after all been the man to encourage Pete to think of rock 'n' roll as art, and to push him from the simple to the complex. However, as far as Pete was concerned he had also been duplicitous in his dealings over *Lifehouse*. Working on *Quadrophenia* was supposed to have been an emotional

Pete My dad welcomes me back to my studio after I've been recording a flock of geese taking off on the river for one of the sound effects on *Quadrophenia*.

and creative reconciliation, with Lambert invited to produce the album. Instead, according to the band, Kit just shuffled around the studio with trays of sandwiches. By mid-1973 Roger, increasingly frustrated with his ailing manager's habit of missing recording sessions, demanded the band get rid of him. The Who finally sacked Lambert and Stamp in 1974, although officially their relationship lasted another two years. It was an awfully sad way for one of the most creatively productive relationships in music to end. But there was no going back, especially after the band discovered Kit had been misappropriating royalties.

Quadrophenia was eventually produced by The Who and engineered by Ron Nevison. Pete also made a huge contribution by making field recordings of train whistles, seashores and brass bands. At one point they had nine different tape machines playing different sound effects – a logistical nightmare, but also testament once again to Pete's crazy ambition.

When *Quadrophenia* was released in October 1973 it was instantly dubbed a masterpiece. Charles Shaar Murray in *NME* called it the 'most rewarding musical experience of the year'. In the US, *Rolling Stone* magazine's Lenny Kaye, soon to become a star in his own right as guitarist for Patti Smith, gushed: '*Quadrophenia* is The Who at their most symmetrical, their most cinematic, ultimately their most maddening.' In *Melody Maker* Chris Welch, a long time fan of the band, caught the mood of the album like no other critic. Saying it was better than *Tommy*, he hailed it as 'more than an LP – a battle cry, and a hammer of heartbeats. For this is a masterpiece – The Who at their greatest, sap flowing from the roots of their creation. In the way that *Tommy* was unreal, an acid trip and finally a monster, *Quadrophenia*, although it deals in aggression, frustration and sorrows, is so real you can almost taste the HP Sauce and smell the fag ash.'

The album was certainly more real than *Tommy*, but it did not have anything like the commercial success. The record went straight to No. 2 in both the UK and the US, but Richard Barnes calls it a failure if *Tommy* is used as a yardstick. '*Tommy* was accessible,' Barnes told Richie Unterberger, 'it was like modern-day Gilbert and Sullivan. It's got light and shade and it's got little ditties in it. *Quadrophenia* was so Wagnerian and heavy. Even when Pete sent me the demos I thought, "Fuck me, it's all very Wagnerian."'

In 2011 Pete Townshend called *Quadrophenia* the last great Who album. 'We never recorded anything that was so ambitious or audacious again.'

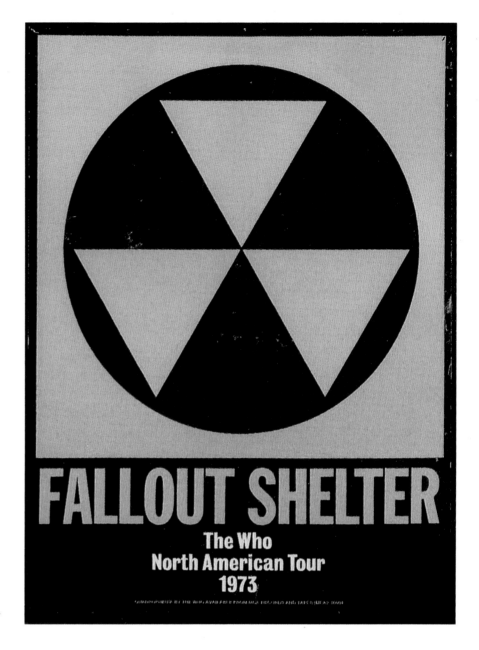

OPPOSITE The Who performing live at Fête De l'Humanité, 9 September 1973, Paris.

LEFT Pete hurls his guitar towards Keith Moon on drums. Just another day in the life of The Who.

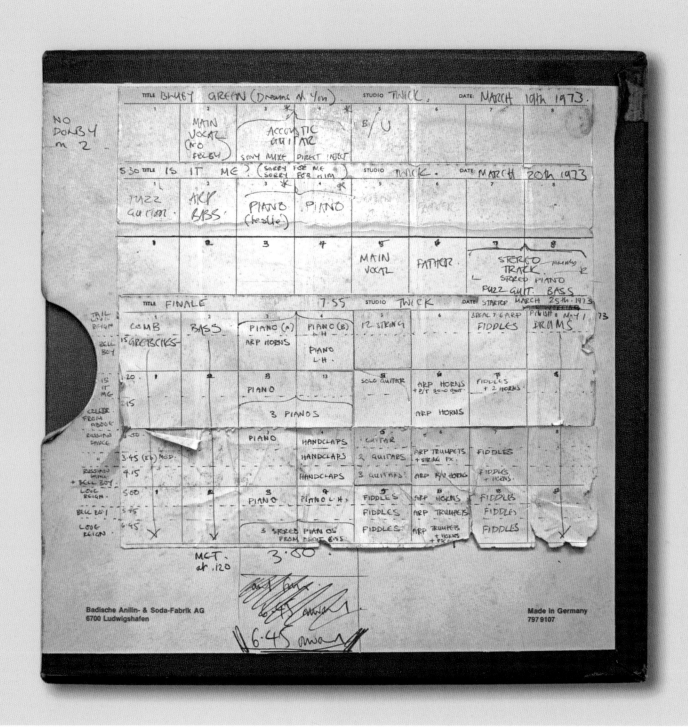

Pete This is a one-inch tape box from my home studio, and the label reveals the complexity of the system I used to compose and demo the pseudo-orchestral elements. In the end we just used these parts of The Who album, and when John added real horns and Keith did his 'orchestral' drumming, the entire score flew like Wagner.

Pete This tape label was designed for my home studio (Eel Pie Sound) by John Davis. Sadly, much of his wonderfully eccentric work has been lost, but if you look closely here you can see that there is a quantity of eels equal to the value of mathematical π (pi). Thus: Eel Pie.

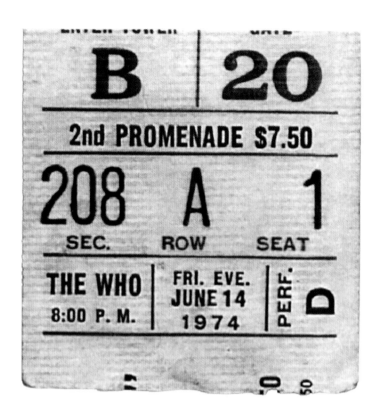

RIGHT The Who's last show at Madison Square Garden, 14 June 1974. After the show The Who threw a party at the Manhattan Center, which featured a magician, snake charmer, fire eater, sword swallower and belly dancers. The 1,500 guests included Elton John, The Beach Boys and Bette Midler.

Pete Charlton is the show that most people I meet in Britain seem to remember. John Wolff created a false 'ceiling' in the sky by using intercrossed laser beams, and as we closed *Tommy*, he slowly lowered it over the crowd. Several people have said that they felt they were levitating.

LEFT Who fans at Charlton. It rained heavily that day.

1975–1978

8

Punk Rock – No Elvis, Beatles or The Rolling Stones

Perhaps if *Quadrophenia*, with its anger and gritty social commentary, had preceded what would become known as the Summer of Hate, Pete Townshend might have felt a little less threatened by punk rock.

As it was, The Who released *The Who by Numbers*, an album of introspective, self-flagellating songs that Pete says were composed 'with me stoned out of my brain in my living room, crying my eyes out … detached from my own work and from the whole project … I felt empty.'

With Pete disengaged, the rest of the band treated the recording sessions with a nonchalance that bordered on the apathetic, often leaving early or not turning up at all. The band had once again recruited producer Glyn Johns, who had done such extraordinary work turning the anarchic *Lifehouse* sessions into the tightly focused *Who's Next*. The recording sessions dragged on, with Pete blaming writer's block and later claiming the band had to record every word and note he had written, otherwise they would have been short of an album. This, remember, is from a man used to being able to throw songs out.

'I felt partly responsible because The Who recording schedule had, as usual, dragged on and on, sweeping all individuals and their needs aside. Glyn worked harder on *The Who by Numbers* than I've ever seen him. He had to, not because the tracks were weak or the music poor but because the group was so useless. We played cricket between takes or went to the pub. I personally had never done that before. I felt detached from my own songs, from the whole record.

'Recording the album seemed to take me nowhere. Roger was angry with the world at the time. Keith seemed as impetuous as ever, on the wagon one minute, off the next. John was obviously gathering strength throughout the whole period; the great thing about it was he seemed to know we were going to need him more than ever before in the coming year.'

When the record was released it left critics utterly confused. The normal distance Pete had on his subjects was completely absent; instead there was a sense of hot, fetid intimacy about the album. Marital breakdown and impotence ('Imagine a Man'), the music business ('They're All in Love' and 'How Many Friends) and alcoholism and womanising ('However Much I Booze') are just some of the subjects Pete grapples with. The only cheerful thing about the album is the cover, designed and drawn by John Entwistle and featuring a painting-by-numbers portrait of the band (he would later complain he only got paid £32 for his artwork.) However, John's one musical contribution,

'Success Story', was a bitterly ironic reflection on stardom. It was a brave, staggeringly honest album, one that is said to have moved Keith Moon to tears. But it wasn't really a Who record. *Melody Maker* called it 'Pete Townshend's suicide note'. *Rolling Stone* wrote: 'They may have made their greatest album in the face of [their personal problems]. But only time will tell.'

Pete has said *The Who by Numbers* should have marked the point where he left The Who and struck out on his own. Certainly *The Who by Numbers* sounds a lot more like a Townshend solo album than it does a Who album. Loyalty prevented him from leaving the band.

In the midst of all this, Pete gave what must surely rank as one of the most ill-advised interviews of all time. Talking to his friend the journalist Roy Carr, he used a long *Melody Maker* piece to attack his fans, his band-mates (Roger came in for a particular bollocking), the music business and all his contemporaries. His favourite target, though, was himself. Pete had turned thirty during the recording of *The Who by Numbers* and was haunted by the battle cries of yesteryear. The line from 'My Generation', '... Hope I die before I get old', which had once excited a generation and moved him to smash his guitar to pieces, now left him frustrated and full of self-loathing. He wondered out loud if he was simply too old for rock 'n' roll.

In London as he was speaking a young band called the Sex Pistols had started playing shows. Within a year punk rock would completely change the face of rock 'n' roll and leave everyone of Pete's generation feeling very old. British punk rock, unlike its slightly earlier American counterpart, was both explicitly and broadly political. The bands it produced, notably the Sex Pistols and The Clash, wanted not only to return rock 'n' roll to its simpler roots but to change society. They combined digs at fascists and the Royal family with rants about the decadence of the hippie generation and rock's aristocracy. Johnny Rotten wore an 'I Hate Pink Floyd' T-shirt and The Clash sang 'No Elvis, Beatles or The Rolling Stones'.

Writing in *The Independent on Sunday* in 1995, one-time *Melody Maker* journalist and early supporter of punk Caroline Coon attempted to describe the febrile atmosphere of the times:

'All through autumn 1975, for a fast-growing network of people who had been wanting and waiting, seeing the Sex Pistols was like instant recognition.

'The years leading up to 1975 I remember as a time of dereliction, squatting, massed riot police protecting National Front rallies, IRA bombings, darkness and strange silence, like after an explosion, when everything blown into the air is falling to earth. The Swinging Sixties party was over. People were reeling in shock. Some were regrouping. Some were watching, wondering what would survive once the debris had settled.

'Street life was nailed down. The spirit of Britain seemed punishing and mean, strung out between two extremes: puritanical Left militancy and loutish Right nationalism. White musicians who had created the hippie soundtrack – those still alive – had traded rebellion for

Establishment. Mega-rich, chummy-with-royalty rock stars were disdainfully out of touch with teenagers. Few resented their making millions, but what they did with the profits mattered. Where was any sense of hippie altruism and community? It was as if white rock 'n' roll had changed sides.'

What Coon does is show just how intimately related in the minds of most punk rock fans were the macro politics of the UK and the micro politics of rock 'n' roll. Rock 'n' roll's royalty needed to be overturned just as urgently as actual royalty. They weren't two separate problems, but the same problem. Thus everything became political. Hippies grew their hair long, punks cut theirs short. Hippies wore colourful flares, punks wore narrow, ripped jeans. Hippies spoke of love and peace, The Clash released a song called 'Hate and War'. The promoter Harvey Goldsmith called it the revolution of the uglies. Pete Townshend remembers feeling genuinely threatened by the movement.

In the documentary *Amazing Journey* Pete describes his fear. 'It was like the French Revolution. I really felt it could have ended with The Beatles, the Stones and The Who being beheaded in public.' The remarkable thing about this recognition of the danger signals is that it shows once again how well he understood his times and the dynamics of rock. Pete grasped punk's existential threat to the old guard because he had, only ten to fifteen years earlier, played a central role himself in disestablishing certain kinds of artist and popular music. The Who, The Beatles and The Rolling Stones hadn't simply co-existed with the jazzmen, crooners and early rock 'n' rollers; they had, for all practical and commercial purposes, wiped them off the face of the planet. Having turned thirty and now being widely known for a film that, as *The Village Voice* had said, looked like a celebration of rock's mindless decadence, he had every right to be worried. The BBC were banning punk rock acts and MPs from both sides of the political divide were asking angry questions in the Houses of Parliament.

In his book *Who I Am* Pete writes:

'Until the British punk rock movement kicked off there were just two contenders for our throne: The Rolling Stones and the upstart, Bruce Springsteen. Bruce had been celebrated in *The New York Times* with the headline "If There Hadn't Been a Bruce Springsteen the Critics Would Have Made Him Up". I concurred. In my mind I had already made him up, and Johnny Rotten too. I saw them both guaranteeing my extinction.'

This wasn't the paranoia of an ageing rock star. This was Pete understanding rock's dialectic, and how youth and anger could genuinely dispose of the older and the more comfortable.

The irony of this is all the more acute because, along with David Bowie, Roxy Music and Marc Bolan, The Who were one of the few bands of the previous generation it was okay to like. Steve Jones, the Sex Pistols' guitarist, remembers a confrontation with Pete Townshend in January 1977.

'Me and Cooky [Paul Cook, the Pistols' drummer] went down the Speakeasy, which was an after-hours place in London. And Townshend was in there, already drunk. We were all a bit tipsy but he was going up to people screaming, "Who are ya, who the fuck are ya?"'

Pete confirms this. 'Yeah, I was there, and I was screaming at them. "Yeah, if you wanna take over come and fucking take over. Just fucking get on with it. You know, good fucking luck."'

There are several accounts of how that night went. Pete claims that after having a go at the two Sex Pistols he told them the music business was corrupt and the Pistols should do their best to destroy it. Others report that he was genuinely disappointed to find that, far from regarding him as the enemy, Cook and Jones saw him as one of their own. 'Here, The Who aren't breaking up, are they, Pete?' said Paul Cook. 'We love 'em, don't we, Steve?' This only succeeded in making Pete more angry, and he took a publishing cheque collected earlier in the day (rumoured to be for nearly

[000,000] and ripped it up in front of the astonished Pistols. Then he stormed off into the night.

Years later in his autobiography Pete would write: 'I met two of the Sex Pistols, and started to preach at them, raging about money. Until the very end I thought Paul Cook, their drummer, was Johnny Rotten … I should have gone home. When I finally did get into my big limo, Tom Jones and the comedian Jimmy Tarbuck pulled alongside in a Rolls. "Any birds in there?" Their faces were full of hope. "No," I replied. "Just a few dead bodies."'

The classic Who song 'Who Are You' was written the very next day. The song is about the business meeting he had the previous day that finally settled matters between The Who,

Kit Lambert and Chris Stamp and also that later, thoroughly bizarre meeting with the Sex Pistols. 'Who are ya? Who are ya?' Pete Townshend was back to doing something he had always done so brilliantly – writing songs about songs. The Who, the meta-Who, were about to produce another classic.

1977 was a year dominated by punk rock. The Who as a band did virtually nothing that year. Touring was out of the question, as Keith's drinking had so badly damaged his health he wasn't capable of performing. The problem was that he wasn't capable of doing nothing either. The band, now with a variety of business interests, made Keith Director of Promotion and Publicity for the Who Group Ltd. Pete and Roger hoped a job of sorts would keep him out of trouble.

Pete was back doing something he had always done brilliantly – writing songs about songs

OPPOSITE Director Jeff Stein filming a promo for the single 'Who Are You' at Ramport Studios in London. The clip was later included in the unedited *The Kids Are Alright*. **RIGHT** Keith sets about editing *The Kids Are Alright* in his own inimitable way, using an axe. **BELOW** Keith outside Shepperton Studios.

The Who were not The Who before Keith and would not be The Who after Keith

In 1978 The Who prepared to release their first album in three years, and their second film, the documentary *The Kids Are Alright*. The sessions for the album, as was typical of the band, took much longer than anyone expected. John was in part busy mixing the soundtrack to *The Kids Are Alright*. Keith was a thorough mess. His time living in Los Angeles had taken a terrible toll. He often didn't just find it hard to keep time, he found it hard to drum at all. At one point Pete became so frustrated with Keith he threatened to sack him. It was an empty threat. The Who were not The Who before Keith and would not be The Who after Keith. But it was an empty threat delivered with the utmost sincerity. The band were at the end of their tether. Shape up or ship out may have been what they wanted, but they knew it was pointless. So they were left with shape up. Neither carrot nor stick.

It was a summer of catastrophe. On 30 July 1978 Pete Meaden, the publicist who had introduced The Who to Mod, was found dead. The news sent shock waves through the band, who had remained close to him. Pete felt particularly bereft, and it would later emerge that every year he had been sending large (undisclosed) sums of money to his mentor as way of thanking him for all that he had done for The Who in the early days.

The *Who Are You* album itself was unusually slick for the time, cut for US FM radio according to the co-producer Jon Astley. Pete Townshend, though, seems to have seen it in part as a way of marrying two conflicting styles, prog rock and punk rock. More bravely, he would come to the defence of disco music with 'Sister Disco'. It was also another attempt to revive some of the ideas in *Lifehouse*. As with *Who's Next*, many of whose songs were also inspired by *Lifehouse*, a lot of the tracks on *Who Are You* feature prominent synthesiser parts and lyrics about songwriting and music as a metaphor for life.

When the album was released, on 18 August 1978, it went straight to No. 2 in the US and Canada and reached No. 6 in the UK. Twenty days later Keith Moon was dead.

ABOVE Keith bows out. This photograph was taken at a privately staged afternoon concert, shot on 35mm at Shepperton in front of a specially invited audience of 500. Among them were members of the Sex Pistols, Generation X, the Rich Kids and The Pretenders.

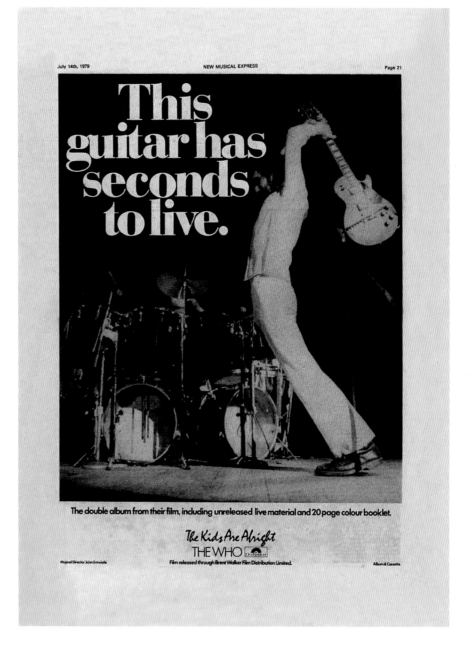

ABOVE Shots from the album shoot for *Who Are You*. **RIGHT** The poster for the film *The Kids Are Alright*. **OPPOSITE** Film can for *The Kids Are Alright*.

"THE KIDS ARE ALRIGHT"

A13/2

TIMER FILM ASSOCIATE

FILM

OPTICALS

To:- SYDNEY ROSE PROD
STORY OF THE WHO.
THE WHO
Dupe from P/C
opt neg from 35mm Print

22 SOHO SQUARE, LONDON, W1V5FJ. 01-4377811

ARTWORK * TITLES * CAMERA * OPTICALS

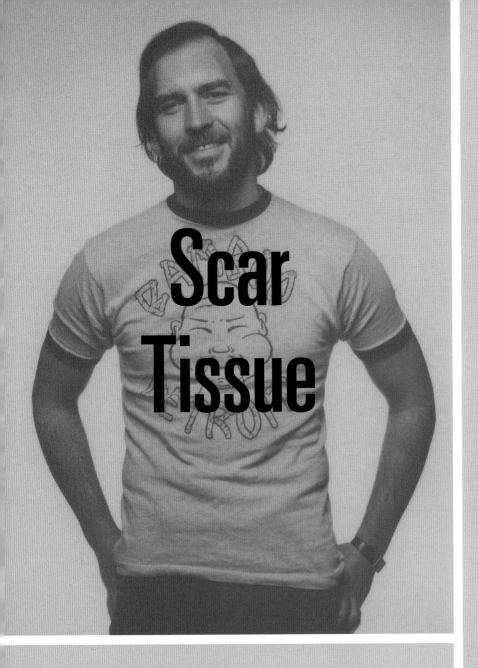

Scar Tissue

The Extraordinary Story of Bill Curbishley and Trinifold

OPPOSITE ABOVE LEFT Bill Curbishley in conversation with Pete Townshend in 1976. 'Pete was initially a little suspicious of me, it took much longer to get to know him. Nowadays we are very close friends.' **OPPOSITE BOTTOM LEFT** Bill Curbishley and film producer Roy Baird in very early talks about the movie *Quadrophenia*, circa 1974.

One of the best days of Who manager Bill Curbishley's life also turned out to be one of the worst. In the introduction to Simon Wells's *Quadrophenia: A Way of Life*, Bill Curbishley writes:

> 'September 7th 1978 was a very portentous day. I was on my way back from Polydor Records, quite elated, having finally signed the contract after many months of negotiation with the record company and their film division to finance two films for me to produce – *Quadrophenia* and *McVicar*. On arriving at the office I was given the stunning news that Keith Moon was dead.'

Bill calls days like that one 'scars'. There have been a lot of scars in the life of Bill Curbishley and of the band he has devoted the best part of forty-five years to looking after. A few months before the death of Keith Moon, uber-Mod Peter Meaden died of a barbiturates overdose. 'Pete was a firecracker of a man, so many ideas, always going off on tangents, very clever.' In 2002 there was the death of John Entwistle. 'No one knew how bad his heart condition was. We knew he had one, but no one, most especially himself, took it that seriously. Mind you, heart conditions and cocaine don't mix.' In 1980 eleven people were crushed to death at The Who's Cincinnati show. 'Still too painful to talk about.' In 1970 Who label-mate Jimi Hendrix choked on his own vomit, also after an overdose of barbiturates.

And there were the deaths of his two former colleagues Kit Lambert and Chris Stamp, with whom he remained friends long after The Who had sacked them both and handed over management of the band to Bill. Kit died in 1981, his death almost certainly related to his drug abuse. Chris died of cancer in November of 2012, after finally winning his own battles with addiction. Stamp's death followed that of Mike Shaw, the man responsible for getting Bill into the music business and a member of a small gang of teenage Mods that included Bill and Chris.

Bill remains almost cheerfully philosophical about all this:

> 'When you solder two pipes together, what is the strongest piece of the pipe? The ridge where the two have been joined. And scars look a lot like that. A lot like the weld in metal. And to me that's what's happened with The Who. We have been made stronger by the tragedies. We have been made stronger by the scar tissue.'

Bill uses fighting metaphors a fair bit, a consequence perhaps of growing up the son of a docker in London's post-war East End. Another one is 'fear' or FEAR, as he would have it. 'FEAR is False Evidence Appearing Real. When you go too far down the road with drugs, that's what happens.'

Kit and Chris had the FEAR. The FEAR is what would eventually be their downfall as drugs and alcohol robbed them of their judgement. The FEAR is what almost got Pete Townshend too. In the months and years after Keith Moon's death, Bill is the man that many acknowledged to have saved Pete from drugs and booze.

Of course it wasn't ever supposed to be like this. Bill was one of six children born to a London docker and his wife, and, like so many of his background and generation, was not expected to succeed. His teachers pretty much hated everything about him and his brothers. Bill the boy returned the compliment by concentrating on extra-curricular ways of making money and losing himself in music, clothes and the street.

'On the cusp of leaving school there was this little gang of us, this gang of Mods. The two I was closest to were Chris Stamp and Mike Shaw. We were Mods, and Mod was all about clothes, clothes, clothes, amphetamines and being out as a gang. We were a bunch of peacocks. We were part of that early sixties explosion of affluence after all the years of negativity. To me that's where the music came from. But as Mods, we didn't follow a certain band. It's a fallacy to say the Mods followed the Small Faces, or the Mods followed The Who. They did not. The Mods followed the Blue Beat bands, like Prince Buster and King Pleasure. We'd go out to the Tottenham Royal, or to the Ilford Palais or to the Lyceum, and we'd end up in Cable Street in some club listening to black music. It was all black music.'

At the age of twenty-eight Bill joined his mates Chris Stamp and Mike Shaw at Track Records.

'People say it's an unusual step, a lad from Forest Gate getting involved in the arts. But for me it was music, and music was in my blood. Music was what we did, that's what we lived for, that's what life was. It was all about the music.'

Bill can't recall the first time he saw The Who. He does, though, remember pretty much everyone dismissing the band.

'I always regarded them as different. For a start none of them were really pretty. Townshend had real appeal, but it wasn't a pretty-boy appeal. Pete asked questions, questions about what it meant to be young, to be alive, to be in love. He asked big, existential questions. He did back then, and he does today.'

By the mid-seventies, The Who were one of the biggest bands in the world but were nonetheless always teetering on the verge of bankruptcy. In 1976 Bill, who had by then established his company Trinifold, took over management of The Who as Lambert and Stamp slid inexorably into addiction. Bill describes their decline as 'almost as glorious in a way as their rise. It had the element of classical tragedy about it'.

'When I looked at Kit and Chris's situation with the band, and realised their deals were not good enough, I changed everything. A lot of people say Peter Grant was the first one to do 90/10 deals for live performance, with Zeppelin. Well he wasn't. I was doing those splits for The Who years before. What Kit and Chris would do was just take the guarantee. That was the safe option. They never fought for the lion's share of the percentage.

'I didn't realise at the time that this apathy was coming from the drugs and booze. I can't stress this enough – so many of the problems they had came from the drink and the drugs. I mean, they raided the account held for Jimi Hendrix's royalties; they raided The Who's accounts. But like all junkies, they never saw themselves as thieves. That's why they were easy to forgive. They didn't feel they were stealing, they felt they were borrowing.

'But the fact is that although the two of them had a tremendously important creative role in The Who, even before the drugs they were not great managers. To begin with, they focused too much on Townshend. I saw this happen with Plant and Page too. [Bill managed the Led Zeppelin vocalist from the mid-1980s until a couple of years ago, and also managed Jimmy Page for twelve of those twenty-six years]. That can have a very unbalancing effect on a band, which in turn can cause tensions between the members.'

One of the first changes Bill made was to get all the money The Who earned paid into an account Trinifold couldn't go anywhere near. 'I made them get their own accountants and they handled their own financial affairs. Trinifold would then bill The Who for their services'. It was not only the best way to establish and maintain trust, it also made financial sense. Pete Townshend says that when Bill took over management he knew he was going to become a very rich man *(The Sunday Times* Rich List puts Pete's net worth at £77 million).

'It has helped coming from where I came from. In fact, it has helped in dealing with people in general. When I first started dealing with record companies, I would go into a meeting or go into a negotiation and I knew I was gonna get what I wanted, 'cos I wanted it so much more than them. I mean, they might've been to university. They might have had the education. But me? I wanted it more. I was also very good with figures and able to think on my feet, which I very much attribute to my upbringing. So when I was in a negotiation I could jump from one thing to another, and they'd agree to things without even being aware they had done. I'd be dancing round them. That's the way it was.'

Robert Rosenberg, who joined Trinifold in the early 80s and now co-manages The Who alongside Bill, reckons that part of their success is due to an artistic sensibility they share with artists:

'I was a musician and song writer myself. I know what it is like to sit on the other side of that desk. I have sat there myself and had A and R men be incredibly dismissive. It gave me an understanding of how you have to pour your heart into it. So whenever I am talking to an artist I am very sensitive to that. I know that I must tread carefully because I am treading on their soul.'

Robert says that the whole Who team has an incredibly strong bond. Like Bill, he calls it a 'family'.

'One of the reasons I know Pete and Roger enjoy touring so much is because they get to see people who they have worked with for decades. A tour is very much like a family reunion. But this isn't just a sentimental thing. It works on a practical level too. For instance, this may sound cruel, but when Bill and I look for new staff in our offices, we often seek out people who can pretty much live and breathe the music business twenty-four hours a day, people like ourselves who essentially never switch off. When I go on holiday I go to LA. My wife and kids go off shopping and swimming. Me, I use the holiday to catch up on all my American contacts. I never switch off.'

Does he ever envisage relinquishing control?

'Well, let's just say that Bill and I are very much thinking about building a company that will be here decades after we are gone. We have been laying the foundations for that, picking the right people, making the right moves, for quite some time now.'

However, with The Who turning 50, Bill and Robert are back on the road. Bill is moving back into feature films and in 2013 he produced the highly acclaimed movie *The Railway Man*, about the traumatised survivor of a Japanese prisoner of war camp. He is also working on a movie about a group of youngsters from Bristol who attend their first festival together. He sees it very much as a companion piece to *Quadrophenia*.

'I always felt great kinship with Jimmy, that much of what happened to him had been a part of my life as well. Mods were industrious, never out of work, obsessed with buying the right clothes and walking the walk and talking the talk.'

And does he ever wonder what Keith would have made of the movie had he lived to see it?

'Of course. I didn't realise it at the time, but in a strange way a part of *Quadrophenia* died the day Keith died. There are quite a few facets of Jimmy that are taken from or mirrored by the antics of Keith Moon. So I have often wondered how Keith would have reacted to the movie had he seen it.'

OPPOSITE ABOVE Bill Curbishley in 1976. **OPPOSITE BELOW LEFT** Bill Curbishley was very insistent that Roger Daltrey play the lead role in the film about armed robber John McVicar. **ABOVE** The Who's co-manager, Robert Rosenberg when he joined Trinifold in the early 80s. **LEFT** Bill Curbishley and Pete Townshend at a charity dinner in New York, 1996.

9

Moon Beams

A Tribute to Keith Moon

When people die young and unexpectedly, and the death of someone young is always unexpected, the manner of their death sometimes helps shed some light on their life.

It is a punctuation mark, at last making sense of all that has come before it. This is true of Kurt Cobain and Amy Winehouse and Jim Morrison. True, in fact, of many of the young stars whose faces grace that gaudy mural on the side of The Prince Albert pub in Brighton. It is only partially true of Keith Moon.

Keith Moon was just thirty-two years old when, on 7 September 1978, his girlfriend Annette found him dead in their bed. He had spent the previous night with Paul and Linda McCartney at the after-party for the Buddy Holly biopic. Many of his friends, including Annette, said that in the period leading up to his death he was finally controlling his many addictions. Many also point to the irony that Heminevrin, the very drug he was prescribed to wean himself off alcohol, was the one that killed him. Here was a man who had spent his entire adult life snorting cocaine and shovelling pills and booze down his throat, only to be killed by a medicine designed to stop him doing all that.

His biographer Tony Fletcher sees it differently. Pondering the apparent contradictions of Keith Moon's death he writes:

> 'There was no irony involved. The fact that, as Annette puts it, Heminevrin was meant to be a "good" drug matters only to the extent that, as Pete later said, Keith might have thought, "If one of these is good for me, eight will be better." (Thirty-two, actually.) Though Keith appeared to understand the dangers of his alcohol and cocaine addictions, he had long thought that anything he got from a doctor must be inherently positive, even though all prescription pills come with warnings and seemingly innocuous over-the-counter drugs can kill if taken in sufficient quantities. His over-enthusiasm or self-perceived high tolerance was, we must accept, always likely to claim him regardless of a drug's intended purpose or effect.'

ABOVE Keith – young, pretty and crazy.

Pete There was a drum wherever a stick happened to land.

ABOVE Keith in his element. **OPPOSITE** 'Fondest memories to a special person who will be sadly missed. Much love from us all Rolling Stones and family.'

Roger Daltrey, who upon hearing of Keith's death rang Pete and said, 'He's gone and done it,' told the makers of the documentary film Amazing Journey that Keith had come to see himself as indestructible. It is certainly true that Moon's ingestion of booze and drugs had gone from prolific to legendary. Moon, however, was not a morbid drug taker. In the words of Alice Cooper, who had come to know Keith well in the last ten years of his life, 'He wanted to make a good time better.' Alice goes on to compare him to other rock 'n' roll stars he knew who had died young. 'I wasn't surprised when Jim Morrison died. I wasn't surprised when Janis Joplin died. I was surprised when Keith Moon died. Because he had no death wish. He was having too much fun living.'

So Keith Moon's death does not say nearly as much about his life as Kurt Cobain's. It was ultimately just a tragic accident. As John Entwistle would later say, 'I think someone looked down and said, "Okay, that's your ninth life."' Pete Townshend would say pretty much the same thing in his official statement. 'Keith has always appeared so close to blowing himself up in the past that we've become used to living with the feeling. But this time, Keith hasn't survived, he hasn't come round, he hasn't thrown himself off the balcony and landed in one piece.' Keith's death, then, was a shock but not a surprise.

Keith's funeral was held on Wednesday, 13 September, at Golders Green Crematorium. The service was kept secret and private to avoid a media circus. Among the mourners were Eric Clapton, Charlie Watts and Bill Wyman. A host of other stars sent their commiserations in the form of flowers. These came from various ex-Beatles and other Stones, from Led Zeppelin and David Bowie, from Fleetwood Mac and The Moody Blues. Keith's favourite charity, Make Children Happy – an apt slogan for his life – sent a display of rosebuds.

Roger cried throughout the funeral. In the early days of The Who he had almost been kicked out the band because of an altercation with Keith. Roger had given Keith such a savage hiding that Moon had said he would 'never fucking work with Roger again'. It took all of Kit Lambert and Chris Stamp's considerable managerial skills to convince the band it was in everyone's best interests that Roger remain their singer. Stamp rang Townshend to say that Roger had promised to never again use violence to win arguments. Pete agreed he should not be sacked. Moon, however, never forgot the incident. 'He was incredibly cruel to me after that,' Roger told the makers of the documentary Lambert and Stamp. 'My God I paid for that day. I had three years of hell. And he would deliberately goad me. He would do anything just to try and make me explode. He gave me hell.' There is a distressing amount of footage of Moon attacking Roger, much of which was broadcast at the time. If this is what was captured on film, heaven only knows what Moon was like to Roger when the cameras were turned off.

And this is another thing Moon will be forever remembered for, his penchant for pranks and wholesale destruction. Keith could not check into a hotel without blowing up the toilets with Cherry Bombs and bangers, and any other explosives he could lay his hands on, and so much the better if a fellow band member or roadie was sitting on them at the time. He celebrated his twenty-first birthday by driving a car into the swimming pool of the Holiday Inn in Michigan, Flint. The band were billed $24,000 in damages and permanently banned from all Holiday Inns. It is some achievement to be banned from the world's biggest hotel chain. On *The Smothers Brothers Show* Keith rigged his drums with explosives, which blew up with such ferocity he was lucky not to incinerate his fellow band members. Footage of the event shows a singed Roger Daltrey going for Moon and Pete looks on astounded. His appetite for destruction was so pronounced he once insisted a car on its way to the airport turn back because he had forgotten something. The car returned to the hotel and Keith jumped out, walked into the foyer, grabbed the nearest TV and lobbed it into the swimming pool, saying cheerfully, 'Almost forgot to do that.' The band missed their flight.

Less amusingly, he would often take to the stage completely off his trolley. During a 1973 performance at the Cow Palace in California, Moon passed out several times on stage while playing 'Won't Get Fooled Again'. He had apparently taken a dose of horse tranquillisers and chased them with brandy before the show, rendering himself unable to play. After a roadie injected him with speed he left his drum riser and started attacking Pete. He was eventually dragged off stage, leaving Townshend to ask, without a hint of irony, if anyone in the audience could play drums so that The Who could finish their set. A young drummer named Scot Halpin got on stage to finish Moon's performance for him.

ABOVE Roger and Keith in the early days having a giggle. **MIDDLE** Keith, looking his 'dear boy' best in a smoking jacket, with John at his country pile. **BELOW** Keith re-imagined somewhat disastrously as a lollipop man. **OPPOSITE** Keith looking svelte.

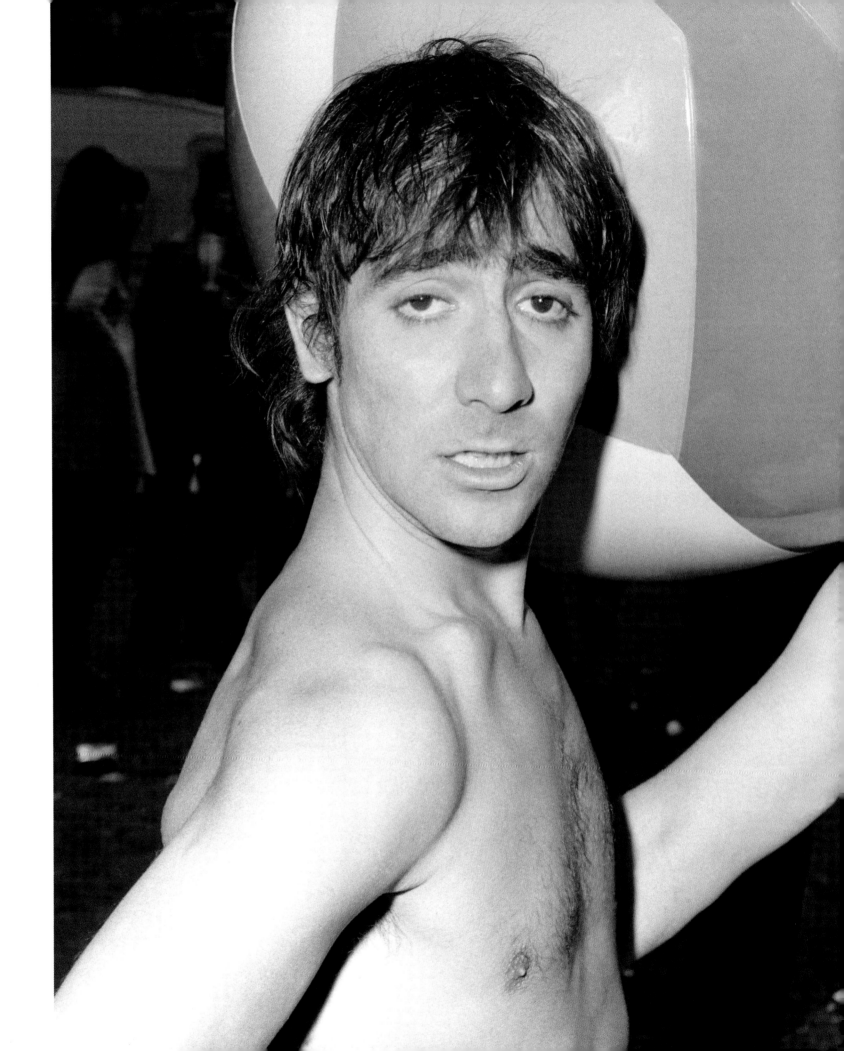

These stories certainly lend a lurid mystique to Keith Moon, who turned excess into a sort of art form. At Keith's funeral service Roger Daltrey supplied the wittiest, and most poignant floral tribute, a champagne bottle embedded in a television set. However, Keith the hell-raiser – Moon the Loon – is in grave danger of eclipsing his contribution to music. As Pete and Roger readily acknowledge, there would have been no Who without Keith. Pete also goes out of his way to call Keith a genius. This is because Moon, more than anyone, including the equally wayward Ginger Baker, changed the way drums are played and perceived. In the words of Tony Fletcher, 'Keith was the first to treat the drums as though they were a lead instrument. He really made the drums an instrument that spoke very much in the same way that a lead guitar does.'

In the days and weeks following Moon's death it must have dawned on the remaining members of The Who just how many fans they and Keith had in a much younger generation. At the Knebworth festival Blondie's drummer Clem Burke kicked over his kit at the end of the group's set, crying, 'That's for Keith Moon.' The US punk rock outfit The Tubes closed their show with a Who medley. Perhaps most significantly, punk Mods The Jam recorded a version of The Who's 1966 song 'So Sad About Us' as the B-side of their classic single 'Down in the Tube Station at Midnight'. The back of the sleeve showed Keith Moon in his young, angel-faced prime. The Jam had never met him, but at a time when so many of the old guard were derided (almost as an article of punk faith) they were paying tribute to a man and a band they owed much to.

OPPOSITE Keith in drag with Larry 'Legs' Smith of the Bonzo Dog Doo Dah Band. He loved dressing up. Bill Curbishley says that he had an uncanny ability to imitate people, taking off their mannerisms and voice within minutes of meeting them. **ABOVE LEFT** Keith as court jester. In the years up to and subsequent to his death there was a danger that his antics, pranks and appetite for destruction would eclipse his extraordinary abilities as a drummer. **ABOVE RIGHT** Keith posing for a nude photo shoot for the Bell Boy tour programme, designed by Richard Evans.

In the 2015 documentary *Lambert and Stamp*, Pete Townshend and Roger Daltrey are filmed in black and white talking about Keith. Pete suddenly remembers that in 1965 Keith's mood changed. Staring at Roger he says:

'Do you remember? He was going through a strange misery of his own. He went through that period when he was on stage and he would cry and he was in deep depression. You could just tell that there was something he wanted that he was never going to get.

'And in a way he wanted us to deliver it. But we couldn't deliver it and he couldn't articulate it. Whenever he was in that state I was always "Aaah, fuck off". You were much more sympathetic, always much more sympathetic. I can remember you going up to him and putting your arm around him, and saying, "What is it, mate? What can we do?" I would say, "Tell him to stop taking whatever stupid shit he's taking," and you would say, "No, there's something wrong with him. There's something deeply wrong here."'

The film zooms in on Roger and we see his eyes cloud with tears. It is an extraordinary moment, almost painfully intimate. A quiet but gut-wrenching testament to just how much Keith Moon meant to them. Of just how much the two loved him. One suspects that in the intervening thirty-seven years not a day has gone by without Roger and Pete mourning their friend.

OPPOSITE ABOVE Keith pretending to practise karate. In his youth he had been a pretty good boxer but had lacked the discipline. 'That was always Keith's problem,' says Bill Curbishley. 'He just lacked discipline. He lacked discipline as an actor, he lacked discipline as a boxer, he even lacked discipline as a drummer.'

Pete This is a glimpse of the Keith–Pete double act. This was usually just for our own entertainment. It was often a running exchange of gags. With John, Keith had a different act, but he used both of us as straight men.

The Strange Story of Esso, Dave, Keith Moon and the Weekend Punks

by Pete 'Esso' Haynes

My brother Dave was two and a half years older than me. One day when I was very small we were about to go shopping with my dad, and my brother just blanked out, he wasn't responsive. I was tapping him on the face and there was nothing, he just stared back. It was very scary. It turned out he had fallen into a deep coma. I remember the day very clearly. I was just nine years old and was ushered into another room by my parents. My brother was in hospital for months. Music was of huge importance to him and he had always loved The Who. In fact, he loved all the music from that era.

My mum, who worked up in Budgens, happened to be friends with someone whose son was roadying for The Who. The feller's name was Roger Searle. Anyway, Roger's mum had heard about my brother and asked if he would like to go and watch The Who rehearse. She said to my mum, 'Roger was saying maybe he can take Dave to watch the band.' Dave was always quite starstruck and was a complete fanatic about The Who. He'd seen them around West London just wandering around, and their van used to be parked around the corner from ours quite a lot. So obviously the idea of seeing his favourite band rehearse, of getting the chance to actually meet the chaps, went down well. He loved the idea. When Mum was told about it she didn't want Dave to go. She was obviously quite protective about Dave, and The Who had a hell of a reputation. But Mrs Searle was like, 'Oh, you needn't worry, the boys will give him a lift to the studio and back.' You gotta remember, these were young men themselves, they would only have been about twenty-two or twenty-three at the time, only ten years older than my brother. It was a bit of a pick-me-up for my brother, these older fellers taking him to meet his heroes. He was so involved with their music. I just thought it was fantastic, these people looking after a kid who was very poorly at the time. And the older I get the more fantastic I think it is.

Anyway, my mum eventually agreed and I remember this feller Roger come down the path and he took Dave off to watch The Who. Drove him

RIGHT Dave Haynes, brother to Pete 'Esso' Haynes, drummer of the punk band The Lurkers. The Who used to take Dave to their recording studio. **OPPOSITE** Keith hanging out with fans in the pub.

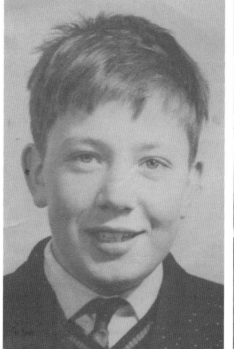

off. We didn't have a car, so for us it was quite a big deal just to see Dave being driven off. So every Sunday Dave would leave in the van to watch The Who rehearsing in Shepherd's Bush. He'd come back with all these little stories. Nothing dramatic, just endearing stories about how well the band were treating him. One time Pete Townshend had bought him a Coca-Cola. Me being so young I was blown away. I imagined it was like sitting in Buckingham Palace with everyone lying about on big couches. One day he tells me Keith Moon came up to him and asked him how he was and Dave said, 'My brother,' referring to me, 'loves drumming too, he practises in front of the radiogram.' Keith loved that, 'cos that's the way he got started, just tapping his legs with his hands in front of an old radiogram. So he gave my brother a whole bunch of sticks to give to me. And of course, over the years, I broke them all. But I did keep one of the sticks – after all, it was owned by the greatest drummer in the world. I stuck it in a draw and I forgot about it.

Many, many years later I was in a group of my own, doing our own West London thing. The Lurkers were one of the original punk rock bands – I am not comparing our little thing to The Who, but at the time punk rock was on the map. Anyway, I was in The Nashville pub next to West Kensington station and this feller came up to me and shouted, 'Oi, what's all this about guitarists with huge fucking noses?'. Cos our guitarist Pete Stride, who I was with that night, much like The Who's guitarist Pete Townshend, had a huge fucking hooter.

The bloke was dressed in a white dinner jacket, properly poshed up. I had no idea who he was. I just thought, 'That's odd, who's this weird old bloke!' I say old, but he was only 32, he just looked old to a young punk like me. Anyway, after doing the big nose thing he starts walking off to join his friends, but gives me this funny look. Like what he used to do with his eyes, making them massive in this cheeky Groucho Marx way. Pete the guitarist in my group says to me, 'Well, that's made your life then.' I said, 'Why's that?' Pete told me that person that had just walked up to me was Keith Moon. 'Fuck me!' I thought. 'That's Keith fucking Moon!' and I thought about how he had treated my brother Dave so well. So I pluck up the courage to go over to where him and his contingent are standing and I say, 'Are you Keith Moon?' And he says yes. So I go, 'Blimey mate, I'm not really one for heroes or ligging or anything but I gotta say hello to you 'cos I am a massive fan of your drumming. I used to bang along to 'Pictures of Lily' and 'I'm a Boy.' Anyway, we get chatting and eventually I tell him the story about my brother Dave, and how he used to go and watch the band rehearse, and how I had got hold of all these drumsticks.

And Keith looks at me – he had these very dark, penetrating eyes, but in pictures you were used to seeing them tinged with humour. But he looked at me really seriously and he said, 'How is Dave?' And I told him he was alright. I was amazed Keith remembered this little boy. But Keith says, 'Yeah, I remember, Roger brought him along.' I was staggered – remember, The Who were one of the biggest bands in the world. All the people Keith had met by then, all the things he had done, and he remembered my brother Dave. So I thanked him for that. I hugely appreciated not just what him and the band did for my brother, but also the fact that he remembered doing it.

He said he remembered Dave saying, 'My little brother wants to be drummer,' and giving Dave that bunch of sticks. Keith then said, 'Where are they, you got any left then?' I said, 'Naah, I fucking broke 'em all. But I kept one.' So he's delighted by this and buys me a drink. He had a quadruple brandy and lemonade and I had a light and bitter. He knocked it back in a second and immediately ordered himself another one. I offered to buy the next one, but he was having none of it and carried on buying the drinks. As he's getting another round in, these two total fucking twats walk up, a pair of boutique, middle-class university educated so-called punk rockers, and they start abusing Keith. Having a go at him for being part of the old guard and other sundry bollocks. One of them, a proper wanker, is going, 'You're Keith Moon, you fascist, capitalist cunt.' So I say, 'Oi, fuck off mate, will ya?' But Keith goes, 'Hang on a minute,' and he takes off his white dinner jacket and he presents it to the bloke who's been swearing at him. And the bloke is like, 'Oh wow. Man. Keith Moon's actual jacket.' And him and his stupid mate went dancing off with it. Keith turns round to me and says, 'That's the way to deal with them, dear boy.' A month or so later he was dead.

Pete Haynes drummed in the seminal West London punk outfit, The Lurkers. He is now a novelist and an animal rights campaigner.

1978–1979

10 ↑

Doctor Jimmy

How *Quadrophenia* Put The Who Back on Top

The Who had confounded Pete Townshend's worst fears by surviving punk rock.

During the period between 1973 and 1978, perhaps the most hectic and traumatic of their lives, they had been working on their second film project, a celluloid adaptation of the band's Wagnerian rock opera, *Quadrophenia*. The movie, which has come to be regarded as one of the most important in the annals of British Youth Cinema – ranked alongside *Trainspotting*, and influential films like Shane Meadows' *This Is England* and Nick Love's *The Firm* – was almost not made. Keith Moon's death had so shaken the band that they wanted to call the project off. According to *Quadrophenia*'s director Franc Roddam, it was the producers Roy Baird and Who manager Bill Curbishley who 'held it together'. For Bill in particular, *Quadrophenia* felt like an extremely personal project. A cinematographic representation of what he and his Mod gang, that included Chris Stamp and Mike Shaw, had gone through in the early sixties as they fought with Rockers on the beaches of Brighton.

Quadrophenia was shot over five weeks in 1978. The movie is in part a love letter to the sixties, part examination of eternal teen angst and part kitchen-sink drama and social commentary. What is less obvious now is that for a great many of the teenagers who went to see the movie when it was released in 1979 it was as much about the late seventies as it was about the mid-sixties.

Quadrophenia could not have been more opportune. The 1970s was a convulsive decade for Britain. Changes were being forced upon the country that were, in their own way, as traumatic as anything that had happened in the previous decade. The seventies, marked by strikes, riots, football hooliganism and latterly punk rock, was singularly aggressive. But also hugely creative. *Quadrophenia* tapped into this like no other film of that era. In *Quadrophenia: Can You See the Real Me?*, the journalist Robert Sandall said that although the film very effectively evokes the early sixties (right down to homes with no bathrooms) it also captures something of the late seventies post-punk violence. 'There was a lot of quite politicised violence at that time between National Front supporters and the far left. And *Quadrophenia* seemed to sum up that very well.'

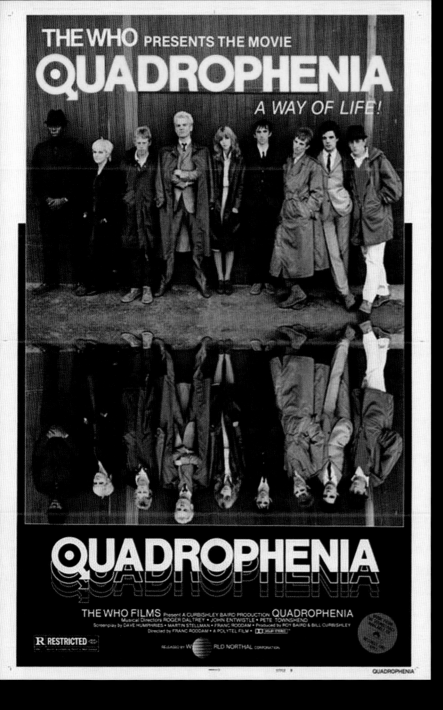

QUADROPHENIA

QUADROPHENIA

Plaza 1, Lower Regent Street,
Thursday, 16th August 1979
7.15 pm for 8.00 pm

Black Tie

J20

OPPOSITE Phil Daniels as Jimmy, trying to chat up Steph, played by Leslie Ash. The scooter he is riding would later be killed. **ABOVE** One of the posters for *Quadrophenia*, which mixed Mod iconography with post-punk aggression.

BELOW The nurses' strike, Newcastle, 1974. **OPPOSITE LEFT** Arrests after a National Front march in Birmingham, 1977. **OPPOSITE ABOVE RIGHT** Football hooligans being arrested, Aston Villa vs Glasgow Rangers, Villa Park, Birmingham, 1976. **OPPOSITE BELOW RIGHT** Drinking by candlelight. Throughout the 1970s power cuts were common.

The seventies, marked by strikes, riots, football hooliganism and punk rock was singularly aggressive. But also hugely creative

Punk rock had led speedily and inevitably to a Mod revival. The Clash, a first-generation punk rock band who mixed reggae, rock 'n' roll and ska, became a major influence on bands like The Specials, The Selector, Madness and The Beat, who dressed in sharp suits in imitation of the Jamaican Rude Boy style.

But the true godfathers of the burgeoning late-seventies Mod scene were The Jam, another first-generation punk band who had adopted a stark Mod look and mixed the energy of punk with the sound of the 1960s. Their debut album *In the City*, released in 1977, mixed R&B standards with originals modelled on The Who's early singles. They confirmed their status as the leading Mod revival band with their third album *All Mod Cons*. In it singer-songwriter Paul Weller created vignettes of contemporary Britain that were both beautiful and violent. Rightly compared at the time to the work of Ray Davies and The Kinks, it paints a picture of Britain riddled with unemployment, casual violence, fair-weather friendships, redundancy and loneliness. It does recall Ray Davies, but a Ray Davies bathed in the political dissent and anger of punk.

OPPOSITE Clockwise from left: The Jam, Madness, and Pete Townshend with Jam singer Paul Weller standing outside The Marquee Club on Wardour Street. Punk-Mod band The Jam were hugely inspired by The Who. **ABOVE** The Specials, another late seventies band heavily influenced by Mod.

ABOVE When The Who played at the Conference Centre, Brighton, on 10 and 11 December 1979, people were lining up forty hours before the box office opened. Fans queuing in the rain were treated to refreshments and live entertainment by the promoters. **OPPOSITE** Pete's handwritten lyrics for '5:15', the song that describes Jimmy's fateful journey to Brighton.

The album, a bona fide classic, helped spur the Mod revival, particularly in London where new Mod bands played small gigs in venues such as the Cambridge and Hop Poles hotels in Edmonton and Enfield respectively, Howard Hall in Enfield, the Wellington in Waterloo and The Bridge House in the East End. By 1979 a whole host of Mod bands – Secret Affair, The Chords, The Merton Parkas, The Purple Hearts, The Lambrettas – had formed and were charting alongside the new wave of Two-Tone and ska bands. The movement even had its own magazine, *Maximum R&B*, its name taken from Kit Lambert's strapline for the early Who posters.

With the Mod revival came the revival of the violence associated with the original movement. In 1978, 1979, 1980 and 1981 there were clashes between punks, Mods, skinheads, Teddy Boys and Rockers every bit as violent as the Mods and Rockers clashes of the mid-sixties. Brighton, Margate, Southend and Clacton all experienced weekend invasions of British subcultures keen to fight it out on their beaches.

Quadrophenia first reflected, then inspired much of this. Just as Who songs had been anthemic, so the film felt like a battle cry. The original album was, unlike *Tommy*, pretty clear in its narrative and its intent. The journalist and broadcaster Robert Sandall said:

'The great thing about The Who was that they were the only band of the sixties to address full on the whole question of youthful identity, and the violence that is inherent in a lot of youth movements and youthful protest. The Who wrote great youth anthems. The Stones and The Beatles didn't really do anthems. They did big catchy sing-along songs, but no one did a song like "My Generation". Or "Anyway, Anyhow, Anywhere" or "Substitute". All of which key in, in different ways, to the very important impulses in youth, particularly in young men.'

Nonetheless when Franc Roddam and Pete Townshend had their first meeting about the film they had very different visions of what it would be. In the documentary *A Way of Life: Making Quadrophenia* Roddam explains the initial awkwardness:

'Pete Townshend is an incredible social chronicler and storyteller. When I first met with him at the studios in Wembley he brought some tapes with him, and the tapes were orchestral versions of *Quadrophenia*. Now *Quadrophenia* is a rock album, but he had brought a string version in. And I imagine he thought I was going to do something similar to what Ken Russell had done with *Tommy*, which is to actually make a film and make an opera. However, I felt it was very important not to follow in Ken Russell's footsteps, because I wanted the film to be very different. But I also felt that this story was much more real. It was much more about working-class culture. It was much more about a street view. It was much more about rock 'n' roll. So I wanted to take a much more realistic approach. A naturalistic approach if you like.

GETS ON TRAIN
DROPS ACID GOES TO SEASIDE.

Girls of fifteen ~~there~~ or so.
~~Sexually~~ ~~knowing~~.
The Ushers are ~~tending~~ sniffing.
~~$~~ Eaude - cologning.
The seats are seductive
~~Nobody's~~ ~~listening~~. ~~Solitary~~ Celibate sitting.
Prettier girls are digging
Prettier ~~men~~ women.

CHORUS Inside Outside leave me alone
Inside Outside ~~You'll never known~~
    "   "   Nowhere is home
               where have I been
Out of my brain on ~~the train~~ IS
Magically doped the $.

         On a quiet street corner
~~Free~~ frustration
          in our minds + our toes.
    Quiet stormwater

        ~~the~~ my generation
Uppers + downers.

BEST † (A secret thats known)
      (~~Either~~ way blood flows)
      ~~the~~
      (Places nobody goes)

        ?

SLOWISH
to allow words to
        breathe.

PREVIOUS The cast of *Quadrophenia*. Left to right: Ferdy (Trevor Laird),
Monkey (Toyah Willcox), Chalky (Philip Davis), Ace Face (Sting), Steph (Leslie
Ash), Jimmy (Phil Daniels), Spider (Gary Shail), Peter (Garry Cooper) and Dave
(Mark Wingett). **ABOVE** John and Roger with lead actor Phil Daniels and
director Franc Roddam. Roger often told Franc there weren't enough white
trousers in the film – 'Loads of the Mods wore white trousers back then.'
OVERLEAF Film stills from *Quadrophenia*

'So I had to say to Pete, at our very first meeting – and it was a difficult moment – I had to say to Pete, "Look, I don't want to do it with this music, I don't want to do the strings. It's gotta be rock 'n' roll, it's gotta be street." And then I said to him, "If you are going to deal in some kind of representation of that period we cannot just have your music, we have to have the music the Mods were also listening to. Your music will be the crowning glory of it, but I have to have other tracks too." I was very straightforward and very clear about it and he was fantastic. He immediately took the tapes and put them back in his pocket. He said, "Look, I did the album. You are going to do the film in your own way."'

The film sticks very closely to the album, and the album itself sticks closely to tried and tested archetypes. By telling the story of Jimmy, a teenage Mod and his mates, Townshend and Roddam run through a series of archetypal situations – getting or not getting the girl, getting or not getting the drugs, wanting to fight and not wanting to fight, feeling like you're a winner sometimes and a loser most of the time. *Quadrophenia* is angst writ large. But it is teen angst with a swagger and style that makes even the most mundane of Jimmy's problems and the most vicious of fights seem impossibly glamorous. Remarkably it achieves this while still preserving a truly gritty sense of the times.

Though the film never labours the notion of Jimmy's quadrophonic, four-way personality split, it does remain faithful to it. What Roddam did want to do was allude to the personality conflicts between Roger and Pete. He saw The Who live as being an exhilarating battle between singer and guitarist. In his view the movie had to be as intense and visceral as The Who live.

'There is a fantastic dynamic between Pete Townshend and Roger Daltrey on stage. They are very, very different people. I try to put some of that dynamic into the film. When you see them on stage they are tousling and arm-wrestling with each other, musically, emotionally and physically. And you see this thing and they create this competition. Roger is trying to sing more and more and Pete won't let him off the hook, and they are going at it and going at it.'

The film does this by perpetually upping the ante and pulling the audience in different directions. Jimmy goes from contemplative to thoughtless, from wide-eyed romantic to vicious thug. When Roddam originally thought of casting the film he had wanted John 'Rotten' Lydon to play the part. Lydon, who in the Sex Pistols had been the sneering, snarling face of youth rebellion and public enemy number one, seemed to perfectly encapsulate Jimmy's rebelliousness. At the time he was shorthand for everything antagonistic and nihilistic. However, the film's insurance company, all too aware of his reputation and of the recent death of his Sex Pistol band-mate Sid Vicious, refused to have anything to do with him.

With hindsight this was a very good thing. Lydon would have brought with him too much very recent baggage. Instead Roddam went for Phil Daniels, who plays the part so well that even at his most desperately unsympathetic there is a poignancy that pulls at the heart-strings. Jimmy's mates were also played by then unknown actors, including Phil Davis, Ray Winstone, Leslie Ash, Gary Shail and Mark Wingett, all of whom are now household names. The only three exceptions were Sting, as the Ace Face, the pop art rocker Toyah Willcox, who plays Monkey, and the British character actor Michael Elphick, as Jimmy's angry and confused father. In the weeks of pre-production Roddam encouraged the cast to spend as much time as possible with one another. He wanted them to act like friends when they actually came to filming. This certainly is a huge part of the film's appeal. You really do feel you are witness to a bunch of mates hanging out together. The sense is so infectious that you often actually feel like part of the gang.

Once he had assembled his cast, Roddam had to decide what the film was about. Roddam knew *Quadrophenia* should have a political edge, in the sense that it deals with the working class, but he chose to make that implicit, rather than explicit. 'I felt that the Mods were not a revolutionary movement, they were a rebellious movement. They were proud of being workers, they liked going to work. They didn't want to change the social order that much.'

He also wanted to reflect a time of massive social change. The Mods weren't simply a youth cult, they were an expression of new-found affluence.

'What happened in the early 1960s was that there was a social revolution in England. The working class started to break out. Suddenly the whole of society was heading towards becoming lower middle class. And it meant that the working class had money in their pocket to spend. So what you had was youth separating itself from the family. They were no longer slaves to their parents, they suddenly had their own rooms, they had their own music, they had their own clothes, they had their own transportation. And this was a social revolution. And one of the main groups that started that social revolution was the Mod group.'

The actor Phil Davis, who plays Jimmy's mate Chalky, thinks that the affluence of the 1960s was for many working-class kids illusory, and that this is what *Quadrophenia* nails and why the movie had such extraordinary resonance in the recession-blighted late seventies. 'The thing about being a kid in the 1960s was that, yeah, you could earn a few bob, but a lot of those kids were just factory fodder. But they'd go down to Brighton dressed in their finery and they were kings for a week. And that was fantastic.'

ABOVE Sting goes from Ace Face to bell boy, tipping Jimmy over the edge.

Eventually, though, the appeal of *Quadrophenia* lies in a simple story told well. Jimmy is any teenager in any time, desperate to prove himself different but eager to be a part of the crowd. Ironically it is Jimmy's dad – often seeming neither to understand nor even like his son – who best sums up the teenager's personality conflict. 'You gotta be part of a gang, aintcha?' he rants. 'You gotta be a Mod, or this, or that. I mean, haven't you got a mind of your own?'

In 1978 this made sense to every punk, Mod and proto-Goth who went to see the film. *Quadrophenia*, by looking back to the 1960s and The Who's humble Mod origins, had seen the band come full circle and yet suddenly acquire a new relevance. Writer Simon Price says:

'The funny thing about *Quadrophenia* is that if it had come out when the album came out, in 1973, it would have looked totally dated on the day of its release. But five years later it looked not just on the ball but ahead of the curve, avant-garde. It captured punk and Mod, and teen angst, and it has pretty much become the most important movie ever made about youth cults. And how these cults have betrayal built into them.

'You know I heard that Pete Townshend wrote the album about a story he had read about a Mod killing himself by driving his scooter off Beachy Head. Now the ending of *Quadrophenia* the movie is ambivalent. But in my view Jimmy doesn't die, he simply trashes his scooter, the symbol of Mod. He has finally got to where he wants to be. He's seen through the cult. He's free of it. In a way *Quadrophenia*, the ultimate Mod movie, is also the ultimate anti-Mod movie.'

The effect of the film, which in the words of DJ Gary Crowley showed youth 'in all its fast-living, sharp-dressing, pill-popping, heartbreaking glory', was to suddenly remind a whole new generation of just how vital and incendiary The Who were. Kids too young to have been born when the band were playing *Ready Steady Go!* took to wearing 'My Generation' T-shirts and swapped their bondage trousers for mohair suits. Just three years after Pete Townshend had assumed punks would want his and Mick Jagger's heads on pikes, he and The Who were suddenly vital again. The critical rehabilitation of The Who, begun a year earlier with the album *Who Are You*, was complete. But how could the band carry on without Keith Moon, the man who everyone agreed had turned a serviceable R&B band into one of the most important forces in popular culture? The Who were back, but not back. There but not there. Critically and commercially they were the biggest they had ever been. Creatively they were, if not nowhere, then certainly in a place they did not recognise.

OPPOSITE The Battle of Brighton fight scene. You get the feeling that for Jimmy life would never get better than that day. ABOVE Peter and Steph on the scooter run into Brighton. They make a lovely couple.

1978–1979 263

ABOVE Jimmy in his bedroom standing next to his 'The Who Maximum R&B' poster.

Pete I never visited the *Quadrophenia* film set, except to eat eel pie and mash. I just left Franc to make his film. There can only ever be one director – I knew that from years of guiding The Who, sometimes entirely against their instincts but with their begrudging trust. I stood back. At first I didn't think much of the film. It has grown on me!

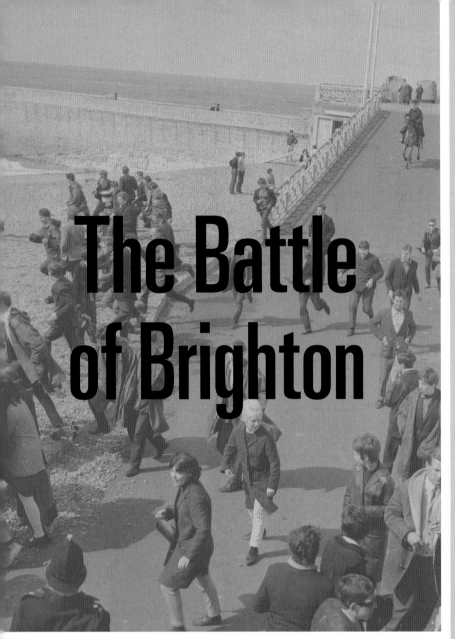

The Battle of Brighton

First-hand account from a Brighton Mod – Brian Muggridge

The first job I ever had was in a scooter shop in Brighton. It was right at the beginning of Mod culture in July 1961. I chose the Mod style 'cos I worked with scooters. Actually, I worked with motorbikes as well, but I preferred scooters. We'd do crash repairs and sell 'em second hand. People were coming in all the time buying and selling scooters and bikes. You could see both sides of youth culture. You see, the Teddy Boy era hadn't really finished. Rockers were essentially just Teds in leathers.

The Rockers were everything that we weren't. They didn't care how they dressed; in fact, the drabber or the dirtier they were, the better. They wore old leather. Never used to come out in shiny leather. The more weather-beaten it looked, the more badges on it, the more they liked it. And we hated that, hated their scruffy clothes and greasy bloody hair. I used to spend every penny I had on looking good. My mother was absolutely horrified by the amount of money I spent on clothes. There was a tailor up the top of Trafalgar Street called Sammy Gordon. Sammy, like the manager of The Who, saw there was a cult developing. A big money pit if you like. And he wouldn't tell you what to wear, like traditional tailors, he would ask you what you wanted. You could have suits with double vents, single vents, no vents. You could have the jacket whatever length you wanted. You could have single-breasted, double-breasted. You could have as many buttons as you wanted. You could have the trousers the style you wanted. And he didn't turn a hair. He just took your money. And if you ever had any money left you'd go to his uncle on Queens Road, who was a wizard with the leather. He'd make you whatever suede of leather coat you wanted. There was none of this off-the-peg crap, every item we wore was unique. Individually tailored. Us lot? We couldn't have been more different to the bloody Rockers. So I saw them coming in, and I saw these much smarter, much younger lads, and I preferred the way they looked.

I spent ten hours a day working with bikes, getting covered in oil and dirt, so when I had time off I wanted to dress up, not dress down. I could never understand why these blokes with their big motorcycles wanted to look like they were working when that was their day off. It was the same with all my mates – we preferred the Mod style and we all bought scooters. We used to congregate round Castle Square in Brighton. This was before they narrowed the pavements, and there was a big lay-by there where we could all park up, sit there and show off. Then we'd go to a coffee bar round Western Road, or you'd go to The Starlight Rooms in Montpelier. But we'd always end up round Castle Square again. We mostly listened to soul music and Tamla Motown. We did listen to The Beatles, Georgie Fame, Geno Washington and of course The Who, but we were quite fixated on Tamla. Normally a Saturday night would consist of going to The Starlight, and then they'd kick us out about midnight, so we'd hop on our scooters and go up to London to carry on dancing. We'd get to Soho about one o'clock, half one in the morning. Most of the clubs up there didn't get going till two, and they would throw you out about ten. We'd drive back down to Brighton, grab something to eat at a transport caff called the Blue Pencil near Gatwick, then go home and crash out till it

was time to go out again on a Sunday night. Of course you wouldn't have been able to stay awake for as long as we were doing without some pills. But the pills were a small part of it – they were just to keep you awake.

By '63, '64 there were an awful lot more Mods. The scene had really taken off. Remember not many of us had TVs and none of us used the phone, so the scene developed very organically. Brighton became a focal point, people came down from all over – Eastbourne, Hastings and particularly London. Us Brighton Mods would do the same. We'd travel all over to meet up. But none of it was planned, it all just sort of happened. We'd pretty much decide what we were gonna do that morning in Castle Square.

The morning of the Battle of Brighton I got up when Mum got fed up with me. She was a widow and she really looked after us. I had a bloody great fried breakfast. Mum always did us something good, she'd never let us go out of the house without something substantial. Some mates of mine, Bob and Jimmy (both of whom are no longer with us), called for me and we all jumped on our scooters, met up with another load of kids and drove into Brighton and parked our scooters up by the Palace Pier [now Brighton Pier].

We all went and sat down on the beach, and we're just sitting about chatting and talking and these reporters from the *Sketch* and the *Sunday Mirror* come over to us and give us ten-shilling notes to throw a few rocks about. They say, 'Throw a few stones, lads, it's a bit quiet round here.' I don't know if that's how it all started, but once it did start it got quite hectic. There were a lot of us, and lot of them got cornered. So it did turn into a genuine confrontation. There were a lot of lads who had come down from London, and they were more violent than us Brighton-based Mods. I think they felt they needed to live up to the capital's reputation. So when things kicked off they upped the ante, quite considerably. If you come from The Smoke you've got a certain reputation to live up to.

We got on our bikes and had been driving about and these Rockers tried to ride us off the road. So we chased them and we caught them and we cornered them down on the seafront. There is a whole sequence of pictures, which I believe the *Argus* has, and if you look at them they had a choice between fronting us out or jumping over the terrace, which is a

OPPOSITE AND ABOVE Mods posing. **LEFT** Rockers on their Triumph and BSA motorcycles. The Rockers called the Mods' scooters hairdryers.

huge drop. And they chose to jump rather than face us. To make matters worse for the poor bastards, the police were waiting for them down below. So they literally jumped into the arms of the police! Us Brighton lot we never carried weapons. The deckchair was my weapon of choice that day, and you'd look a bit bleeding stupid walking around with a deckchair under your arm. Hard to conceal, a deckchair. I'd paid for that deckchair, and I definitely got my hour's worth out of it!

None of our little mob, about twenty or thirty lads, were arrested. Most of the Mods that were nicked were Londoners. I went home dancing that night. Never really realised the significance of the day until years later. Those pictures of me are in every print shop and every trendy restaurant in Brighton. I get asked to autograph them a fair bit. So glad my mum didn't find out, though.

First-hand account from a London Mod – Barry Simner

My family are from Peckham but by the early sixties we'd moved to the suburbs, Epsom way. So Brighton was only an hour on a scooter. Our mob came from the south-West London suburbs, Richmond, Kingston, Epsom. I was still at school in 1964. I had been lucky enough to get to a grammar school, which was great for my future but it meant that unlike a lot of my mates who had started full-time work at fifteen, I never had much money. My clothes were bought from markets, where you could get decent off-the-peg clobber for not too much.

We were into soul, ska, The Who, Blue Beat. A lot of my musical education came from the Jamaican Rude Boys. There were these guys who would bring their sound systems down from Brixton and play all-night parties at a boozer in Chessington called, weirdly, The Blackamoors Head. Brighton was a weekend place for us. We would often go down there on a Friday night and hang out at the clubs. We'd dance all night and then catch a couple of hours' sleep on the beach. That's where the parkas came in handy. We were always trying to get hold of drugs. Hours wasted trying to get hold of this pill or that pill. Never with much luck, to be honest. People sold us all sorts of rubbish telling us they were Purple Hearts or Black Bombers – normally they were just some slimming aid.

At home I never had too much of a problem with Rockers most of the time. But one night we came out of our youth club and someone had knocked down all our scooters. They'd gone down like dominoes. We were convinced it was the Rockers, so we went to their pub in Malden Manor, we went through the car park and smashed all the cars' headlights, and then we chucked chairs and dustbins through the pub's plate-glass windows. Not much coming back after that sort of thing.

On the way down from Epsom we'd bump into loads of Mods from East and South London. There was one bloke, hugely tall, long leather coat and dyed blond hair – just like Sting in *Quadrophenia* – and he would take the lead. He was known as The General. He was from the East End and him and his lot were seriously intimidating. They looked amazing but they were violent blokes. Anyway, we'd all meet on the A23 and one day as we were driving down some of the cars weren't giving us much

room. So The General steps off his scooter, walks out into the middle of the road and brings all the traffic to a halt. Then he waits till all the other scooters have caught up, orders us all to get back on our bikes and we take up the whole of the road, completely blocking the cars. There must have been about fifty to a hundred of us in that one little group. And we drove down doing about 20mph – any faster would have messed up our hair. We had the traffic backed up all the way to London.

I never saw any reporters give money to anyone to start a fight. I can completely believe it happened, but I honestly don't think that's what caused the fights. The fights would have happened anyway, there was just an inevitability about the day. See, up until '64 the Rockers had outnumbered us. They were older than us, only by about five or six years, but when you're sixteen or something, that's an age. So we would always get the worst of it. Then in '64 it just changed. There were so many, many more of us than them and I think it was payback time – we wanted to give them a hiding. I can't remember how it all started, I just remember people would be saying, 'We've seen a bunch of them [Rockers] on West Street' – or 'We've spotted 'em down by the West Pier!' And we'd all tear down there. The crowd moved in this very organic way. There was nothing organised about the violence, not like the hooligans of today, who sort things out by mobile phone and on Twitter and things. This was just happening. And that's what made it so exciting. 'Cos any second you and your mates could turn the corner and you'd be confronted by a hundred of them. There was this sense of freedom really. This idea that we, the young, had taken over. It felt great – we had the run of Brighton.

At one point we were chasing these Rockers and I whacked one of them with a deckchair, and – I remember this like it was yesterday – this old woman turned around to me and said, 'You Mods. You don't fight fair.' For some reason that still makes me giggle. That day was pure dumb fun. None of us wanted to change the world. I got home that night and I was really pleased we'd made the evening news on the telly. We didn't get the papers, so I never saw the Battle of Brighton headlines. My mum and dad weren't remotely aware of what I had gotten up to that day. Four years later, though, I made the front cover of the papers when I was nicked outside Grosvenor Square where I'd been demonstrating against the Vietnam War. In a way I like to think The Who and I followed a similar trajectory. From rebelliousness to revolution

1979—2000

11

When You
Do It Alone

The Who Go Solo

In the initial days after Keith Moon's death, The Who seemed almost bizarrely bullish.

The three remaining members told people they were in a sense more free than they had been in years. This must have been some crazy silver-lining thinking, a way of turning a negative into a positive, a gloss put on the tragic loss of their friend and drummer. But they really did make a pretty convincing case.

'In a way, it was like a sacrifice,' Roger Daltrey told *Rolling Stone's* Dave Marsh, who had flown to London upon hearing of Keith's death and was granted an interview with the grieving group. 'We can do anything we want to do now. I have very odd feelings. I feel incredibly strong, and at the same time, I feel incredibly fragile.'

The implication in those early, tear-stained days was that Keith Moon, so much larger than life, had somehow trapped the band into sounding a certain way, and living up to a certain image and lifestyle that Roger, John and Pete had long since left behind. Without him, and his heavy, heavy baggage, The Who would be free of those constraints, inspired to be something different, to sound in some way new. To be The Who, but The Who Mark II.

Maybe it was the shock and maybe they really believed it. Certainly their first move was to replace Keith with a much, much more conventional drummer. In November, The Who hired Kenney Jones, who had been the drummer with The Small Faces and later The Faces. 'There was nobody else, in my opinion,' declared Pete emphatically. It did make a sort of sense. The Small Faces had been contemporaries of The Who. Like The Who, they had helped to lead the London Mod scene. One of their albums, *Ogden's Nut Gone Flake*, even seemed to share Pete's beautifully lofty ambitions. Furthermore the two bands had toured together and on a personal level they really liked one another. Roger in particular had been very friendly with Kenney.

But Kenney was not Keith. He didn't play anything like Keith. In fact, he could not have been any more different. Keith was so exceptionally talented and imaginative he was able to tear up the rule book and throw technique out the window. Kenney was reverential – a stickler for the rules. Like The

RIGHT The Who minus Keith at the premiere of *The Kids Are Alright*. Keith was indisputably the star turn in that movie, making his absence even more painful.
BELOW Kenney Jones replaced Keith on drums, but he never quite worked. No one could replace Keith on drums.

Beatles' Ringo Starr he kept solid, tight time. He was classic back-line. Pete especially seemed to welcome this, having convinced himself that a certain amount of orthodoxy from the rhythm section would afford him a new creative liberty. He was so keen on this idea, and by extension on Kenney, that he insisted he be made a full member of the band.

Roger, who despite his friendship sensed from the off that Kenney's regimented style wouldn't suit the band, attempted to talk Pete out of what was undoubtedly a momentous decision, made while still grieving. 'I just never thought he was the right drummer for the Who,' Roger Daltrey would tell *Musician* magazine in 1989. 'Kenney was simplicity itself … Kenney was not capable of doing any more than he did.'

Ten years later Pete attempted to explain his thinking to Charles Young of *Musician* magazine: 'He [Roger] wanted Kenney on salary. I said, "No, I'm not ready for that. It means we're still running The Who. It's like we're on a pilgrimage to find Keith. To be really unpleasant about it, I'm kind of glad Keith is gone. He was a pain in the ass. The band wasn't functioning. This is a chance to do something new."' He didn't mean it. But it was typical Pete – committing himself to a decision, and burning bridges by taking his old mate's name in vein.

Eight months after Keith's death The Who Mark II, with new full-time member Kenney Jones on drums, made their debut at the Rainbow in London on 2 May 1979. But even at that moment they were thoroughly eclipsed by The Who Mark I. The documentary *The Kids Are Alright* premiered at Cannes the following week. Scriptless, and without narration or even apparent direction, it presented the band at their anarchic, explosive best. Keith Moon dominates the film, he is its star. A legend in his lifetime, his death made him immortal, and the film only helped to enhance the feeling that rock and popular culture had lost a true one-off. *The Kids Are Alright* was a fitting eulogy to Keith Moon.

ABOVE The artwork for the *Face Dances* album. The design was conceived by Peter Blake. In the wake of Keith's death the skull imagery seems oddly macabre. **OPPOSITE** The Who play Live Aid, one of many sporadic reunions.

The documentary was followed that summer by *Quadrophenia*, which further elevated The Who and reminded the world just how subversive a band they had been. In 1980, just over a year after Kenney Jones had joined the band, The Who Mark II went into the studio to record their ninth studio album, *Face Dances*. Boasting one great single, 'You Better You Bet', and a magnificently strange and macabre cover, it suggested there was real hope for the band post-Moon. The sleeve carried portraits of the band members painted by some of Britain's most famous artists, including Bill Jacklin, Tom Phillips, Colin Self, Richard Hamilton, Mike Andrews, Allen Jones, David Inshaw, David Hockney, Clive Barker, R.B. Kitaj, Howard Hodgkin, Patrick Caulfield, Peter Blake, Joe Tilson, Patrick Procktor and David Tindle. The original concept had come from Peter Blake, the pop artist responsible for the cover of The Beatles' *Sgt. Pepper* album. The *Face Dances* sleeve is considerably darker, the faces of the band looking ghoulish and skull-like, almost as if they were ghosts. The album came out in March 1981 and reached No. 2 in the UK charts and No. 4 in the US.

Just one month later, news reached Pete Townshend that his old mentor and muse Kit Lambert had died. The exact circumstances of Kit's death remain a little mysterious, but it is likely that a beating he received at a gay club two days earlier caused the brain haemorrhage that killed him. In the space of just twenty months, Pete, Roger and John had lost three of the most important influences on them: first Pete Meaden, then Keith Moon and now Kit Lambert. And all of them from 'fucking around with drugs and alcohol', as Pete later defined Keith's cause of death. He sank into a self-destructive depression. In *Dear Boy*, his biography of Keith Moon, Tony Fletcher describes Pete's desperate state of mind: 'Townshend became the fool instead of the teacher, the gadabout in place of the spiritualist, the destroyer rather than the seeker and the adulterer where once he was the family man.'

In 1982 The Who released *It's Hard*. They had hated recording the album, and it has been described as soulless and even pointless. However, *Rolling Stone* magazine's Parke Puterbaugh wrote a polarising review of the record, calling it 'their most vital and coherent album since *Who's Next*'. Puterbaugh also wrote that the song 'I've Known No War' was 'a song that could become an anthem to our generation much the way "Won't Get Fooled Again" did a decade ago'. A tour followed, but it lacked the aggression, magic and chaos The Who had become famous for. Later that year The Who quietly split up. They made no official announcement, but Pete bought himself and Kenney Jones out of the contract they had just signed and the band sold off, or wound up, all the companies belonging to The Who. In 2014, in an interview with Adrian Deevoy for *Event* magazine, Roger Daltrey said it was he who split the band. 'Pete's drinking had got very bad by '82,' Daltrey contends. 'That's why I stopped the band. Two bottles of brandy a day and who knows what else. It was going to kill him. And I didn't want to kill Pete Townshend. So I went to see him, tell him I love him.

Why are you doing this to yourself? It wasn't pretty but he listened and went into rehab the next day. I think we still all had a lot of guilt about not saving Keith.' And that was pretty much the end of The Who Mark II.

They would get back together again in 1985 for Live Aid with Kenney Jones on drums. It was a brief and noisy appearance, but it did once again prove that The Who had an uncanny knack for being in the right place at the right time. They had played the first ever festival at Monterey, and the two most famous with Woodstock and the Isle of Wight. After Live Aid, however, they went their separate ways. The group reformed again three years later, but only to receive a BPI Lifetime Achievement Award. This would be the last time Kenney Jones performed with The Who.

Then in 1989 Pete, Roger and John embarked on a real tour, to mark their twenty-fifth anniversary. This time they made no attempt to replace Keith; instead they wisely chose to augment their sound with three session singers and several extra musicians including drummer Simon Phillips, whose jazz training allowed him to successfully ape Keith Moon's extraordinary rhythms. The tour also included spectacular performances of *Tommy* in LA, New York and London with celebrity guests including Elton John, Steve Winwood, Billy Idol, Phil Collins and Patti LaBelle. It turned into one of the biggest money-spinners of the decade.

Exactly ten years later The Who re-formed once more to play a gig at the MGM Casino in Las Vegas – and became an unwitting part of a huge financial scandal. Although Pete had determined he would never play with The Who again, he agreed to re-form the band after he was told that the show in Vegas would be the first ever to be broadcast live over the internet. The concert, with a line-up that also included Kiss and the Dixie Chicks, was supposed to have been witnessed by millions across the globe. As it turned out, it was only seen by the people in the theatre. Upon returning to the UK it quickly transpired that the concert's organisers, Pixelon, were using technologies that were, in fact, fake. Pixelon's founder, 'Michael Fenne', was actually David Kim Stanley, a convicted crook involved in stock scams who was, in his own words, 'on the lam and living out of the back of his car' when he had arrived in California two years earlier. The Who had been one of the few acts to receive their fee up front. Manager Robert Rosenberg even made sure the money was in the bank before he even bothered putting the band on a plane to the US. When The Who finally released the concert as a DVD, they called it ambiguously *The Vegas Job* – a 'job' being London slang for a bank robbery.

The incident would surely have amused Keith Moon. Back in 1972 the drummer had looked into the future and concluded that The Who would always need to have some point. 'Once we feel we've achieved all we can together, then there's no point in carrying on because we'd have nothing more to give.' From now on this would be the pattern. The band would come together rarely. And then only to make a point.

12

The Ox

A Tribute to
John Entwistle

In 2002 The Who were preparing themselves for another US tour.

The previous couple of years had, by the band's standards, been very busy. In 2000 they had set out on a two-leg US tour that ended with four consecutive nights at Madison Square Garden. This was followed by an eleven-date British tour that climaxed on 27 November at London's Royal Albert Hall with an all-star gig for the Teenage Cancer Trust. In addition to The Who, the show featured Nigel Kennedy, Paul Weller, Eddie Vedder, Bryan Adams, Noel Gallagher and Kelly Jones.

The following year the band were back in New York to perform a four-song set at the Concert for New York in aid of victims of the September 11 Twin Towers atrocity. Then in the winter of 2002 they played five UK dates, including a further two charity gigs at the Royal Albert Hall. In the summer of that year the band flew out to the US to start another lengthy tour. They were genuinely enjoying themselves in a way they hadn't done in years.

On the 27 June 2002, just one day before their first US show, bassist John Entwistle died in room 658 of the Hard Rock Hotel and Casino in Las Vegas, Nevada. He had spent the previous night with a friend. She had awoken at ten in the morning to find John lying cold and unresponsive next to her. The Clark County Medical Examiner would later determine that John's death was due to a massive heart attack brought on by cocaine.

In some ways John Entwistle's death seemed utterly unexpected. Certainly Dougal Butler, who spent years partying with and looking after Keith Moon, seems to suggest this. In the documentary *Amazing Story* he says, 'John died at nearly sixty with a woman in his bed after snorting cocaine. And you think, "Hold on John? You should've done this in the seventies."' Pete Townshend suggested that 'John only had one addiction: "H" – Harrods' – referring to the bassist's penchant for hugely expensive shoes and clothes. The implication is that John, always known as the quiet one of The Who, had up until his death led a relatively normal, drug-and-booze-free life. In fact, ever since the early days John had liked to party. When by the late sixties Roger and Pete found themselves fairly settled, John would accompany Keith on his havoc-making jaunts

across the West End. It is certainly true that he didn't share Keith's rapacious appetite for drugs and destruction. But then no one did. Frankly, no one could.

Despite John having always been Pete's best friend, the relationship that developed between the bassist and the drummer became so strong that at one point the two even thought of leaving The Who. This came after the pair recorded the instrumental 'Beck's Bolero' with Jimmy Page, John Paul Jones and Jeff Beck. The track came out well, and they tossed around the idea of forming a new band. Moon allegedly said the band would go down like a lead balloon. Years later John claimed it was he who said it. Whoever said it, Page remembered the joke two years later when he created Led Zeppelin. It is hard, and perhaps best not to imagine, just how debauched Led Zep would have been with the inclusion of Moon and Entwistle.

The fact is, The Who's rhythm section was also its party section. Pete seemed to accept this when, shortly after John's death he said: 'The coroner's report is quite clear. He shouldn't have been there, he shouldn't have been doing what he was doing. I mean it was crazy. But it was what he chose to do. That's just how he was.' Kenney Jones, who had grown to know John well in his short tenure as The Who's drummer, said simply, 'If he was gonna go, he couldn't have gone in a better way, doing all the things he liked doing and being around the things he liked best.'

OPPOSITE Cheeky, boyish John in the brief psychedelic phase. **ABOVE** The Ox carrying his drinking buddy Keith off stage.

'John is a fucking genius, a fucking genius on bass guitar, what he did was beyond conception'

John was nicknamed the Ox. It's now widely assumed this is because he was quiet, and had a very still presence on stage (are oxen unnaturally quiet?). In reality he was awarded the nickname because of his astonishing constitution. He could imbibe virtually anything without it having too much of a deleterious effect. Drink, drugs, food, anything. And that really is just how he was. Right up until the day he stopped being that.

That said, John's death came as a huge shock. As manager Bill Curbishley would later say, 'If Moon was predictable, then John was unnecessary. A great, great loss.' Bill is still visibly shaken and upset when he talks about the loss of his friend John Entwistle. John had been Pete's school-friend, and the two of them had been in bands together since their mid-teens. John had been the guy who joined Roger's band The Detours and who had invited Pete in as second guitarist. He had from a solely logistical point of view been central to The Who's very existence.

Then there was his talent. Pete has spent his entire adult life praising John. 'John is a fucking genius, a fucking genius on bass guitar. It wasn't something we were particularly aware of at the time, but Jesus Christ, what he did was beyond conception.' What John did was revolutionise the art of playing the bass guitar in as radical a way as Moon had revolutionised the art of drumming. John, the only one of The Who with any formal musical education, could play piano, trumpet, guitar and pretty much anything else dropped in front of him. He refused to see the bass as simply an accompaniment. In this, by the way, he had a good deal in common with Roger and Keith. Roger had ceded artistic control of the band to Pete, but never gave up his role as The Who's focal point. Keith was a drummer who wanted to be a front man. Only Pete, the main songwriter, was able to take a step back.

John's technique involved pressing down on the string hard and releasing it to produce a trebly sound. He was he said trying to imitate the sounds of Duane Eddy, Gene Vincent, and the American soul and R&B bassists he and Pete had been so obsessed with in their teens. He also developed something now known (with a distinct lack of poetry) as the 'Typewriter'. This meant positioning his right hand over the strings so that all the four fingers could be used to tap on the strings, causing them to strike the fretboard with a distinctive twangy sound. This gave him the ability to play three or four strings at once, or to use several fingers on a single string. It allowed him to create passages that were both percussive and melodic.

But maybe what pushed John to innovate more than anything else were the other egos in The Who. Bill Wyman, The Rolling Stones' bassist, described Entwistle as 'the quietest man in private but the loudest man on stage'. John was indeed one of the first people to make use of Marshall stacks in an attempt to hear himself over the noise of his band-mates. With Pete Townshend and Keith Moon smashing their instruments on numerous occasions, John felt he needed to stand out. Townshend later remarked that Entwistle started using Marshall amplifiers to hear himself over drummer Keith Moon's rapid-fire drumming style. This in turn meant Townshend himself also had to use them, just to be heard over Entwistle. It was a volume arms race that at one point earned The Who the title of the loudest band on the planet (and nearly cost Pete his hearing).

OPPOSITE & ABOVE John with his French horn and on bass guitar. He was astonishingly versatile, able to play bass guitar, guitar, French horn, trumpet and piano.

John also lent The Who a wry dark humour that they might otherwise have lacked. Although Pete was the primary songwriter, John supplied quite a few of the band's best-known tunes and lyrics, including 'Boris the Spider', 'Uncle Ernie' and 'Cousin Kevin'. That humour, in fact, (along with the single 'Squeeze Box') is all that lends a little levity and light to the great but blackly introspective album *The Who by Numbers*. John designed the cover, a series of pencil-drawn caricatures of the band. And to his dying day he never abandoned art. Between 1996 and 2002 he attended dozens of exhibitions honouring his cartoons and caricatures. Always inordinately gracious, he would spend hours signing his work for collectors, often with a drawing of Boris the Spider.

John Entwistle's funeral took place in Gloucestershire, at St Edward's Church, Stow-on-the-Wold, on 10 July 2002. He was cremated and his ashes were buried privately. A memorial service was held in London on 24 October at St Martin-in-the-Fields, Trafalgar Square. On Pete Townshend's website, he and Roger Daltrey published a tribute, saying, 'The Ox has left the building – we've lost another great friend. Thanks for your support and love. Pete and Roger.' John's massive collection of guitars and his mansion were sold in order to meet the demands of the Inland Revenue. Ironically, John had begun his working life as a tax collector working for that institution.

The Who elected to continue with the remainder of their US tour with Pino Palladino on bass alongside Roger and Pete, with Zak Starkey (Ringo Starr's son) on drums, John Bundrick on keyboards and Simon Townshend, Pete's younger brother, on second guitar. As Bill Curbishley says, 'If we had just split up and gone our separate ways it would have been very difficult to perform again together.' On their opening night at the Hollywood Bowl, Pete turned to look at John, only to realise, with an awful lurch, John was no longer there. 'I can tell you now, with my hand on my heart, that when I looked over and he wasn't there I wanted to die. I just wanted to die.' Despite this, Curbishley's call was the right one. For all that pain, for all that scar tissue, The Who are still with us.

Roger said simply, 'I miss him so much, I can't tell you how much.' The three men had known one another since they were children.

ABOVE The main tribute at John's funeral. **OPPOSITE** John the Mod.

The final word goes to John's son, Chris.

'My younger memories of him are Sundays and old movies. *Ivanhoe, Robin Hood* – the Errol Flynn version. Lots of black-and-white movies. The movies of his youth. And he loved introducing me to them, and back when I was a kid they were the movies that were shown on a Sunday on TV. Sunday was pretty much the only day I would get to see him because he would work late into the night. He would get up long after I had left for school, and obviously I would be in bed before he got home. Sunday was a day when he would do nothing, it was the day he would spend with me. Those are my formative memories. And I credit my love of films to my dad – I now have a film collection that is vast.

'I really do think he was a genius. He started out playing in the Boys Brigade, and he could play French horn, trumpet and piano before he took up the bass. With the bass he wanted more noise, that's the way he would describe it to me. He wanted to make the bass more of a front instrument rather than just a part of the back line. He was an utter perfectionist.

'When I was twenty-five I moved to Quarwood, in Gloucestershire, to look after his estate. The Quarwood Estate was a fifty-five-room mansion house and seven 'cottages' set in 42 acres of field, woodland and gardens. I lived in one of the cottages. Not exactly with him but the other end of a very long drive within the same estate. For the last five years of his life I saw him pretty much every day, and that was wonderful for me because I got to know him as both friend and father. I worked for him. He could occasionally be difficult, but that was the perfectionist in him. He wanted things done right. There is not a day goes by when I don't think of him. One of the main problems is that I keep seeing him everywhere. I don't want to forget, but it would be almost impossible to if I did, because The Who are everywhere. He is everywhere. New pictures of him appear constantly.'

Pete This was the period with John that I enjoyed the most. He was defiantly rock 'n' roll, and defiantly resistant to change. His playing got crazier and wilder, more flashy, but his temperament was always the same: calm, restrained, ironic and affectionate.

2006

13

The Who Search for
the Big Truths Again

Almost a quarter of a century after 'It's Hard', The Who released their eleventh studio album.

Endless Wire was not simply another Who record; it was, after a gap of more than thirty-three years, a return to what Pete Townshend and the band had made their name with, the grand concept. Essentially it constitutes the band's third rock opera and returns to themes explored in *Tommy* and *Lifehouse* – loneliness, isolation, rock stardom, addiction, the search for spiritual identity and salvation, interconnectivity and even the infamous 'Grid' that Richard Barnes, Kit Lambert and other Townshend confidants had been so dismissive of.

Lifehouse it seems had never really left Pete, as his description of *Endless Wire*'s first track, 'Fragments', makes clear.

> 'This song is based on one of the very first experiments by Lawrence Ball, a composer I commissioned to create a system, and software, that would recreate the "Method" music [music accurately reflecting an individual via a website] described in my three interlocked rock-opera projects; *Lifehouse*; *Psychoderelict* [Pete Townshend's solo album of 1993]; *The Boy Who Heard Music* [his 2005–6 novella]. In *The Boy Who Heard Music* a group of three young people form a band – The Glass Household – and their first big hit is this song.'

Endless Wire contains nineteen songs. Many revisit the past, or rather use the past to examine the present. For instance, with 'It's Not Enough' Pete looks back to the French New Wave movies that so inspired Kit Lambert and Chris Stamp. Writing on his website at the time of the album's release, Pete explained his thinking: 'Watching *Le Mépris*, the '60s film by Jean-Luc Godard starring Brigitte Bardot, I found myself wondering why it is that we choose people to partner who we feel aren't quite right. Bardot asks her lover, "Do you adore my legs?" He nods. "My breasts?" He nods. "My arms?" He nods. She goes over her entire body. He nods every time. When she's finished she gets up and tells him, "It's not enough."'

ABOVE Set list lying on the production desk side-stage during the 2006/07 US tour, on which The Who played some of their most loved songs.
OPPOSITE Still crazy after all these years.

Elsewhere the album moves from the temporal to the spiritual, and clearly recalls Pete's devotion to Meher Baba. 'In my novella *The Boy Who Heard Music,* the narrator is Ray High, a rock star whose drug abuse has led him to a sanatorium. While there he learns to meditate and begins to sense that someone is interfering with his quietude up in the place where he allows his mind to go. It seems almost as though they are using a ham radio, an old-fashioned long-wave radio that was the specialist precursor to the modern internet chatroom. He may sense another presence, but this song reinforces how lonely it is to be spiritual. If the intention of the *spiritual* aspirant is to "become one with the infinite", and yet life is almost the universally finite antidote to the infinite, isn't he likely to get very lonely?'

Meanwhile, the title track of *Endless Wire*, says Pete, 'refers to a crazy scheme to use the global wire network Ray saw as a young man to spread unifying music to everyone. (This matches my own vision for The Lifehouse Method, a computer-driven website through which people can commission their unique musical portrait.)'

Endless Wire is in many senses a musical adaptation of *The Boy Who Heard Music.* And both are also to some degree an autobiography of The Who, albeit one told in an extremely elliptical fashion. The novella, which in its musical adaptation contains all the songs from *Endless Wire*, is about three young musicians, all from different ethnic and religious backgrounds, who meet and form a band. The three live in the same neighbourhood but are of different religious faiths: Gabriel is Christian, Josh is Jewish and Leila is Muslim. The narrator Ray High resembles Townshend himself and the band's history parallels that of The Who before and after the hiatus in the band's active working career.

In his autobiography Pete says that he enjoyed making the album. Despite its darkness it certainly sounds utterly committed. It also got the best reception given to any Who record since 1978's *Who's Next*, everyone lauding its ambition and imagination. The *Guardian*'s rock critic Alexis Petridis was especially impressed by the way the album was able to look back at past triumphs while sounding resolutely contemporary.

'It's tempting to point out that Townshend has neglected to include the piece of information about "Fragments" most vital to prospective purchasers – it sounds a bit like "Baba O'Riley" off *Who's Next* – but at the very least, you could never accuse him of thinking insufficiently about what he does. That is a definite point in his favour, given that most of his peers seem content to shuffle into retirement, making vague attempts to replicate their classic sound. Townshend doesn't entirely eschew references to The Who's golden era on *Endless Wire*: as well as the "Baba O'Riley" synths, something approximating to the hard acoustic guitar sound that opens "Substitute" is everywhere, as are Beach Boys-influenced harmonies, while whoever is drumming on "Sound Round" has a game stab at some Keith Moon-ish fills. Crucially, however, you never feel like you're being cravenly invited to wallow in nostalgia: all these elements are pressed into the service of something undeniably modern.'

That *Endless Wire* happened at all was something of a surprise. That it should have been so madly ambitious was a shock. That it mostly worked was truly amazing.

RIGHT The backstage rider looks somewhat different to Keith's days: tea and mineral water. Bill Curbishley convinced Townshend to stop drinking in 1994.

14

What's Next

The Who Hits 50

It has been just over fifty years since The Who formed.

In that half-century The Rolling Stones have released twenty-four studio albums, Bob Dylan has put out thirty-six, Neil Young thirty-five and David Bowie twenty-four. Since 1964, The Who have released just eleven studio albums. The Beatles, who only just made it into the 1970s, released twelve in seven years – one more if you count *Magical Mystery Tour*, the EP that became an LP. The Who, even in the 1960s when it was quite common for bands to release a couple of albums a year, were never especially prolific. In fact, their inaction came very close to bankrupting them on several occasions.

This comparative lack of output makes the band's achievements all the more extraordinary. The Who are seen as part of a sixties Holy Trinity, together with The Rolling Stones and The Beatles. With just eleven albums to their name they have had staggering cultural impact. Having sold well in excess of 100 million records, they are regularly cited as one of the most important rock 'n' roll bands in history. A cliché frequently trotted out is that The Beatles had better songs, and the Stones were sexier. The implication, intentional or not, is that The Who didn't really write tunes and weren't really that alluring as pop stars. It is a nonsense, and easily seen as such when you listen to a song like 'Baba O'Riley', or watch footage of them from their Mod days or see Daltrey in the *Tommy* days, tanned, long-haired, bare-chested and every inch the rock god. He practically invented that look. Seven of the group's albums appear on *Rolling Stone* magazine's 500 greatest albums of all time. That is more than any act except The Beatles, The Stones, Dylan and Bruce Springsteen. The fact is that The Who had great tunes, were fiercely, menacingly sexy and deeply, dangerously subversive.

TOP Keith cracking a joke with the band on the photo shoot for *The Kids Are Alright*. **OPPOSITE** Early, early days. The Who as Mods, and Roger is right – at least three of them are wearing white trousers.

The Stones and The Beatles, and so many after them, happened upon subversion. Rebelliousness was thrust upon them by a press and a public eager to be outraged. The Who, thanks to Townshend and the svengalis Chris Stamp and Kit Lambert, worked on the art of outrage and subversion. In the early black-and-white BBC footage of The Who, Pete Townshend – an acutely intelligent man – does a brilliant job of providing interviewer after interviewer with surly quotes and a distressingly convincing impression of teenage nihilism and lethargy. The effect is accentuated by the fact that, gangling and sullen-eyed, he looks about fourteen years old. Truly he is the person your mum and dad warned you about. Some of that footage, such as the time when he tells a journalist that The Who don't need to take pills on stage because they take pills 'all the time', still has the power to shock. Back then there was no distinction between, pop, rock and indie. So Pete matter-of-factly mentioning The Who's drug consumption would be like One Direction doing the same on *The One Show*. Except The Who did it first. There was no precedent for this stuff. Tactics like these have influenced everyone from the Sex Pistols, through The Jesus and Mary Chain to The Stone Roses and Oasis.

The power chord, the Marshall stacks, the windmilling arm of a guitarist – these are all now rock 'n' roll tropes. And yet they were invented by The Who. Pink Floyd only began to use feedback as a deliberate part of their sound in 1966 after they saw The Who. Jimi Hendrix was so impressed and astonished by Pete Townshend's use of the guitar that after he saw The Who he visited the Marshall music shop and demanded an amp set-up like Pete's. John Lennon says that he took the guitar sound for 'Polythene Pam' from 'Pinball Wizard', and Paul McCartney says that 'Helter Skelter' was inspired by 'The Who's heavy sound'.

The band's later excessive volume would go on to inspire heavy metal, punk and proto punk. Motörhead, the Sex Pistols, Iggy and the Stooges, MC5, Green Day and The Clash all owe a huge debt to The Who. Their earlier sounds inspired The Jam, Blur, Oasis, the British Mod revival and Brit pop. Meanwhile, the pioneering use of synthesisers to produce both melody and rhythm has had a huge aesthetic and technological influence on dance music.

The Who's most enduring impact came via their most esoteric ambitions. Long before anyone of their generation dared to see rock 'n' roll as an art form The Who were talking openly about how one day pop would rival, or even eclipse, classical music. Every aspect of their work, from the music to the lyrics, the sleeves they had designed and the clothes they chose to wear, was an art statement. Pete's embrace of pop art led him to describe The Who as Power Pop. The band's destruction of their instruments, for many little more than vandalism (albeit visually compelling vandalism), was for Townshend, a student of Gustav Metzger, a genuine act of creation. David Stubbs who wrote the award-winning book *Krautrock*, attributes The Who's enduring influence to their 'lunatic pretentiousness'.

'I want to be clear,' says Stubbs, 'this is not a criticism. Quite the reverse in fact. The reason I am so interested in bands like Kraftwerk is because they are clearly a group interested in both the sound and artifice of pop. This is very much the case with The Who. Destroying a guitar recalls the Swiss Dadas and paradoxically is both reverent and irreverent as a gesture. It is reverent because it so clearly and obviously turns pop into something else, something bigger and more dangerous. And it is irreverent because it says that instruments, which are costly and precious and beautiful, are just tools to be used in any way you choose.'

That The Who would eventually take this attitude all the way to the stage and the cinema by inventing the rock opera speaks volumes about just how serious their intent was. Stubbs sees this as both the best and worst thing about the band.

'I am glad someone was bold enough to say this, to say that pop could be put right up there with the best of classical music, but I am also disappointed they chose the word "opera". For me it is one step too far. Pop can be art without renaming itself opera. The irony of course is that once you forget the label you realise what great records these [*Tommy, Quadrophenia*] were. I am also fairly convinced that had they not done that, or at least thought in that way, they would not be as influential as they are.'

OPPOSITE The very, very best of friends. **OVERLEAF** left to right: John at home with his bass guitars; Roger looking every inch the rock 'n' roll messiah; Pete loved being in the studio; Keith the joker and drummer.

Or as ubiquitous. Walk around London or Brighton and every print shop you pass will be festooned with framed Who artwork. In Brighton, which has become the spiritual home of Mod and therefore The Who, it is perhaps inevitable that every pub, shop, café, hotel and hairdresser's should be festooned with *Quadrophenia* posters and Who memorabilia. What is more extraordinary is just how far The Who have permeated all popular culture. Their music has been used in films as diverse as *Almost Famous*, *Apollo 13* and A*ustin Powers: The Spy Who Shagged Me*. On TV they have been used to soundtrack *The Simpsons* and *Top Gear* and their music features as a theme to the three most popular US crime shows – *CSI: Crime Scene Investigation* uses 'Who Are You'; *CSI: Miami* 'Won't Get Fooled Again' and *CSI: NY* 'Baba O'Riley'. A new series, *CSI: Cyber*, uses 'I Can See for Miles', at last turning it into the international hit Pete always felt it should be.

The Who's career has been called, after one of their own songs, an amazing journey. One of the more amazing things about it is how four such strong, often volatile personalities were able to stay together so long. The war, and a sense that a generation had survived the worst the world could throw at them, brought many unlikely people together. Chris Stamp and Kit Lambert are one example; The Who are another.

Chris Entwistle, John's son, says that his dad was 'never happy taking a back seat and being just part of the rhythm section'. Keith Moon was certainly never happy being just a drummer. Roger was never going to relinquish his role as the band's focal point. Ironically, it was Pete who gave each of them that space and, as chief songwriter, accepted he was in a band that had four people who wanted to be a front man. So he stepped back, and in doing so allowed The Who to sound the way they sound.

Only Pete and Roger remain now, and yet they have a new album and a huge world tour. It is banal to say we will never see their like again, but it is nonetheless true. This is certainly not something that can be said of the vast amount of pop music being made today. We will most definitely see its like again. And again. And again. The Who invented things that are now so common to pop and rock'n'roll we assume they were always there. Even the rules they broke and the way they broke them have become tropes in themselves.

Pete and Roger, who have known one another longer than they have known their own wives and children, or even knew their parents, and who have outlived so many of their friends and peers, have something more than a friendship. They are the last two people on earth to have been there for the full story of The Who. They are like the survivors of some war or cataclysm, or the last remaining witnesses to a tumultuous historical event. Amazing journey hardly covers it.

Pete We have known each other for a long time, maybe many lifetimes – who knows – but we are still very, very different. Even the music we like, and want to make, is different. Maybe that difference is what makes it possible to return over and over to the same music and the same process. Even that process is changing, with Roger having more creative control – and therefore an additional responsibility – over our recording method and our stagecraft. Sadly, it would be disingenuous to pretend that we are not at an end. Our inability to let go of our old ways on stage will eventually stop us dead. But it is hard to change, to slow down, to accept we are too old to do what once came so easily. We drag our past along with us, and in a book like this there may always be a final chapter …

So, we were four, and now we are two. Who will get the last word? Who will get to revise the entire history of The Who and tell the story again without any refutation? It's either me, or Rog. Whichever one of us is left is going to have a lot of very funny stories to tell, with new endings, new context, new meaning. Because for each of us the journey – sometimes amazing and sometimes downright stultifying – was seen through a different pair of eyes. Prepare for the elaboration of the myth.

— Pete Townshend

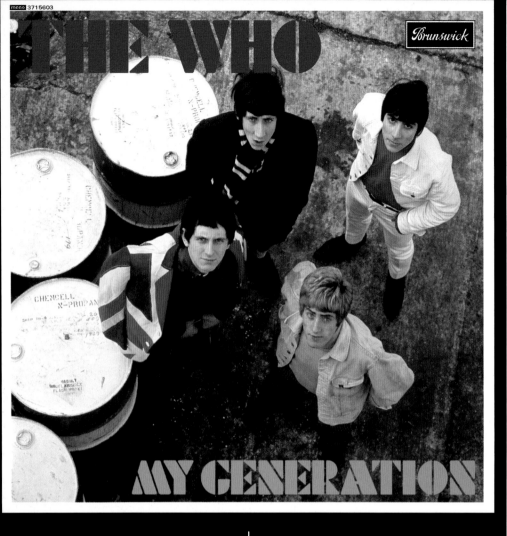

mono 3715603

THE WHO

Brunswick

MY GENERATION

My Generation

1. Out in the Street
2. I Don't Mind
3. The Good's Gone
4. La-La-La-Lies
5. Much Too Much
6. My Generation
7. The Kids Are Alright
8. Please Please Please
9. It's Not True
10. I'm a Man
11. A Legal Matter
12. The Ox

The Who's debut album was produced by Shel Talmy and first issued in the UK by Brunswick Records in December 1965, and in the US under the title *The Who Sings My Generation* in April 1966. It was recorded in short bursts in April, October and November 1965, and for many tracks The Who were joined by Nicky Hopkins on piano. Assisting Talmy for the most part was engineer Glyn Johns.

The UK release featured an iconic front sleeve, taken at Surrey Docks in south-east London by Decca Records' photographer David Wedgbury, featuring an aerial view of the four members of The Who gazing skywards, a pose that other bands, Blondie, The Jam and The Undertones amongst them, copied in almost perfect pastiches years later. In the US American Decca attempted to jump on the British invasion bandwagon by using a different yet similarly iconic Wedgbury shot, picturing The Who with London's Big Ben in the background.

My Generation reached #5 in the UK charts, but flopped in the US. Polydor, who would release The Who's recordings in the UK over the next two decades, didn't own the rights to the album, which went out of print in the UK within twelve months of its release. For years no company seemed inclined to reissue it in Britain until Virgin picked it up in 1980. This issue had good sound quality, but was pressed on inferior vinyl and disappeared at the end of its meagre print run.

Decca kept the US version available domestically throughout the sixties and, when MCA reorganised in the early seventies, *The Who Sings My Generation* was issued as a double budget package with the US-only *Magic Bus – The Who on Tour*. MCA first issued the album on CD in the States in the early eighties, but was criticised for the mastering job and a better version followed yet with the same catalogue number.

In 2002 a Deluxe Edition of *My Generation* was released on two-CD and double vinyl, adding several bonus tracks including the singles and B-sides of 'I Can't Explain' / 'Bald Headed Woman', 'Anyway Anyhow Anywhere' / 'Daddy Rolling Stone' and thirteen out-takes, instrumental versions and a cappella versions of the album's tracks.

As part of The Who's fiftieth year celebrations, in 2015 *My Generation* was reissued in mono on 180 gram heavyweight vinyl.

A Quick One

1. Run Run Run
2. Boris the Spider
3. I Need You
4. Whiskey Man
5. Heatwave
6. Cobwebs and Strange
7. Don't Look Away
8. See My Way
9. So Sad About Us
10. A Quick One, While He's Away

The Who's second album was produced by Kit Lambert and released on Reaction Records in December 1966. In the US it was held back until May 1967 and retitled *Happy Jack*, partly because the 'Happy Jack' single had been a

THE WHO
A Quick One

minor hit for The Who there, reaching #24 the same month, and also because their US record company objected to the double entendre in the title. To make room for the hit single, the American version lost 'Heatwave'.

The album was recorded between August and November of 1966, mostly at IBC Studios. It made #4 in the LP chart.

Two remastered versions of *A Quick One* were subsequently released, the first with ten bonus tracks in June 1995 and the second, including bonus tracks, in stereo in the US in 2002 and on Polydor in the UK in 2003. Both reissues were produced by Jon Astley.

In 2015 *A Quick One* was reissued in mono on 180 gram heavyweight vinyl.

The Who Sell Out

1. Armenia City in the Sky
2. Heinz Baked Beans
3. Mary Anne with the Shaky Hand
4. Odorono
5. Tattoo
6. Our Love Was
7. I Can See for Miles
8. I Can't Reach You
9. Medac
10. Relax
11. Silas Stingy
12. Sunrise
13. Rael 1 & 2

The Who's third album was produced by Kit Lambert and released by Track Records in December 1967. In the US *The Who Sell Out* was released in January 1968. A remastered CD version, produced by Jon Astley, was released in 1995. The 1995 CD used the stereo mixes of the tracks until a Deluxe Edition of *The Who Sell Out* was released in 2009, when both the mono and stereo mixes plus a host of bonus tracks were added.

Accurately predicting the modern-day trend for commercial sponsorship of rock, the songs on the first side of *The Who Sell Out* are linked together by spoof commercials similar to those heard on contemporaneous offshore pirate radio stations. The eye-catching sleeve design by David King and Roger Law, and photographed by David Montgomery, also enforced the sell out concept.

For all its imagination *The Who Sell Out* reached only a disappointing #13 in the UK LP charts, and failed completely in the US despite the heavy touring schedule that the band were undertaking there. Because of the touring, the album was recorded variously in London, New York and Los Angeles, and there were even some sessions in Nashville.

In 2015 a 100 gram heavyweight vinyl version of *The Who Sell* Out was reissued that included the original 20" × 30" psychedelic poster insert by Adrian George.

Tommy

1. Overture
2. It's a Boy
3. 1921
4. Amazing Journey
5. Sparks

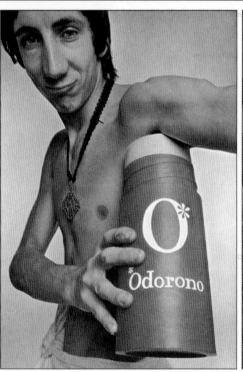

THE WHO SELL OUT

Replacing the stale smell of excess with the sweet smell of success, Peter Townshend, who, like nine out of ten stars, needs it. Face the music with Odorono, the all-day deodorant that turns perspiration into inspiration.

THE WHO SELL OUT

This way to a cowboy's breakfast. Daltrey rides again. Thinks: "Thanks to Heinz Baked Beans every day is a super day". Those who know how many beans make five get Heinz beans inside and outside at every opportunity. Get saucy.

6. Eyesight to the Blind (The Hawker)
7. Christmas
8. Cousin Kevin
9. The Acid Queen
10. Underture
11. So You Think It's Alright?
12. Fiddle About
13. Pinball Wizard
14. There's a Doctor
15. Go to the Mirror!
16. Tommy, Can You Hear Me?
17. Smash the Mirror
18. Sensation
19. Miracle Cure
20. Sally Simpson
21. I'm Free
22. Welcome
23. Tommy's Holiday Camp
24. We're Not Gonna Take It
25. See Me, Feel Me / Listening to You

Produced by Kit Lambert, the double album *Tommy* was released in the UK in May 1969 by Track Records.

Recorded at London's IBC Studios between September 1968 and March 1969, The Who's first official performance of *Tommy* was at a press preview at Ronnie Scott's Jazz Club in London's Soho on 1 May 1969, the same month the original double album was released. The final *Tommy* performance, until their 25th Anniversary reunion tour in 1989, was at London's Roundhouse on 20 December 1970, when they dedicated it to their support act, an upcoming singer-songwriter/pianist called Elton John. In between, The Who took *Tommy* across Europe and America, performing it over 160 times. Despite the perfect timing – its mystical themes were ideal for 1969 – and the general hullabaloo surrounding its release, *Tommy* stalled at #2 in the UK charts. In America it eventually reached #4 on re-entering the charts. Overall, it re-entered the *Billboard* charts several times for a total of 126 weeks, far longer than any other Who album.

A remixed single CD of *Tommy* was released in 1996, followed by a Deluxe Edition SACD hybrid in 2003 with many bonus tracks of

out-takes, demos and in-studio banter. In 2012 a lavish five-disc box set of *Tommy* was released with an eighty-page hardback book in a slipcase with an essay by Richard Barnes, and including the original remastered album, a CD of Pete Townshend's demos, a 5.1 mix hi-fidelity Pure Audio Blu-Ray version and a live 'bootleg' album.

In 2015 *Tommy* was reissued on two 180 gram heavyweight vinyl records in its original triptych sleeve designed by Mike McInnerney with accompanying libretto, true to its original LP format.

Who's Next

1. Baba O'Riley
2. Bargain
3. Love Ain't for Keeping
4. My Wife
5. The Song is Over
6. Getting in Tune
7. Going Mobile
8. Behind Blue Eyes
9. Won't Get Fooled Again

Who's Next was first released by Track Records in August 1971, although it started life as a Pete Townshend concept entitled *Lifehouse*, which contained enough songs for a double album, but the project was eventually reduced to a single LP. Recording for the album began in New York with Kit Lambert as producer, but the band weren't satisfied with the results and returned to London to re-record them at Olympic Studios in Barnes with Glyn Johns. Most of the songs recorded with Johns appeared on *Who's Next,* while the leftovers appeared on singles and later on *Odds & Sods*, a 1974 album of

Who's next

immaculately packaged in a handsome black-and-white gatefold sleeve, photographed by Graham Hughes, with extensive liner notes outlining the story and a twenty-two-page book of evocative black-and-white photographs illustrating the central character Jimmy's personal odyssey with photos taken by Ethan Russell.

A remastered double CD of *Quadrophenia* was released in 1996. In 2012 Pete Townshend assessed his archive of material on *Quadrophenia* resulting in the release of a beautiful five-CD Quadrophenia box set which housed the original album on two CDs, two CDs of Pete's demos and a fifth disc of 5.1 surround sound mixes. Included in the package was a 100-page book with a 20,000 word essay by Pete plus several inserts and a poster. A cut-down two-CD version of the album plus demos was also released, followed by 180 gram heavyweight vinyl in its original gatefold sleeve with twenty-two-page booklet.

The Who by Numbers

1. Slip Kid
2. However Much I Booze
3. Squeeze Box
4. Dreaming from the Waist
5. Imagine a Man
6. Success Story
7. They Are All in Love
8. Blue, Red and Grey
9. How Many Friends
10. In a Hand or a Face

previously unreleased material from the Who's vaults. *Who's Next* became the only Who album to make #1 in the UK charts. It peaked at #4 in the US. Sleeve design by Kosh. Photography by Ethan Russell.

A remixed and remastered CD of *Who's Next* was released in 1995. Later, in 2003, a Deluxe two-CD and three-disc vinyl version with several bonus tracks, including many live tracks from the Young Vic sessions, was released. Then in 2015 the original nine-track album was reissued on 180 gram heavyweight vinyl.

Quadrophenia

1. I Am the Sea
2. The Real Me
3. Quadrophenia
4. Cut My Hair

5. The Punk and the Godfather
6. I'm One
7. The Dirty Jobs
8. Helpless Dancer
9. Is It in My Head?
10. I've Had Enough
11. 5:15
12. Sea and Sand
13. Drowned
14. Bell Boy
15. Doctor Jimmy
16. The Rock
17. Love, Reign O'er Me

The double album *Quadrophenia* was originally released by Track Records in November 1973 (October 1973 in the US). The album was recorded at Ramport, The Who's own studio in Battersea, South London, in May and June of 1973. It was

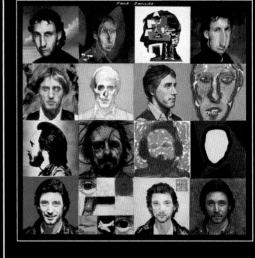

The Who by Numbers was released in the UK on 3 October 1975 and in the US on 25 October 1975. Produced by Glyn Johns, all the tracks on The Who by Numbers were recorded on the Shepperton Sound Stage using Ronnie Lane's Mobile Studio. Recording began with a jam session on 4 April 1975, continued throughout May and overdubs were done in June. Mixing was done by Glyn Johns at Basing Street Studios in London's Notting Hill during July and August. Packaged in an individually numbered, self-deprecatory join-up-the-dots cartoon designed by John Entwistle, it reached #7 in UK and #8 in the US. It was released with bonus tracks as a remixed and remastered CD in November 1996 and the original album was reissued on 180 gram heavyweight vinyl in 2015.

Who Are You

1. New Song
2. Had Enough
3. 905
4. Sister Disco
5. Music Must Change
6. Trick of the Light
7. Guitar and Pen
8. Love is Coming Down
9. Who Are You

Who Are You was released in the UK on 18 August 1978 where it reached #6. It was released simultaneously in the US where it reached #2. Keith Moon's accidental death on 7 September 1978 completely overshadowed the release of Who Are You. Ironically, he is photographed on the cover sitting on a chair with the words 'Not to be Taken Away' emblazoned on its back. All the tracks on Who Are You were originally produced by Glyn Johns and Jon Astley, and mixed by Jon Astley at CTS Studios in Wembley. It was reissued as a remixed and remastered CD with bonus tracks in 1996. Sleeve design by Bill Smith. Photography by Terry O'Neill. A 180 gram heavyweight vinyl LP of Who Are You was reissued in 2015.

Face Dances

1. You Better You Bet
2. Don't Let Go the Coat
3. Cache Cache
4. The Quiet One
5. Did You Steal My Money?
6. How Can You Do It Alone?
7. Daily Records
8. You
9. Another Tricky Day

Face Dances was released in the UK in March 1981. After the death of Keith Moon, The Who

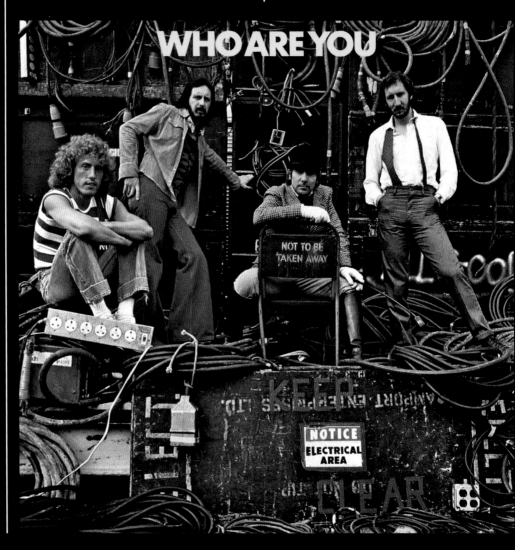

regrouped with Kenney Jones on drums and, initially, concentrated on live work. The new look Who launched themselves in a barrage of publicity, playing their first concert at London's Rainbow Theatre on 2 May 1979. It wasn't until over a year later that work began on *Face Dances*. Aside from the arrival of Kenney Jones, there were other changes in the traditional Who modus operandi: John 'Rabbit' Bundrick played keyboards and on some of the newer numbers Roger played guitar on stage for the first time since the days of The Detours in 1962.

The album cover concept by Peter Blake featured sixteen portraits of the members of The Who painted by the elite of Britain's contemporary fine artists including Blake himself, David Hockney, Patrick Caulfield, Richard Hamilton and others. *Face Dances* was produced by Bill Szymczyk and reached #6 in the UK LP charts, and #2 in the US. The album was recorded at Odyssey Studios, London, from June 1980 and mixed at Szymczyk's own Bayshore studio in Coconut Grove, Florida, at the end of that year.

A reissue of *Face Dances* including four bonus tracks was produced, remixed and remastered by Jon Astley and Andy Macpherson with Bob Ludwig in 1997. The original LP, including the 24" × 24" colour poster insert, was reissued on 180 gram heavyweight vinyl in 2015.

It's Hard
1. Athena
2. It's Your Turn
3. Cooks County
4. It's Hard
5. Dangerous
6. Eminence Front
7. I've Known No War
8. One Life's Enough
9. One at a Time
10. Why Did I Fall for That?
11. A Man is a Man
12. Cry If You Want

It's Hard was released in the UK and US in September 1982, and a remixed and remastered CD with bonus tracks was issued in 1997.

It's Hard, The Who's final studio album until *Endless Wire* in 2006, was released to coincide with what was billed as The Who's farewell tour of America, which included two nights at Shea Stadium in New York. It reached #11 in the UK charts and #8 in the US.

It was recorded at Turn Up-Down Studio at Glyn Johns's home in Surrey in June 1982, where it was also mixed. Original sleeve design, concept and photography by Graham Hughes.

In 2015 *It's Hard* was reissued as a 180 gram heavyweight vinyl edition.

Endless Wire
1. Fragments
2. A Man in a Purple Dress
3. Mike Post Theme
4. In the Ether
5. Black Widow's Eyes
6. Two Thousand Years
7. God Speaks of Marty Robbins
8. It's Not Enough
9. You Stand By Me
10. Sound Round
11. Pick Up the Peace
12. Unholy Trinity

13. Trilby's Piano
14. Endless Wire
15. Fragments of Fragments
16. We Got a Hit
17. They Made My Dream Come True
18. Mirror Door
19. Tea & Theatre
20. We Got a Hit (Extended Version)
21. Endless Wire (Extended Version)

Endless Wire was released in the UK and US in October 2006 and as a Deluxe Edition with a bonus disc *Live at Lyon*. Recorded at Pete Townshend's home studio and Eel Pie Oceanic between autumn 2002 and summer 2006, *Endless Wire* was the first album of new material to be released by The Who since *It's Hard* in 1982.

The album was produced by Pete Townshend, with Roger Daltrey's vocals produced by Bobby Pridden and Billy Nicholls. In the UK, it reached #9 in the charts, and in the US, #7. Sleeve design by Richard Evans, utilising elements created with the Visual Harmony software designed by Dave Snowdon and Lawrence Ball. A double album of *Endless Wire* was released on 180 gram heavyweight vinyl in 2015.

LIVE ALBUMS

Live at Leeds

1. Young Man Blues
2. Substitute
3. Summertime Blues
4. Shakin' All Over
5. My Generation
6. Magic Bus

Acclaimed as the best live album by a rock band ever, *Live at Leeds*, produced by The Who and recorded on 14 February 1970 at Leeds University, was released in the UK on 27 May 1970 on Track Records.

Live at Leeds was designed to emphasise The Who as a rock band as opposed to opera singers, and its packaging was also an antidote to the splendour of *Tommy*: a plain buff sleeve rubber-stamped with the band's name and designed by Graphreaks to resemble a bootleg. Within could be found an envelope containing all sorts of facsimile Who ephemera and a record on which there was a handwritten warning that crackles heard throughout were not the fault of your record player. The remastered 1995 CD amended the note to say that the crackling noises had been corrected!

The original album consisted of just six tracks. The 1995 reissue added another eight tracks (everything except *Tommy*) and in 2001 a Deluxe Edition added a second CD of the *Tommy* segment of the concert.

A fortieth anniversary box set of *Live at Leeds* was released in 2010, which included the complete concert at Leeds University plus the complete concert from Hull City Hall recorded the following night.

The Monterey International Pop Festival

1. Substitute
2. Summertime Blues
3. Pictures of Lily
4. A Quick One, While He's Away
5. Happy Jack
6. My Generation

Released in October 1992, this four-CD box set includes The Who's entire twenty-five-minute performance from 18 June 1967. On a smaller scale than Woodstock, Monterey played a pivotal role in building The Who's credibility across America.

Live at the Isle of Wight Festival 1970

1. Heaven and Hell
2. I can't Explain
3. Young Man Blues
4. I Don't Even Know Myself
5. Water
6. Overture
7. It's a Boy
8. 1921
9. Amazing Journey
10. Sparks
11. Eyesight to the Blind (The Hawker)
12. Christmas
13. The Acid Queen
14. Pinball Wizard
15. Do You Think It's Alright?
16. Fiddle About
17. Tommy, Can You Hear Me?
18. There's a Doctor
19. Go to the Miror!
20. Smash the Mirror
21. Miracle Cure
22. I'm Free
23. Tommy's Holiday Camp
24. We're Not Gonna Take It
25. Summertime Blues
26. Shakin' All Over / Twist and Shout
27. Substitute
28. My Generation
29. Naked Eye
30. Magic Bus

In the mid-nineties, film director Murray Lerner dug out his film of this concert, and the original eight-track tapes (along with some of the other festival acts) were found in Pete Townshend's tape archive. Negotiations finally resulted in the release of a double CD and a VHS video in 1996, with a triple vinyl and DVD release following in 2001. Design by Hugh Gilmour at Castle Communications. Front cover photography by Claude Gassian.

The Who Live – The Blues to the Bush 1999

1. I Can't Explain
2. Substitute
3. Anyway Anyhow Anywhere
4. Pinball Wizard
5. My Wife
6. Baba O'Riley
7. Pure and Easy
8. You Better You bet
9. I'm a Boy
10. Getting in Tune
11. The Real Me
12. Behind Blue Eyes
13. Magic Bus
14. Boris the Spider
15. After the Fire
16. Who Are You
17. 5:15
18. Won't Get Fooled Again
19. The Kids Are Alright
20. My Generation

Released in April 2000, *The Who Live – the Blues to the Bush 1999* is a selection from The Who's low-key comeback performances (in October 1999 at Chicago's House of Blues, and December 1999 at London's Shepherd's Bush Empire) as a sensibly stripped-down five-piece featuring Roger, Pete, John, John 'Rabbit' Bundrick (keyboards) and Zak Starkey (drums). Design and art direction by Richard Evans. Photography by Graham Hughes.

The Who Live at the Royal Albert Hall

1. I Can't Explain
2. Anyway Anyhow Anywhere
3. Pinball Wizard
4. Relay
5. My Wife
6. The Kids Are Alright
7. Mary Anne with the Shaky Hand
8. Bargain
9. Magic Bus
10. Who Are You
11. Baba O'Riley (Violin: Nigel Kennedy)
12. Drowned
13. A Heart to Hang Onto
14. So Sad About Us (Pete Townshend with Paul Weller)

15. I'm One (Vocals: Eddie Vedder)
16. Getting in Tune (Vocals: Eddie Vedder)
17. Behind Blue Eyes (Vocals: Bryan Adams)
18. You Better You Bet
19. The Real Me
20. 5:15
21. Won't Get Fooled Again (Guitar: Noel Gallagher)
22. Substitute (Vocals: Kelly Jones)
23. Let's See Action (Vocals: Eddie Vedder with Roger and Pete)
24. My Generation
25. See Me, Feel Me / Listening to You (with Eddie Vedder and Bryan Adams)
26. I'm Free
27. I Don't Even Know Myself
28. Summertime Blues
29. Young Man Blues

The majority of this 2003 CD was recorded at a charity performance at London's Royal Albert Hall on 27 November 2000, most of which had previously been available on DVD. The four tracks on the Bonus Disc emanate from a Royal Albert Hall show on 8 February 2002, which unfortunately marked the final onstage appearance of John Entwistle.

Greatest Hits Live

1. I Can't Explain – recorded December 1971, San Francisco Civic Auditorium
2. Substitute – recorded December 1971, San Francisco Civic Auditorium
3. Happy Jack – recorded February 1970, City Hall, Hull, England
4. I'm a Boy – recorded February 1970, City Hall, Hull, England
5. Behind Blue Eyes – recorded December 1971, San Francisco Civic Auditorium
6. Pinball Wizard – recorded June 1976, Vetch Field, Swansea, England
7. I'm Free – recorded June 1976, Vetch Field, Swansea, England
8. Squeeze Box – recorded June 1976, Vetch Field, Swansea, England
9. Naked Eye / Let's See Action / My Generation – recorded May 1974, Charlton Athletic Football Club, South London, England

10. 5:15 – recorded December 1973, The Capital Centre, Largo
11. Won't Get Fooled Again – recorded December 1973, The Capital Centre, Largo
12. Magic Bus – recorded February 1970, Leeds University, Leeds, England
13. My Generation – recorded 1965, BBC Sessions
14. I Can See For Miles – recorded August 1989, Universal Amphitheatre, Los Angeles
15. Join Together – recorded August 1989, Universal Amphitheatre, Los Angeles
16. Love, Reign O'er Me – recorded August 1989, Universal Amphitheatre, Los Angeles
17. Baba O'Riley – recorded August 1989, Universal Amphitheatre, Los Angeles
18. Who Are You – recorded August 1989, Universal Amphitheatre, Los Angeles
19. The Real Me – recorded January 2002, Watford Civil Hall, Watford, England
20. The Kids Are Alright – recorded February 2002, Royal Albert Hall, London, England
21. Eminence Front – recorded March 2009, Brisbane Entertainment Centre, Brisbane
22. A Man in a Purple Dress – recorded March 2007, Nassau Coliseum, Uniondale, New York

Twenty-two recordings of the band's biggest and best-known hits – most of them never widely available or unreleased and twenty of them newly mixed by the band and its production team – were collected on *Greatest Hits Live* released exclusively on the iTunes Store on 19 January 2010. Just a few weeks later, on 7 February, The Who took the stage to headline the Super Bowl XLIV Halftime Show at Dolphin Stadium in South Florida.

Pearl Jam's Eddie Vedder has said that 'The Who quite possibly remain the greatest live band ever' (*Rolling Stone*, 2004) and *Greatest Hits Live* justifies that statement with scintillating tracks ranging from 1965 to 2009, from London's Royal Albert Hall to the San Francisco Civic Auditorium.

The Who Live at Hull 1970

1. Heaven and Hell
2. I Can't Explain
3. Fortune Teller
4. Tattoo
5. Young Man Blues
6. Substitute
7. Happy Jack
8. I'm a Boy
9. A Quick One, While He's Away
10. Summertime Blues
11. Shakin' All Over
12. My Generation
13. Overture
14. It's a Boy
15. 1921
16. Amazing Journey
17. Sparks
18. Eyesight to the Blind (The Hawker)
19. Christmas
20. The Acid Queen
21. Pinball Wizard
22. Do You Think It's Alright?
23. Fiddle About
24. Tommy, Can You Hear Me?
25. There's a Doctor
26. Go to the Mirror!
27. Smash the Mirror
28. Miracle Cure
29. Sally Simpson
30. I'm Free
31. Tommy's Holiday Camp
32. We're Not Gonna Take It

Recorded the day after the famous *Live at Leeds* album on 15 February 1970, *The Who Live at Hull 1970* was released as a stand-alone CD in 2012. Regarded by many, including Roger Daltrey, as a far superior concert to Leeds, the Hull tapes were found to be missing John's bass parts on the first six tracks. By 'flying in' the bass parts from the Leeds tapes, producer Bob Pridden and engingeer Matt Hay at FX in Acton managed to repair those tracks. Sleeve design by Richard Evans.

Index

Charlesworth, Chris 176

musical tastes, youthful 17, 28, 30, 35, 39, 48

'My Generation' and 91, *92*, 93–4, 115

pop art style and 112, *113*, *114*, 144, *145*

Quadrophenia and 193, *195*

Quadrophenia film and *256*, 257

Ready Steady Go!, first appearance on *84*

relations between members of The Who improving after US touring, comments on 150

rock 'n' roll as inspiration to 28, 30, 35

Rolling Stones Rock and Roll Circus and *156*

solo albums 214

'Substitute' and 115

Teddy Boys and 40, 48

The Who Sell Out and 137

Tommy album and 153, 158, 160, 166, *167*, *212*

Tommy film and 160, *161*, 166, 212, *213*, 214, *214*, *215*, *217*

Townsend and *40*, 48, **51**, 56, 218, 257, 274–5, *297*, *300–1*, 301, **301**

transformation of character 'Peaceful Perce' 148

US, 1968 tour of *140–3*

Who by Numbers and 210

Who's Next and *174*, *189*, 190

Woodstock and 162, *163*, 165

Daniels, Phil 72, *244*, *246*, *247*, *255*, *256*, *257*, *258*, *259*, 261, *264*, *265*

Davies, Ray 51, 250

Davis, John 201

Decca Records 83, 89, 115, 119, 308

Detours, The 39, *44*, *46*, *47*, 48, 51, **51**, 52, *52*, *53*, *54*, 55, 56–7, 62, 280, 313

'Doctor Jimmy' 193, 311

'Dogs' 148, 149, 182

Donegan, Lonnie 17, *34*, 39, 47, 52

Druce, Bob 52

Dunlop, Frank 186

Picture Credits

Alamy 56 © Tracksimages.com, 68 Tracksimages.com, 76/77 © Pictorial Press Ltd, 117T Pictorial Press Ltd, 122 Pictorial Press Ltd, 145B Pictorial Press Ltd, 171T Trinity Mirror/Mirrorpix, 236T © Pictorial Press Ltd, 256 © Moviestore Collection Ltd. **Richard Barnes** 69 bl, 71br. **BBC Copyright material reproduced courtesy of the British Broadcasting Corporation. All rights reserved** 87 **BBC Photo Library** 90 T&B. **Courtesy of The Beachcombers** 22btm, 36, 39t, 39b. **Adrian Boot** 270. **Peter Blake / UMG** 274. **Courtesy of Brunswick Records / UMG** 28, 83. **David Edward Byrd** 166r. **Corbis** 116 © Jacques Haillot/Apis/Sygma, 163 © Henry Diltz, 164 © Henry Diltz, 165 © Henry Diltz. **Courtesy of the Daltrey family** 12t, 16, 17, 40. **Courtesy of Decca Records US / UMG** 91. **Len DeLessio** 298R **Michael English and Nigel Waymouth** 126. **Courtesy of the Entwistle family** 12btm, 18, 19, 44, 46, 47, 49, 50, 52, 53, 54. **Josh Emmett** 140, 141. **Richard Evans** 2, 93t, 93b, 136t, 136b, 188, 200, 201, 225. **Getty Images** 2 The Visualeyes Archive, 4 Jack Robinson, 8 Hulton Archive, 11T Popperfoto, 13T Fox Photos, 13B Fox Photos, 15B Keystone, 24 George Douglas, 27T GAB Archives/Redferns, 27B Mondadori Porfolio, 30 Robert W. Kelley, 31 The LIFE Images Collection/Charles Trainor, 34TR RB/Redferns, 34BL Micheal Ochs Archives, 34BR V&A Images, 38BL Bert Hardy Advertising Archive, 41TL Popperfoto, 41TR Joseph McKeown, 41B Popperfoto, 42T Joseph McKeown/Picture Post/Hulton Archive, 42BR Alex Dellow, 43T Popperfoto, 79 GAB Archives/Redferns, 84 Monitor Picture Library/Photoshot, 85 Chris Morphet/Redferns, 86 Michael Ochs Archives, 88/89 The Visualeyes Archive/Redferns, 98 Chris Morphet/Redferns, 100 Chris Morphet Redferns, 101 Chris Morphet/Redferns, 102/103 The Visualeyes Archive/Redferns, 104T Fincher/Express/Hulton Archive, 104BL King Collection/Photoshot, 104BR Rick Hardy, 105T Archive Photos, 108T Rick Hardy, 109 SensorSpot, 114B Bentley Archive/Popperfoto, 118 Philippe Le Tellier/Paris Match, 124 Chris Morphet, 129T John D. Kisch/Separate Cinema Archive, 130 Paul Ryan/Michael Ochs Archives, 131 Paul Ryan/Michael Ochs Archives, 137 David Montgomery, 146 Archive Photos, 156B Mark and Colleen Hayward/Redferns, 157TL&R Hulton Archive, 157B David Cairns/Express, 172B Chris Morphet/Redferns, 173C Robert Altman/Michael Ochs Archive, 177 Michael Putland, 195TL Chris Morphet/Redferns, 197 Michael Putland, 208 Terry O'Neill, 213R Mondadori Portfolio, 214 C Michael Ochs Archives, 214B Anwar Hussein/WireImage, 215 Stanely Bielecki Movie Collection, 216/217 Stanley Bielecki Movie Collection, 221B John Downing, 229 B Time & Life Pictures, 244 Jeremy Fletcher/Redferns, 250T Clare Muller/Redferns, 250RB Janette Beckman, 251 Chalkie Davies, 263 Central Press, 266T Ron Case/Keystone, 275T Phil Dent/Redferns, 291T Jo Hale, 292 Larry Busacca/Clear Channel, 297R Rick Diamond, 299R Chris Morphet/Redferns, 300/301 Kevin Mazur/WireImage, 303 Jan Persson/Redferns, 304 Christie Goodwin/Redferns, 306/307 Chris Morphet/Redferns. **Hipgnosis** 239tr. **Marcelle de Kreuk van Beek** 142, 143. **Chris McCourt** 176, 178, 179, 180–181. **Mike McInnerney** 125 tr, 125br, 154, 168–169, 171btm, 173 btm, 168–169, 170btm, 173 btm. **Barrie Meller** 158. **Mirrorpix** 26, 32 & 33, 34TL, 38TR, 43TR Arthur Sidey, 43B Alan Grist, 74/75 King, 75B Eric Piper, 94 Eddie Waters, 109T Freddie Cole, 120 L & R Charles Ley, 145T Mike Maloney, 148T Tony Eyles, 149 Tom King, 156T Peter Stone, 170, 172T, 204B Mike Maloney, 204T Mike Maloney, 213TL &B George Phillips, 218T, 226 Edward Sanderson, 230 Ron Burton, 235 Peter Case, 236C Tom King, 239 Kent Gavin, 241T Allan Olley, 241B, 242 Tony McGee, 243B & T Tony McGee, 248 NCJ Archive, 249L, 249RT, 249RB NCJ Archive, 250 Kent Gavin, 252 Hill, 260T Geoffrey Day, 260B Geoffrey Day, 262 Geoffrey Day, 264R, 265 Alisdair MacDonald, 266B Cyril Maitland, 267B, 269B King, 272, 273B, 275B, 283 George Phillips, 298L George Phillips. **Courtesy of the Moon family** 11 btm, 22 top, 23 tr, bl, br. **National Portrait Gallery, London**/David Wedgbury 110. **Press Association Images** Mark Humphrey/AP 7. **Photofeatures** 127 © Chris Walter, 148B © Chris Walter, 150 © Chris Walter, 151 © Chris Walter, 186 © Chris Walter, 193T&B © Chris Walter, 278 © Chris Walter, 295 © Chris Walter, 305 © Chris Walter. **Picture Desk** 212 RBT Stigwood Prods/Hemdale/The Kobal Collection, 214T RBT Stigwood Prods/Hemdale/The Kobal Collection. **Polydor / UMG** 222. **REX** 29T&B Associated Newspapers, 95 David Magnus, 106T George Konig, 131 Bruce Fleming, 132/133 Barry Peake, 173 T Everett Collection, 268/269, 273T Associated Newspapers. **Ethan Russell** 174, 189. **Will Schoenke** 297L. **Barry Simner** 267T, 268B. **Topfoto** 37 © Colin Jones, 61 © Colin Jones, 78 © Colin Jones, 80 © Colin Jones, 82 © Colin Jones, 92 © Colin Jones, 105B © Colin Jones, 106B © Colin Jones, 107B © Colin Jones, 113 © Colin Jones, 119 © Colin Jones, 144R © Colin Jones, 184L © Colin Jones, 232 Colin Jones, 237 UPP, 254/255 © United Archives, 264L © United Archives, 282B, 294B © Colin Jones. **Courtesy of the Townshend family** 10, 20, 21. **Pete Townshend archive** 153, 155 Photo by Pete Cook, 159l, 162, 166, 194, 253. **Pete Townshend** 195t, 196btm. **Trinifold archive** Gus Christie: 276, Chalkie Davies: 2, Ian Dickson: 202–203, Aubrey Dewar: 62, 64, 65, 66, 67, 72, 108btm, 283, Bush Hollyhead: 205, Graham Hughes: 198–199, 264, Vincent McEvoy: 211, Terry O'Neill: 224t, 224btm, 294t, Peter Saunders: 185, Kevin Stein: 220, 221t, 223, William Snyder: 286, 288, 289, 290, 291 both, 302, David Wedgbury: 2, 58, 81btm, 96, 97, 104t, 107t, 145c, Tom Wright: 125tl, 139tl, 138nr. **Trinifold archive** 63, 70, 73, 79, 81t, 99btm, 104bl, 117, 120tl, 120tr, 121, 123, 134, 138tr, 138bl, 161, 183, 185, 190t, 190b, 191, 196, 219, 224r, 233, 234, 236btm, 238, 239l, 240, 279, 280, 281, 282. **Universal Music Group** 167, 274, 308-313. **Nigel Waymouth and Michael English** 126 **Weidenfeld & Nicolson**, Arfur © 1970 by Nik Cohn, Jacket design by Bentley Farrell Burnett, photography by **Ray Rathbone** 159b. **The Who Films** 246, 255, 257, 258, 259, 261. **Barrie Wentzell** 152 bl, br, 153 br **Baron Wolman** 152t.

The publishers would like to thank Richard Evans for all his help in compiling this book.

The Who: 50 Years: The Official History

Published in 2015 by
Harper Design
An Imprint of HarperCollins*Publishers*
195 Broadway
New York, NY 10007
Tel: (212) 207-7000
Fax: (855) 746-6023
harperdesign@harpercollins.com
www.hc.com

Distributed throughout the world by
HarperCollins Publishers
195 Broadway
New York, NY 10007

ISBN 978-0-06-239636-5

Library of Congress Control Number: 2015943466

Editorial Director: Lorna Russell
Editor: Elen Jones
Production Manager: Phil Spencer
Consultant and Archive: Richard Evans
Picture Research: Claire Gouldstone
Copyeditor: Steve Dobell
Design by Barnbrook
Colour origination by Rhapsody Ltd London

Printed in China

First Printing, 2015